Nine Jewels of Night

One Soul's Journey into God

Beverly Lanzetta

BLUE SAPPHIRE BOOKS

SAN DIEGO

Note: There is no other way to narrate the development of a spiritual life than to tell the stories of those one encounters. However, privacy also must be honored and thus—for this reason—I have changed personal and institutional names, and/or places in the book, with the exception of known historical, literary, and academic figures, and those of my immediate family.

Similarly, because confidentiality is a core principle of spiritual direction and healing, while all I describe in my case studies is drawn from real situations, the characters I write about in these spiritual direction and healing narratives are not modeled on real individuals, but are constructs influenced by the many people I have been privileged to serve over these years.

Scripture Quotations from the New International Version of the Bible are copyrighted © 1973, 1978, 1984, 2011 by Biblica, Inc., published by Zondervan. Reprinted by permission.

Blue Sapphire Books website http://bluesapphirebooks.com

Cover and interior design: Nelson Kane

PUBLISHER'S CATALOGING-IN-PUBLICATION
(Provided by Quality Books, Inc.)
    Lanzetta, Beverly.
      Nine jewels of night : one soul's journey into God /
    Beverly Lanzetta.
      pages cm
      Includes bibliographical references.
      ISBN 978-0-9840616-1-7

      1. Lanzetta, Beverly. 2. Spiritual biography.
    I. Title.

BL73.L369A3 2014   204'.092
            QBI14-600123

Printed in the United States of America

CONTENTS

This book is dedicated to my beloved children

Maya
Gina
Tobin
Shana

Who taught me the meaning of unconditional love

As the image grew more vivid, I saw the entire spiral contained multiple factors of wisdom and multiple stages of soul development that were neither linear nor hierarchical. The nine jewels represented three divisions of three degrees of spiritual growth. Yet the number "nine" was not mathematically precise. Each jewel was a limitless mystery of divine-human possibility.

Suspended in the divine milieu, the glistening jewels were called "nights," their fiery light turning to ash our distorted habits and beliefs, plunging the soul in darkness. But these nights of surrender were also "jewels," because every degree of spiritual development guides us to a new future, to a more whole and embodied understanding of our place in the sacred web of life

Author's Journal, 1980

PROLOGUE

W HAT FOLLOWS IS A PERSONAL ACCOUNT of my search for a new expression of the eternal quest for truth. The story chronicles my growing restlessness to answer a spiritual call until on a gorgeous autumn day in my twenty-ninth year, I am converted by a series of revelations beyond the boundaries of established religions to the one reality at the heart of all religions, and to an entirely singular path of contemplation.

Leaving behind worldly influences, comfort, and convention, over the next thirty-eight years I practice this radical path of devotion, serving as a teacher and soul guide of the inner life. During this same period and as a mother of four children, I eventually become a professor of theology, building a bridge between classical accounts of the soul's journey and the universal call of the spirit, later leaving academia to found an interspiritual seminary and monastic community outside monastery walls.

Of course, every age finds women and men of faith who risk reproach to venture into the unknown. Not content with mere appearances or half-truths that prey on the gullible, they search for the real, the ultimate concealed within the everyday. They have not torn their feet and spilled their blood to claim a prize or to lead others on the clear path. No, in the first instance, the longing was all their own: not a conscious choice, not even a thought in the mind, but a flame of passion burning in their souls.

Like them, I was not to follow the path of commitment to a stable ideal but to break loose and break free of every kind of stereotypical containment, to tremble and burn in my own fire. And it was then that I realized that my journey, and that of many other people, differed from traditional categories of spiritual growth. Over time I would learn how the details of everyday life was the stuff of mystical transformation.

Nine Jewels of Night is a testament of gratitude for God's infinite mercy, and for the blessings I have received from innumerable people who entrusted their souls to my care. Despite my theological studies and spiritual training—what I have learned and still have yet to know—a shattering, life-changing experience of divine love informs all that I say and don't say. While my language may be limited, and my heart may be incomplete, the Holy One is not.

Oh Beauty, how I do adore you! So weary am I and so habituated to the old ways. Grant me the courage to abandon all, to savor your sweet call that fills my whole being with the delicate ardor of love. Call me again and again and I will come. Ask me what you will and I will answer. Give me a task and I will fulfill it. Ask me to go hungry, send me away in thirst, I will not abandon you. It is your will that my love commands. It is your desire that my life is for.

Show me what you need and I will do it. Show me what you wish and I will find it. Ask me to give myself away and I will lay my heart upon stone tablets for all to tread. For you there is nothing I will not do. You, Beloved, who wants my freedom, who leads me through the valleys of despair to a Light brighter than any sun, you who have given me the gift of Love: what else can I do to show my gratitude?

Author's Journal, 2002

PART I

LOW PLACES BRING LIGHT

* *1* *

I Counted My Solitude

THE CLOCK READ 5 A.M. Sliding out of the covers, I found pants and shoes at the foot of my bed and slipped them on. Reaching for the wool coat I'd left on my desk chair, I tucked my arms in and buttoned up. Then I tiptoed down the stairs, hoping our new puppy wouldn't hear me and wake my parents, and holding my breath, soundlessly opened the door, passing into the still dawn.

Our old dog, Trixie, lifted her mustard-colored head, eyeing me sleepily as I stepped off the porch. Shaking herself, she trotted beside me, tail wagging, ears twitching, and then darted ahead to chase a baby rabbit zigzagging across the field. Beyond the boundary of lawn, where the tall trees began, I picked up my pace, turning with false bravado onto a dirt trail that led deeper into the woods. The sky, a star-jeweled dome above, was a swirl of midnight blue and pale yellow, alerting me that daybreak was not far away.

I made my way to the lean-to I'd built in the woods, without getting permission from my parents, and knowing my sister was too proper for such a venture. After reading about the exploits of St. Francis in the church library, I had decided to build a cave of my own, away from argument and noise, and spent weeks dragging materials to the site. I usually

I COUNTED MY SOLITUDE   15

came after school to my hideaway, which I soon started to call a "hermit-age" in imitation of Francis, and stayed for hours, my mother too repelled by the dark forest to venture after me.

But this morning was special. I was intent on starting a novena, a nine-day prayer of petition that the priest had talked about during his homily, for my grandmother who had cancer.

I passed the ancient oak tree, gnarled bark and broad limbs, and turned left at the moss-covered boulder that marked the way. Around the next bend, tucked under a rock overhang, was my shelter, constructed of stone and covered with an old plastic tarp. Bending down, I crawled in. Sweeping leaves out with my hand I found the tin box of matches and lighted the votive candle, my hand shaking. Eventually I settled down, legs crossed, back straight, silently watching the flame flicker and glow, overwhelmingly happy. I counted my solitude like other girls collected shells or tiny porcelain figurines. No one invaded my thoughts, telling me what to believe or how to feel. I was safe, guided by a living presence that suffused me with tenderness.

I could be, just *be*.

On the walk back to the house, I wondered: Did my parents know why I clung to solitude? It wasn't my position to tell them and even if I had wanted to, I wouldn't have known what to say.

Yet the disparity between the secret worlds I inhabited and what I was allowed to speak took its toll. I was kicked out of Sunday school for asking questions about logical inconsistencies in the Baltimore Catechism. When someone was criticized on the basis of morality or social custom, I retreated to the public library to test the truth or falsehood of the claim. At night I prayed my thoughts into secrecy: *Dear God Please, don't let me talk in my sleep so my mother won't know what I am thinking.*

I grew sullen and secretly rebellious. I had mysterious fevers and suffered with colds, propped up with four pillows and Vicks VapoRub smeared over my chest. Even these maladies led me deeper into solitude, deeper into my nature.

Once, at five years old, I'd come down with a severe case of chicken pox and was on fire with a high fever. On the second or third day of being confined to bed, in the evening when the television was turned off and the house quiet, I was twisting around in my sheets unable to get comfortable. A faint breeze was rustling the curtains on the window next to my bed. Reaching for the glass rosary on the nightstand, I poked my head out of the covers. Soundlessly, an immense figure of light as tall as the ceiling appeared in the corner of my room. A glowing, pulsating vibration that was wise and calm and protective expanded in the air the way helium filled a birthday balloon. Robes shimmered blue and gold. Eyes, deep brown, looked into me with piercing gentleness. I was transfixed. Instantly a sweet feeling of comfort filled me, an electrical current humming at a precise rate.

The Special One spoke: *You cannot die. You have work to do. We will be with you.* I wonder if I heard these words as sounds, with my ears? Or were they inner words, transmitted silently? How long did the Special One stay with me? I still can feel the clock ticking, 2:15 a.m., 2:30 a.m., 3:05.

Lulled to sleep by the soothing vibration, hours later I woke, sunlight on my face. The Special One was gone. Yet, throughout my childhood and into my late twenties, whenever I was sad or lost, joyful or serene, the energy returned to remind me I was not alone.

I heard things no one said and saw things everyone hid. The Special One whispered through the veils: *Remember, Remember.*

THE VISITATION from the Special One heightened my sensitivity. I became more silent, an observer. Yelling, loud noises, punishment were unbearable. I sought refuge in books, at night reading under the covers by flashlight. Rising before dawn, I spent hours alone jumping rope or hanging out with my dog.

How tender is a child's spirit, living between worlds, not yet fully established in the earth realm, not yet fully torn from the divine heart!

My vulnerable status escalated when that same year, 1952, my father was hired to build a hospital for the Mexican government and our family moved from Long Island to Mexico City. Driving around the central zocolo, on our way to a tourist attraction at a local church, I couldn't take my eyes off vendors in tattered clothes pressing greasy bags of fried worms against our glass-protected faces. On street corners, women dressed in vibrant swirls of color picked lice out of their children's iridescent black hair. I caught glimpses of a beggar missing a leg holding a tin cup. Rail thin children, with no shoes and darkened by soot, plied unsuspecting tourists for money, crying, "*Dame un centavo!*" As my father turned a corner, extricating our car from the tangle of donkeys, automobiles, and buses clogging the roadway, my heart constricted in my chest as a businessman in a tan suit kicked a rag-covered body on the sidewalk. "Too much tequila," someone said.

Finally at our destination, I fled from the car. Clutching my mother's hand, I descended beneath the church to an underground crypt, over-whelmed by cloying moisture dripping off the walls. When my eyes ad-justed to the dark, I became paralyzed with fright. Cooped up in rows of glass cases were skeletons of priests dressed in black vestments, peering with their blotted out eyes on our sorry lot of tourists. Boney relics of the faithful lined up on shelves in liquid-filled jars and tiny golden boxes sent me bolting up the stairs into the sunlight.

Not long after, between my fifth and sixth birthdays, an awareness of our economic and social circumstances formed in my mind, and although my parents urged us to be model foreigners, the disparity between our lives and the majority of Mexicans affected me deeply. I felt ashamed for having an overabundance of food and nice dresses. I started to help our housekeepers, Marta and Silvia, who couldn't have been much older than teenagers, with their chores. I saw sadness in their eyes. Perhaps for this reason I was embarrassed to accept their kindness and refused to let them bathe or dress me.

Mexico introduced me to suffering. It was then that I began to recog-nize the bond between souls, how sorrow and love were shared equally in the spirit. I grew serious, troubled by the cruelty I witnessed in the streets and among my schoolmates. In a way, I became a critic of my parents' world, an outsider in my own family.

Portends of our Mexican adventure quickly became evident: my sister, Carol, contracted typhoid fever; Pop was plagued by nosebleeds and faint-ing spells; my parents narrowly escaped death, hit head-on by another car while negotiating a mountain pass. I became frighteningly sick with dysentery, losing weight precipitously and spending much of the next year under medical care.

* * *

Bᴀᴄᴋ in the States, we rented a house in the predominately Jewish com-munity of Long Beach, Long Island, where I attended first through fourth grade. I played dreidel with my friends, ate latkes and matzo ball soup, and took advantage of extra school holidays during Passover and the High Holy Days. While priests and rabbis may have fostered segregation, we kids simply lived and played together, moving seamlessly between cultures and religious practices.

Eventually, my parents saved enough to purchase land, and we moved further east on Long Island to Suffolk County. Old Barto Road, where my father built our home in the middle of forty acres, extended from Montauk Highway through the property of a mysterious neighbor and dead-ended in marshlands coming off Great South Bay. Separated from us by tracks of the Long Island Railroad was a burned-out house that reminded me of gloomy Miss Haversham from *Great Expectations* and raised the hair on my arms whenever I approached it. Deeper into the forest, headstones overgrown with poison ivy and thickets of weeds marked the site of a colonial family's cemetery.

When I wasn't at school or reading, I followed trails through the woods, crouching by the stream's edge for a glimpse of a doe's night eyes. Quivering lights across the water's eddies or maple leaves rustling in the morning's cool wind quieted me. Abandoning myself to nature, I found solace with my more-than-human kin. I felt cellular bonds with stately oaks and white tailed deer. I spent hours rambling through storied dwellings built of bark, limb, and leaf by burrowing critters—hedgehogs, possum, and beavers. When the wind blew northwest off the bay, the spicy scent of sassafras trees enticed me under their canopies. I loved those days, living not by the yardstick of this world, but in a dreamy, timeless domain.

Little by little, through my daily excursions into the woods, I fell in love with solitude, suddenly aware that it was my vocation and not merely an escape from pain.

Through this irresistible longing for communion, I discovered a living theology within the cellular and spiritual energies that made me, reminding me of our undivided origins in the mother womb of spirit. In the beginning of creation was not a punishing god or a painful exile, or even the word of god as it was written in the Gospel of John, but *intimacy*. This was not the genesis story I had been taught in Sunday school but something *wholly other*. Here began my search for the one reality at the heart of all religions.

A few weeks after my ninth birthday a quote by Albert Einstein in the *Sunday Herald Tribune* attracted my attention: "I am truly a 'lone traveller' and have never belonged to my country, my house, my friends, or even my immediate family with my whole heart; in the face of these ties I have never lost a sense of distance and need for solitude—feelings which increase with the years." I carried that column in my wallet until it shred from wear years later.

* *
*

WHEN I was not alone in my room or wandering the woods, my mother was nearby, often yelling, scaring me to death with her emotional intensity. And yet her spirituality helped shape me as well. An avid student of the psychic and spiritual, she accepted every faith and championed the latest social outcast: gays, artists, raunchy comedians, or the poor. She also disdained religious politics that crippled the whole person, the vow of celibacy an example of how out of touch The Church was with the human condition. "You can't put a lid on your emotions and not expect to explode one day!" she'd say. No doubt her parochial school experience (she was beaten with a ruler because she was left-handed) contributed to my mother's pledge never to send her children to Catholic school. Her early life was scarred, as well, by the divorce of her parents, unheard of for an Italian family in those days.

Her father's refusal to support the family left psychic wounds, which she worked out in the perfection of her children. Carol and I were taught to be independent and strong-minded; we had souls that needed tending, an obligation to something greater than childish concerns. The more rebellious daughter, I was the usual recipient of instruction in public rectitude. Once, when I was four, I forgot to answer the phone in the proper manner, "Who is calling, please?" Quickly reprimanded and sent to my room, I never made the mistake again.

In spite of my mother's upbringing or perhaps because of it, style was as important to her as good manners and a healthy dose of humor. Tall and slender with a movie star's face, her only physical flaw was her "baby" hair, which was infant fine and refused to grow below her ears. She carried herself with an imperial air and smoked with a cigarette holder like Bette Davis in a film noir. She washed laundry or swept floors dressed in a caftan, high-heel slippers, and one of her favorite turbans—a pink or green (she had several) confection of silver dollar–sized circles made of some type of gauzy material.

Pursuing her from room to room as she folded clothes or put on makeup, I plied her with questions. "Why do you know so much about God?" I listened with rapt attention to her stories about the White Light of the Holy Spirit or the apparition of her long-dead grandfather standing beside her bed. Never shy about her connection to the supernatural, she would ask the waitress (or grocery clerk or butcher) taking our order: "What's your sign, honey? You're an Aries? Oh, the best sign, mine too!" God was a good friend.

I don't know if her good friend approved of the stories she told about me as a difficult infant who cried too much. Sandwiched on the sofa between Aunt Linda and Uncle Tom one afternoon when I was about eight years old, I knew what was coming and shrank into the cushions. She was telling again how she broke my will and turned me from an unruly infant into an obedient daughter.

"One night," she said leaning forward, "when Bev was about three months old, her crying was driving me crazy. Determined to break her of the habit (*crying? hunger?*) I took the *Reader's Digest* off my nightstand, leaned over her crib, and hit her over and over, screaming, 'Go to sleep, Baby! GO TO SLEEP!'"

Thomas Merton once conjectured that his monastic bent was the result of a stern mother. I've wondered if the same were true in my case. Was my need for solitude survival or salvation? Many years later I will realize that silence was more than an escape from the quivering tenderness of childhood—it was beckoning me toward a limitless horizon, toward God.

*
* *

L IKE many first- and second-generation Italian-Americans, my parents wanted us to be assimilated, modern Americans. We routinely were cautioned about *gavone* who greased their hair and wore gold chains or belonged to the underworld and in every way gave the noble Italian culture a bad name. Our family was dignified and discreet. We scrubbed our almost-spotless house before the cleaning lady came so she would know we weren't slobs.

Saturday was cleaning day. Carol and I vacuumed and changed sheets while Pop tended his roses. As soon as Mom left for the grocery store, my sister and I would dash around looking for burns in the carpet caused by glowing embers falling from my father's pipe. We warned him when smoke was wafting out of the pocket of his sports jacket, and tried to shield him from the fit my mother would have if she were to see the burned rug. While we worked, Pop turned the stereo up to full volume, better so we should hear the popular Mario Lanza belt out Neapolitan tunes. (I still can't erase "O Sole Mio" and "Funiculì Funiculà" from my brain.) On our knees, scissors in hand, we cut carpet fibers from behind the couch and glued them over the singed offense.

My father was baptized Guglielmo Lanzetta; everyone called him Bill. The third son and first child born in the United States to Vincenzo and Maria, my father revered his parents. Arriving in Ellis Island in 1905 during the great wave of Italian immigration, Vincenzo worked as a stone-mason while Maria mothered thirteen infants, of whom only six survived into adulthood. My grandmother died before I was born and I only knew grandpa in a spare way because he spoke almost no English.

His parents' immigrant experience of hard work and personal sacrifice was ingrained in my father's personality. A lifelong champion of the underdog, Italian or Jew, Chinese or Irish, American Indian or African American, Pop had a motto: Do the right thing; all life deserves respect. I still can hear him rooting for Black leaders as we watched a newscast on the civil rights uprisings, saying, "Give 'em hell." Aside from these rare bursts of emotion, Pop was a quiet, thoughtful man, handsome in an understated way, who enjoyed reading the morning paper while dunking bread in coffee, and the occasional good round of golf.

Usually up before dawn, except on cleaning days, Pop and I would make toast and then head for the garden to prune trees or plant tomatoes. On occasion we would drive the thirty miles to the Shinnecock Indian reservation, where I learned that much of eastern Long Island had been the tribe's ancestral lands. A student of history, Pop wanted me to understand the injustices suffered by the Shinnecock nation during the white settlers' expansion into their territory. But it was Pop's reading of their creation story that I loved most: the goddess who descended from the sky was their mother; it was she who caused the land to form on the back of Great Turtle and filled the sky with birds, the bays with fish and mollusks.

Pop and I shared other adventures. A civil engineer, he taught me how to estimate material costs for bidding on construction contracts. Adept in calculating cubic yards of concrete and lineal board feet of two by fours, I accompanied him to job sites where he showed me off. I loved to wrap my arm around his sleeve as we walked to the beach or strolled the boardwalk. His sole desire, or so it seemed from my child perspective, was to make us happy. Perhaps it was his humor that won over my mother, the elegant and beautiful Evelyn Acampora, even after he presented her with a twenty-five cent cookbook on their first date.

Though spirituality was important to him, my father was no churchgoer. Yet the Catholic faith in which he was raised permeated his life in mystifying ways. Two stories he told still give me chills. In the first, Pop was seated in the back pew of St. Mary's of the Isle Church waiting for mass to start. All at once he had a vision of Jesus standing in front of the altar in long, flowing robes with one arm outstretched, pointing directly at him. Their eyes met. He never spoke in greater depth about this vision except to say that it made a lasting impression.

Many years later, when Pop was dying of cancer, he told me another story. He was a teenager rushing down the sidewalk, behind schedule in his job of distributing shopping leaflets. Pop remembered an old man wearing tattered clothes touching his shoulder and asking for help. My father told him he had no time to talk, but sixty years later, as we sat arm in arm, he wondered, "Bev, was that old man Jesus in disguise? Was he asking me for help, and I turned away?"

We had to drag Pop to church on Christmas Eve and Easter Sunday, yet he lived its true meaning: to be simple of purpose and pure of heart. His whole life was bent toward the good: family, work, integrity. Concerned for the disenfranchised and poor, Pop was uninterested in material goods for their own sake. It was always possible, he said, to achieve spiritual well-being and financial security without compromising one's principles. My father was a gentle person, who by his actions ushered love into our lives.

If I had followed the path of my ancestors and behaved as my parents wished, I would have turned into a good housewife and mother, polite and intelligent. Perhaps I would have had a late-life career. If the world's happiness were all I desired, I never would have left home in search of the divine realm. But I felt a different pull from the beginning.

* *
*

OF my four grandparents, I knew only my mother's mother well. Like a small, delicate bird with a broken wing, Nana, as we called her, came to live with us a few years after my sister, Carol, was born. I recall sitting on her lap, an embroidery hoop stretched over the blue-stenciled x's on a linen napkin. "Here's how you make the first stitch, up through the left corner of the x and down through the right. Good, *filia mia* (my daughter), you see how it goes?" I stroked her soft hand, rested my cheek on her ample bosom concealed behind a lace-trimmed buttoned-up blouse. I watched her make *cavatelli*. Laying a long white strip of cloth on the mahogany dining table, she sprinkled it with flour and rolled the sticky pasta dough into a thick sheet. "Pinch off a piece, dolly, press down and flick like this with the thumb. *Bene*. We let them dry and cook later."

I prayed to take away her sadness. Raised as a traditional woman, my grandmother's marriage had been arranged between the two families and blessed by the local priest. In her wedding picture she was radiant in a satin gown with a wreath of flowers in her hair, clasping a long veil. When my philandering grandfather divorced her, a light in her heart died.

Within a year of our moving to Old Barto Road, Nana was diagnosed with breast cancer. She was fifty-eight. The lively red and white bedroom we shared was turned into a grim hospital ward. I moved my books and pillows in with Carol. A tremendous sadness settled on me. I wanted to make amends for her sacrifice. At night I read books on cancer and vowed to find a cure. I contemplated and just as quickly abandoned the thought of becoming a nun. I didn't know why I was drawn to the idea. Perhaps a call was stirring.

Every Sunday, Nana took me to mass, dressed in hat and gloves. When it was time for communion, I lined up behind the other supplicants and waited to receive the body and blood, the papery wafer dissolving on my tongue, the droplets of wine burning my throat. Walking back to my seat, head bowed, thoughts evaporated in a timeless eddy until the aroma of incense mingled with my senses, and I was raised above myself heady and faint. Then, unbidden, the words came: *I want to know you. I want to be like you, God.*

When Nana was too weak to take me to church, I retreated to the secret altar I had constructed of round stones and pine cones. Kneeling on the moist, cold earth, I made the sign of the cross—Father, Son, and Holy Spirit—and breathed the luscious silence into my lungs. For a moment, I felt myself transported to a side chapel at Mary Immaculate, wafts of incense stinging my eyes and making me cough. The soulful Madonna looked down on me. She knew where I ached.

The worry brought me back to the present, to the melting snow wetting my knees. I placed my palms together and prayed: *Dear God Please don't let Nana suffer. Please don't let her suffer.*

Nine days later Nana died. My mother's anguished cry fell into my soul. I wasn't allowed to see my grandmother's body or attend her funeral. "You're too young," I was told. Ten years old, a new hole was punched into my heart.

THE NEXT WEEKEND, after my mother returned from the burial at Pine Lawn Cemetery, I asked her to take me to confession. She drove in silence to Mary Immaculate and once there, waited for me in the car.

I opened the door to the confessional booth and knelt, the musty order of incense and dank cold overwhelming.

"Forgive me, Father, for I have sinned."

"Yes, my child. What is your confession?"

"I haven't been to mass in nine months. My grandmother was dying."

"You haven't been to church in almost a year?" bellowed the shrouded figure on the other side of the wooden grate. "You will go to hell for this sin!"

"Forgive me, Father."

The penance (was it ten Hail Marys and twenty Our Fathers?) rolled out of his mouth into the dusty air and settled on my heart. I bolted from the confessional booth, hardly aware of my surroundings, and knelt at the front altar. Unwinding the rosary off my wrist, I gazed at the merciful statue of Mary and prayed with breathless haste, "Hail Mary, full of grace, blessed art thou amongst women, and blessed is the fruit of thy womb, Jesus." I barely got through the first stanza before I choked up with tears and, stuffing the rosary into my coat pocket, ran from the church to the car.

"What's wrong?" my mother asked.

"I'm never going to church again!"

"Why, what happened?"

"Do you know what that priest said? He said I'm going to hell because I didn't attend mass for nine months. That's not true! *I'm just a little kid!*"

It would be more than twenty years before I entered a church again. I knew that cruelty and punishment were against the Divine Mother's law. I didn't understand the betrayal. I was told to love, and love would be reciprocated. Why did they tell us to love when they had no love to give?

Is it any wonder there are so many people without a rudimentary understanding of the interior life, forced to flee their religious heritage in search of meaning and love? No doubt my defense of the defenseless took root here, not through my own will but through the One who gave me the courage to stand against falsehood. And not long after, I was illuminated by a thought: it was not religion that brought me to God, but solitude. The divine Presence came to me when I was alone, in the silence of my soul.

Yet I was grateful that my parents and grandmother wanted me to have a religious foundation, even if it led to rebellion and dissent. Years later, when I wound up at a Jesuit university, I was able to push beyond the superficial sermons and petty sins that occupied too much of religious life, into the deep current of wisdom that flowed through the history of Christian thought and by extension through much of Western civilization. Even as I left behind membership in the formal church, I would take refuge in the mystics who knew me better than any living person.

* *
*

M Y grandmother's death deepened my mother's unsteadiness. Generous and charming with others, she was often harshly critical and aloof with my sister and me. Slight offense rendered the perpetrator expendable, torn from her safe harbor like a wooden skiff shattered in a storm. Often the target of her explosive moods, I remember Carol, who was four years older, whispering to me from an adjoining bed, "Don't upset her. You know she's going to come in and beat you up."

Refusing to admit her mental anguish, Mom dismissed her moods as dramatic venting. "I'm an actress," she liked to say.

I began to run away from the agitation in the pit of my stomach, from the church's hypocrisy, the fear of my mother, and the pain I felt over my grandmother's death. To escape, I sewed and knitted or painted and wrote poems. Incisive and intense, I annoyed my family and schoolmates. When I called the girl next door and asked if she wanted to play, I heard her muffled plea to her mother, "Do I have to play with *her*?" Sometimes my mother wouldn't speak to me for a week, punishment for some infraction. I endured, but silently withdrew, choked with desolation.

Even at Southaven Elementary, events furthered my outsider status, segregating me from the majority of my classmates. A two-room school-house populated by blond-haired children of local farmers, I was the Italian girl not from these parts whose father must be in the mafia, kids whispered. My dear Pop would have laughed.

Our teacher, Mrs. P, not up to the rigors of long division and barely competent to teach grammar, left us to fend on our own. Perhaps to cover these inadequacies, she embellished her teaching style with references to opera. Shortly after my grandmother died, she declared Opera Week, requiring students to ask and answer every question in song. Even at that age, I was uninterested in the quaint for its own sake. I refused to sing. Unnerved by my silence, Mrs. P called in my parents for a conference, declaring that I was an introvert. Whatever that meant.

But friendly gestures disquieted me as well. Delbert, a nice-looking, gentle boy a grade older, had a bit of a crush on me and one day asked if I wanted to go to the movies. Tongue-tied, I stared stupidly. That night I wrote him a note saying we were far too immature to be going out, and I couldn't waste my time on a relationship since I had so many books to read! Whatever made me think this was a relationship or whether my mother put me up to the note, I don't recall. But I have a strong feeling I never revealed the invitation to her. The superior tone must have been my own.

WHEN IT WAS time for me to start junior high and Carol was an eleventh grader, my parents transferred us to better schools in Port Jefferson. By the first enrollment period I was placed in the honors program. Sired by genius parents working at Brookhaven National Laboratory, my classmates were years ahead of me. I became even more interiorized, consuming books like a person possessed in the hopes that reading would ward off the inevitable aloneness. My nervousness reached new peaks. I peeled the skin on my fingers down to the backside of my knuckles and laughed impolitely.

The fact that we lived over an hour round trip from school, and the bus schedule did not extend to extracurricular activities, meant my parents frequently had to take us in the morning and pick us up. As a result, my father eventually bought a used pink and white Pontiac for Carol to drive us to school. A hulk of a car, it handled the thirty miles with ease. Most afternoons Carol coaxed it under the Carvel sign, neon lights gleaming off the fins, to fill up on hot fudge sundaes on our way home—our secret ritual. Without Nana's home-cooked meals, we were starving. My mother was still figuring out how to navigate a kitchen, and there were only so many times a week that pasta e fagioli (pasta and beans) was tempting to us teenagers. I lingered over every spoonful of ice cream, cringing at the thought of my mother's rages that awaited at home.

In my sophomore year, the universe provided me with a quixotic savior. Mr. S was my irreverent, iconoclastic honors English teacher. He came to class dressed in a black turtleneck, bolo tie, and tattered sports jacket. He wore a goatee. He picked his ears with a pencil eraser while elaborating on obscure points in an e.e. cummings poem or infuriated us with his positions on the superiority of insects in the evolutionary scheme. Most students thought he was rude and crass. I loved him for putting truth above rules. Handing me a copy of Summerhill: A Radical Approach to Child Rearing, he encouraged questions and affirmed my need to find a college far away from my family. One Friday our assignment was to go home, lock ourselves in our rooms, and not come out until we had re-created ourselves.

He also told me I was good, that I had everything I needed inside, and challenged me to find the meaning of my life.

I wasn't interested in sports or clothes or the latest matinee idol. I wasn't a cheerleader or a popular girl. I resisted high school proms and teenage girls' infatuations. What I wanted to know, but didn't have the nerve to ask was, Is there a place for me to stand not sullied by falsehoods, a place that is steady and sure? *Why am I on earth?*

When I took my first breath, a spiritual formation process already was stamped into my soul. Did you, God, enter me then? Or did your Spirit flow out of me?

It would not matter how lost I became or how many mistakes I made. I was drawn to your power, even as I would sink further into lowliness.

Around this same time, I discovered the power of literature to shape my moral universe. Working my way through Mr. S's reading list, I spent whole weekends and every school night with books piled next to me. Among the great novelists, W. Somerset Maugham, Fyodor Dostoyevsky, and Hermann Hesse exposed me to a search for self-knowledge and to an emotional depth that saved me from the banality of high school. I would later associate my desire to be a writer with this period in my life, when language was used to illuminate the tragedy and grandeur of the human condition. "In each of us spirit has become form," Hesse wrote, "in each of us the created being suffers, in each of us a redeemer is crucified.[1]"

By spring, I had a boyfriend, another small saving grace. Since he was going away to college in the fall and I was only fifteen, my parents' logic was "What would he see in Bev?" He picked me up in his blue sports car and had an aristocratic-sounding English name, complete with roman numerals at the end. Everyone called him Bert.

We became fast friends. Best of all, he made me laugh. He brought me gifts: a book of John Donne poetry, a wool beret. We took the train to Manhattan, dined on coq au vin at a fancy French restaurant, pretended I was eighteen, and ordered wine. We roamed the alleys of Chinatown, Little Italy, and Soho, attended the Broadway show about Sir Thomas More, *A Man for all Seasons.* He brought me an article in *Time* magazine about a college I will call Kresher, which had a program for early entrants, and encouraged me to apply. He was ballast against the harshness of my mother and the silence of a father afraid of his wife. I filled out the college paperwork, gathered together transcripts, test scores, and application essay, and sealed the mailer.

I needed to get away from home. *Dear God Please let me have a different life.*

* 2 *

Disgrace

REDEMPTION AND REPRIEVE arrived in a large white envelope. I was accepted to Kresher College as an early entrant after my sophomore year, at age fifteen. I believe my parents would have come to their senses and prevented me from going more than a thousand miles away from home if it hadn't seemed like such an honor. My first night in the dorm, I had a faint longing to rub my puppy's head and run my fingers through her thick fur. Other than that, I feared no loneliness.

The 1960s were in full force on campus. Students tumbled whole sacks of marijuana in the laundry room dryers; blues musicians came to campus with their sultry guitars; Bob Dylan's old-man voice scratched lyrics out of vinyl; and free love was the rage. Before long I joined friends to wander the rocky banks of the Mississippi River (careful not to step on rattlesnakes), hitchhiked around Illinois farm country, rode Amtrak into Chicago to attend a Simon and Garfunkel concert at Orchestra Hall, hung out with faux beatniks and wannabes, and listened to girls in my dorm discussing sex. I knew I had feelings, but I couldn't connect with them very well. Mostly still mute, I reveled in the freedom to make my own decisions. But I also was a ship unmoored from harbor, unguided in the tumult of the times. Little did anyone suspect that before another

September rolled around, I would be called home in disgrace.

My roommate was an offbeat slip of a girl who wore white lipstick and ironed her hair flat. Three years older than me, Charlotte had spent most of her teenage years in foster care. Black tights and loose smocks hung in her wardrobe. These, along with worn jeans and leather lace-up boots, were her uniform. My closet was stuffed with cotton dresses, button-down blouses, circle skirts, fluffy sweaters, stockings and garter belts, and the occasional pair of tights. I didn't wear sneakers.

It didn't take long for me to transform my dress habits and along with them my sense of right and wrong.

Boys were the main topic of conversation among my older and more knowledgeable dorm mates. I was unsure how to handle their excessive interest in the opposite sex, or even if I understood what being sexually active meant. My experience of males was limited to the nightly kiss or to furtive touches in movie theatres and cars. Before the winter was over, I convinced myself I had fallen in love, or at least as much in love as a teenager could be. Antons, a senior, was brilliant and witty, and we soon became inseparable. Since everyone who knew anything was seeing a doctor in Chicago for oral contraceptives, I went along, not knowing if I wanted to be one of "those girls."

On the basis of a vague notion that I intended a future in international affairs, I declared language as my major and enrolled in Spanish Literature. Señor Karkowsky, as he preferred to be called, invariably arrived for class in a stained sweater-vest, his bulbous nose swollen from too much drink, and began to mangle the melodic timbre of Unamuno or Cervantes while scratching conjugations on the board. He gave grades based on chest size—which in retrospect makes me wonder what he saw in me—and placing an age-spotted hand on my knee, assured me that under certain circumstances I surely would pass his course. His disturbing advances raised bile in my throat and a few months into the semester I not only dropped out of Spanish, but also wrote off my future career as a linguist.

I mention this minor event as a cautionary tale about how easily the tender aspirations of youth can be crushed by the sordid advances of the less than noble among us.

MY SIXTEENTH BIRTHDAY, I hunkered in a floppy chair in the student lounge waiting for a call from my parents, which never came. Too shy or choked up to tell my new friends that I'd like to celebrate, I spent the rest of the day alone wandering around campus and reading. Even now, I can taste the low spirits that gripped me once I realized my parents were not going to phone.

Little more than a month later I stumbled into the student lounge, hair tousled and eyes swollen, to grab some crackers, surprised by the number of people standing around the television set. Joining them, I was transfixed by the news that President Kennedy had been shot in Dallas, my chest seized by a dull, persistent pain. None of us knew what to say. Images of Jackie Kennedy, her tidy suit splayed with blood, and of the President slumping over in the backseat of his limousine played over and again on the gritty black and white screen. As the newscaster groped for words to explain the unfolding tragedy, not yet declared an assassination, the camera panned the horrified faces of onlookers and the grim determination of the Secret Service men.

I can still recall the November light coming in the windows, the green plaid couch near where I was standing, and the rangy black table holding the small TV. Everyone spoke in hushed tones, and I wondered if anyone else's heart was torn like mine.

It has been said that large historical events affect the soul, changing the orientation of a people or society. This surely was true in my case. The assassination of President Kennedy fueled a growing disaffection with what I perceived as moral hypocrisy and heightened my distrust of convention. This violent rend in the social fabric of America during my first semester away from home, when I already felt abandoned by family, magnified my outsider status and deepened my resolve to forge my own way.

Without guidance in tempering my choices, feelings of betrayal intensified the assertion of my own desire. I think now that every college should provide spiritual guidance for the sole purpose of tending to the development of students' souls. Even though I prayed to God, I doubted its efficacy and began to follow my own will, believing that was sufficient to direct my future.

Through all this, I still wanted to be a good daughter, to be faithful to my family. Yet I knew that in some fundamental way I was unfit for the task. By asking to leave home to attend Kresher, I had transgressed against an unspoken rule to never voice dissent, even though my parents allowed me to go. Without realizing it, I was being forced to develop fortitude, fortitude that would be my anchor in the years to come.

*　*　*

I LASTED at Kresher for one year. I wrote my parents that I was not coming home for the summer; that I had transferred to the University of Wisconsin in Madison. Furious at my independence, my mother stopped sending living expenses. Waiting for summer session to begin, when I would have a dorm room and a paid assistantship in the Department of Botany, I survived at the YWCA on saltines and peanut butter. What I didn't tell my parents was my reason for moving. I wanted to be with my boyfriend, Antons, as he entered graduate school. I registered at the dorm, but many nights I stayed at his apartment above a noisy pizza parlor.

Somehow my secret was discovered, though till this day I don't know how or by whom. My mother demanded that I come home. On a hot and humid August day I stepped off the plane at LaGuardia Airport, wearing a loose blue muumuu dress and sandals, to confront my parents and sister.

"What kind of outfit is that?" my mother seethed. "Don't you wear a girdle anymore? You look like a slut."

The ride home on the Long Island Expressway was tense. We were barely inside the house before my mother began her interrogation.

"Who are you sleeping with? How old is he? How many times did you sleep with him? Are you pregnant?"

"No! I'm on the pill."

She screamed at me and I yelled back. Pop hid behind Newsweek. I was given an ultimatum.

"He's twenty-one and you're underage. I'll report him to the police," my mother threatened. "You can get married, or you can leave college and go to Europe with me."

In an era when marriage was the usual course demanded of pregnant teenagers, my mother's insistence that I marry when I wasn't pregnant was a vindictive act. And her enticement to travel was a ploy—my parents didn't have the funds for such a trip. Every fiber within me was in revolt; to concede to her demand was to lose my own integrity.

Yet how passive I was! I didn't want to cross her. For the rest of the day and into the next, she assailed me with an incessant barrage of questions. Worn down and cowed by fear, I countered with my own pathetic ultimatum, "I'm not going to get married until I am seventeen years old," which was only a few months away.

My mother dug into her closet and collected my baby book and pictures. Throwing them at me, she screamed, "I don't want these in my sight anymore!"

Bending down, knees weak, I listlessly gathered these childhood memories into my lap. Ripped apart by my mother's anger and my father's silence, I lacked words to express the tumult of emotions drowning my voice or the flush of thoughts invading my mind: the innocence of my relationship with Antons; college, an escape from my mother's suffocating criticism; I can't go to Europe with her, it will ruin me—I will never find my true way; I won't give up my education; there is NO REASON for making these demands.

Suddenly, a fiery resistance exploded from my gut. Dropping the photos, I rushed out of the house and into the woods. Circling my arms around my favorite maple tree, pressing my chest against its sturdy bark, claiming its warmth, I sobbed, "Why? Why, don't they love me?" Have I done something so wrong? *Dear God Please show me what to do.*

My body began to shiver. Rising up from the soles of my feet and out the palms of my hands was the pulse of the earth calling me home. Yet I wouldn't understand until it was too late that the forests and salty marshes of Great South Bay had been my teacher, nurturing the formation of my moral universe. When I removed my feet from the land before my inner development was complete, I lost my center. Making my way back to the house, I knew I would never walk in my woods again.

If I hadn't been so young, I would have asked my mother why she was making these ultimatums, why she did not offer guidance or discuss how to handle sexuality with her teenage daughter. Or perhaps I would have laughed and walked out, to do as I pleased. But my mother's angry demand, to which my father's silence acquiesced, struck a forceful blow. I took a stand, albeit an impetuous, raw stand, to choose marriage over emotional abuse, without even a thought of a third way. But I made my choice nonetheless and I was forced to stand by it. My teenage mind believed no one had the right to control my destiny. No one, not even God could do that, and God was silent that night.

* * *

CAST out, but never really let go, I was surprised when my sister Carol asked me to be her maid of honor a few months later. I loved my sister, but I didn't want to return home. Yet I was incapable of saying no. The pain I felt over no longer having a family who cared about me turned into buried grief. Shaken, I flew back for the wedding. At the reception, Uncle Tom, my mother's brother, pulled me onto the dance floor and asked me if I were pregnant.

"No."

Recently, my brother-in-law told me that my father wanted Carol's wedding to be the most beautiful and lavish of all weddings. He poured money into the choice of location and the extravagance of food and dresses. Looking through their wedding album, I was drawn to a picture of my mother and father, arm in arm. Mom is wearing a floor-length white satin skirt and black jacket with her hair swept up in a fake chignon on top of her head. Pop is in a tuxedo and bow tie, his hair slicked back, with a joyous smile on his face. In the next picture, Carol, radiant in her elegant gown, cuts the wedding cake. All my cousins and aunts and uncles are gathered together. I alone am the disgrace.

Years later, when I reconnected with a cousin, he mentioned in a casual conversation how surprised he was that I was such a together, competent person. From his father's description of me as "crazy," he expected to meet someone who would have confirmed the stories my mother told all her relatives and friends about her impetuous, strong-willed daughter who, against her wishes, insisted on getting married.

Antons never opposed marriage, claiming if he were going to marry anyone it would be me. New Year's Day, 1965, we wed at City Hall in front of a justice of the peace and quickly jumped into our Volkswagen bug for the drive back to our apartment in Madison. My mother demanded proof of our marriage before she would release the one thousand dollar bond my parents had bought for me when I was an infant. Soon after the wedding I received weekly letters from her, written in longhand on yellow lined legal pads. The tone varied from week to week, but my mother's central message remained the same: *You are a selfish person who doesn't know what love is and never will. You are without remorse and your marriage is a sham.*

The trauma carved an indelible groove in my heart, from which I constantly averted my face. What I perceived as my mother's callousness perpetuated a self-erasure that would shadow me for years. In having my life direction invaded against my will and injured by someone I trusted to care for me, I became homeless in my own body. But lacking understanding of the great harm that befalls the person whose autonomy is assaulted, I didn't have a conceptual framework to explain how much my soul suffered.

It would take more than twenty years before I made a direct association between being female and the fateful choices made on the stifling August day I was forced into a marriage. If I had been my parents' son instead of their daughter, my supposed transgression would have been celebrated as conquest, virility. Instead, we played out in our middle-class kitchen the theatrics of virginity, reinforcing the ancient code that a woman's body belonged to someone else. Perhaps our drama was nothing more than a family psychosis, where my mother's illusion of purity found the perfect foil in me. But I cannot deny the fierce loyalty I now have to all women who are ostracized, humiliated, branded, tortured, or killed for their right to choose freedom of self.

Yet I am certain that the formation of what would become a significant part of my life's work was established during these dark days of grief and despair. Without conscious awareness, I stood on the side of freedom of conscience and dignity of personhood that true authority, of parent or clergy or nation, was dependent on the renunciation of power. Harsh behavior, coercive demand, and cruel insult simply were pitiful refusals to love and to be loving.

Although I must have understood the violation I had been subjected to, I also carried guilt, shame, and humiliation. I had "ruined" my life, a life that could have been so neat, orderly, and consistent, like my sister's. I had created, as my mother used to say, a "schmear."[1]

* * *

M Y mother and I never spoke about these events until she was in her eighties and growing more infirm. Over the years she had intimated that she was less than virginal when she married Pop, and I couldn't understand what had prompted her impetuous, cruel ultimatum when I was so young. On one of my visits after my mother was widowed, we were alone eating chocolate cake at the dining table.

"Why didn't you come home again for Christmas after you left for college?" she asked. "Pop and I missed seeing you and the kids during the holidays."

"Mom, getting married as a teenager had devastating consequences for me. I felt cast out from the family. I had no idea that it mattered to you and Pop because you never said anything or encouraged us to visit at Christmas."

"Really?"

"Yeah. What I don't understand is why did you insist I get married?

Why didn't you discuss sexuality with me or guide me to alternatives? Why did you alter the course of my life?"

"Because I had an image of my pure, untouched girls and I wanted everything to be perfect."

We were so silent I could hear the clock ticking in my mother's bedroom. Minutes passed. Carol always said that our mother lived in a fantasy world, but until that day I never truly understood.

"What else is there to say after you say you're sorry?" my mother added in a derisive voice.

RECENTLY, I WAS relating this story to a friend who wanted to know why I hadn't given up on my mother, why I had worked so hard to maintain a relationship. "Weren't you bitter?" she asked.

I thought about her questions for some time. My answer surprised me. I said I was more crushed and pained than angry. But deep down, the real reason was that I wanted to be a person of love. If I couldn't love my mother and open my heart to her through all this, I would never be true to myself.

Love was the highest teaching. Perhaps even on her deathbed, my mother didn't realize how much I loved her or she, me. But months after she passed away she appeared to me in a dream, placing her face next to mine. "I'm sorry, Bev," she said. "I'm so sorry."

3

Hidden Hand of Fate

A TURNING POINT IN LIFE not infrequently occurs through choices we will live to regret, but which spirit uses to spur growth of the soul. What we're not told is that too often we choose wrongly, giving our hearts away to the wrong people, never realizing that love and integrity are inseparable. But, oh the young do not know this! Their hearts, bursting with affection, squander love, never realizing that it, of all things, cannot be bartered or sold.

By our second anniversary, Antons and I were settled in a house that was biking distance to campus. Occupied by my senior project in Botany, I painstakingly gathered Dutchman's breeches (*Dicentra cucullaria*), Wild columbine (*Aquilegia canadensis*), and other native Wisconsin plants, which I pressed dry and added to the Herbarium collection. Less adept in my other courses, I'd set a record for breaking the most glassware in Organic Chemistry. Calculus was a jumble of symbols and numbers, taught by an incoherent graduate student strung out on equations. The Humanities were no easier. I barely squeezed out a C in creative writing, incapable of crunching a meager four sentences onto a page. Daily I thought about dropping out as my self-esteem plummeted.

Despite these inadequacies, I secured a paid assistantship in the

Department of Genetics, working the 5 a.m. to noon shift. I was the only woman and only undergraduate in the lab, and my male colleagues were less than welcoming. Many mornings I unlocked my research notebook from its cabinet, ready to record the overnight results, only to discover my experiments had been unplugged and ruined by an anonymous graduate student. Even the fellow assigned to sterilize glassware for the lab refused to clean my equipment because I was a "girl and should do it myself."

I graduated January 1967, but didn't attend the ceremony. My parents never asked to come. Recently nineteen, I was old enough to drink the 3 percent beer served in Der Rathskeller, but not sufficiently interested to try. I had won a prestigious job in the new Electron Microscopy Department, which would help Antons complete his doctoral studies and support our growing expenses. I still didn't know how to drive.

Looking back, I have little recollection of how I got through those years, how I finished my Bachelor's degree, or what kinds of things went on in my heart and mind. I remember it all as a kind of deep sleep in which sparks of light appeared, only to be extinguished by greater darkness. I was dormant, like a tulip bulb in winter. I no longer could depend on Dear God to light the night lamp of my stunned heart with hope.

* * *

MARRIED life was difficult. I had no idea how to be a girlfriend, let alone a wife. I mimicked the things women did—shopping, cooking, laundry, mending—but I didn't know why I was doing them. I spent an inordinate amount of time creaming butter and rolling dough. I didn't know how to gauge boundaries with Antons. What was appropriate behavior? Did women ask for what they needed? I doubt he was aware. When he wasn't studying, he spent three or four hours a day practicing Mozart or Chopin on the grand piano he had moved from his parents' home. I was desperate for affection, viscerally pained over the deficits in my marriage.

Traumatized, I lived on the surface. It was too painful to look deeply at my relationship or myself. I didn't express my feelings or ask for help. I developed various maladies; doctors worried, plying me with antibiotics for recurring bouts of strep throat, sinus infection, and bronchitis. Looking back, illness was my body's way of shouting, "Speak truth, listen to your feelings, heal your heart!" No one suggested counseling as a way to help me unravel the turmoil I experienced daily. Unskilled in sorting through heartbreak and psychological stress, and struggling with my role as a married teenager, I was convinced that my only option was to leave.

Perhaps the drama was a convenient foil. One afternoon, on my way home from the lab, I heard a voice clearly ask, "*Is this all there is to life?*" I hadn't been able to expel the question from my thoughts. It struck a deep anguish, a query that I unconsciously must have been asking myself for years: What is the purpose of my life? Why am I on earth?

The guilt I felt over my confused emotions became the catalyst for escape. Another running away, I had invested no moral responsibility in my choices, a condition that would persist for years. I resigned my job, sold or gave away most of my possessions, and left Madison. I was terrified, but made no promise to Antons that I would come back. I wrote to my parents that the path I now had chosen was more radical than anything I'd done before. I had to find out: who am I?

I was estranged from family and functioning with a teenager's mind when a friend from Kresher College, Kevin, invited me to Chicago. I took the next bus south, my meager possessions in a suitcase. Once again, I hoisted myself from trouble to follow the unbidden call. No one told me to believe, no one told me I had to leave; it all came from the mysterious whirlwind of light twisting inside me, until I gave up and gave in: I will find You.

If only I had known then that the divine call is person-to-person, reserved for one's self, alone. It was a lesson that would be branded into me over and again. Truth cannot be bartered. It must be taken fully, unconditionally. To do otherwise is to stumble through life with the false belief that there is nothing Real against which your soul is measured. I can attest that if once you have been touched by the hidden hand of fate and still persist in thinking you can gamble on life in the usual, undisciplined way, it will haunt you. Forever.

* *
* *

KEVIN and I settled into an easy pattern of adventure, touring the country in his blue Chevy van. We survived off meager savings, which in 1967 wasn't difficult. Milk was 33 cents a gallon, gas during the frequent price wars could be as low as 19 cents a gallon, and movie tickets were $1.25. We went to concerts by BB King in Chicago, Jim Morrison and the Doors in a small Manhattan club. Wading along the shore of the Maine coast, we dug longneck clams out of tidal mudflats and cooked them for dinner.

The atmosphere in the country was tense. Race riots erupted in Detroit over police brutality against African Americans; 7,000 National Guard troops were called to quell the violence. Almost half a million military personnel were in Vietnam, and Martin Luther King, Jr. supported the anti-war movement on moral grounds. Students for a Democratic Society (SDS) ignited college campuses with protest, and in June 10,000 students demanded that Secretary of Defense McNamara provide a program of alternative service for those opposed to war.

I aroused suspicion—red bandanna tied around my forehead, pierced ears, and flowered skirt—especially in the South. In an Alabama campground, cooking crabs on a two-burner propane stove, the dour face of a police officer standing at the open van door startled us. Shining a flashlight in my face, he asked, "What are you doing out here in the sticks? Are you a runaway?" The light glinted off his holstered revolver. Hoping to avert a standoff, we invited him to share dinner with us, handing him a crab plate.

Increasingly conflicted about leaving Antons, I was wracked with guilt. I stuffed quarters into a pay phone and spoke to Mr. S, my beloved high school English teacher, who suggested that if my mother had not forced a marriage I probably would be a graduate student now.

My mind chatter was constant. I thought about war, nonviolence. Was passive resistance different from my inability to take a personal stand? I wondered if victims of racial segregation felt the way I did: numb, unable to make changes. Accepting rejection as the way things are. Not challenging injustice. Is this what happened to the abused soul?

In the middle of the night, unable to sleep, I prayed: *Please give me courage. Help me to find my way.*

College friends invited us to spend a week at their Missouri farm. I was treated as an outsider. I didn't like the taste of wine, which signaled that I was "no fun." Not up on the latest bands or philosophical trends, I was left out of the conversation. The subject that interested me—what are we doing here on this earth?—had no traction. I resisted feigned sophistication. Desperate to escape the table one evening after dinner, I offered to wash dishes, overhearing whispered conversation.

"Beverly is so naïve, Kevin! What are you doing together?"

"I like her, she's sweet."

"She's not just sweet, *she's different.*"

"Yeah, you're probably right. We won't be together for long."

Our relationship was doomed, and I was paralyzed to do anything about it. Unable to combat another loss, rejection compelled me in ways I seemingly could not control.

*
* *

W E drove west across the Great Plains, Rockies, and into Arizona. The grandeur of the landscape loosened a knot in my soul. I was in love with the jagged mountains, purple and orange sunsets, and giant saguaro cactus of the Sonoran desert. In January, we crossed the lower pass of the Sierra Nevada range into Sequoia National Park. Laden with snow, magnificent redwoods soaring 250 feet (and more than 2,000 years old) reminded me of the wise beings I saw in dreams.

Early February 1968, we arrived in San Francisco, invited to stay in Haight-Ashbury at the apartment of Charlotte, my former Shimer College roommate. A worn-out neighborhood, faded colors of once-stately Victorian row houses were barely visible beneath the gray soot. The Summer of Love, when an estimated 100,000 young people converged here, was only months old. Guys in ponytails, beards, and grimy plaid shirts stood in groups talking to their ladies. Distracted by a toddler's cry, a mother bent down, wiped a nose, and offered a cracker. The smell of marijuana wafted off the pavement. Down an alley, a homeless man lay on a pile of newspapers.

Swapping stories of our adventures since Charlotte and I last met, we piled into the van to attend an art fair in Golden Gate Park. Hippies were playing guitars, throwing Frisbees, smoking dope, and hanging out with their kids. I didn't know what motivated the Free Love movement, but a palpable energy disrupted the status quo, the so-called "sexual revolution" as much about exposing the racist, sexist, anti-gay agenda as it was about the relaxation of social mores.

What stands out about the 1960s from my current vantage point is that it was a time of civil unrest that ushered in a new type of planetary consciousness, one in which individual actors claimed the right to challenge a wide range of social ills, while simultaneously rejecting the personal morality that had guided our parents' and grandparents' generations. This freedom from social constraint came at a price, swept up as many of us were by the ethos of a social movement for which we were neither emotionally nor spiritually prepared.

Yet the 1960s were significant for another reason: a revolution was taking place within religious communities that would lead to radical changes in centuries-old practices and behaviors. In addition, a rush of gurus, lamas, and roshis descended on the American mainstream, converting celebrities and ordinary folk to the virtues of yoga, Zen, and other meditation practices. Mired as I was in a sea of confusion and doubt, I was unaware of these new voices, or that my future doctoral mentor was attending the Second Vatican Council (1962–65) in Rome, helping to establish a commitment to interfaith dialogue that would become central to my life's work.

For the most part I remained on the fringes of the foment, in a few years to become a mother occupied with changing diapers while my contemporaries were burning bras and protesting war on college campuses.

* * *

On a whim, Kevin and I left San Francisco in March for Mexico, stopping in San Blas, a fishing village on the Pacific about 275 kilometers south of Mazatlan. We parked the van on a deserted beach near a straw-thatched hut that had coconuts and grilled fish for sale. The sand was fine and white, the sea pure blue, empty of tourists or hotels. Juan Ramón, the proprietor, invited us to set up our tent under his awning, regaling us with wild tales and sharing his tequila bottle with Kevin. The warm sea breezes were healing, even though my extremities were covered with countless bites from nasty no-see-ums. Before dawn, fishermen dotted the shore with lines or pushed wooden boats out to sea, returning hours later with the day's catch, which they grilled over wood fires and sold on the beach.

During the weekend the roar of a silver and red homemade racecar awakened us. Curious, we were introduced by Juan Ramón to Alejandro, his thin, suave amigo from Mexico City. Before long we were sharing fish, rice, beans, tortillas, and Alejandro's ensalada muerte, a concoction of lettuce, cabbage, tomatoes, and cilantro drenched with dressing and then allowed to wilt.

Alejandro invited us to his home in Mexico City, where his aging mother plied me with more food than I could eat in a month. Jefa (chief), as her children called her, was a Michoacán Indian with a dignified face and bright blue eyes. Leading me by the hand into the kitchen, she taught me how to make refried beans, a recipe I still use today. A framed photo of John F. Kennedy shared a prominent place on her altar, next to a statue of the Virgin of Guadalupe and an icon of the Pope. With sadness she pointed to Kennedy's picture, "`el era un buen hombre." Then she made a prophecy about Robert Kennedy: "lo asesinarán también." He, too, will be assassinated. While Kevin and Alejandro sparred about sports, she whispered, "Ke-veen no es bueno para ti."

Kevin is not good for you.

* * *

O UT of money, we'd sent in applications for teaching positions, and were finally hired as first-grade teachers at a remote Reservation school in Northern California. While driving to the border and tuned to an American radio station, we heard the frantic newscaster recounting the scene outside the Lorraine Motel, where Martin Luther King, Jr. had been gunned down in Memphis. "His dream of a nation more concerned with racial segregation and poverty than with war," the announcer said, "is stillborn." I was sick with outrage and grief. *Jefa's* prediction came true as well. Two months later, after winning the California primary election for President, Robert Kennedy was assassinated while walking through the kitchen of the Ambassador Hotel in Los Angeles. These events, along with the assassination of President Kennedy five years earlier, defined the fate of our generation, injuring our collective heart.

As we followed the curve of the highway deeper into US territory, an impulse was taking shape in me. I had to consider what made for brutality and hatred and greed. I had to find a way out of the collective illusion. I knew that neither social rules nor religious ethics were enough to stem the tide of racism and other forms of gratuitous violence. What was needed was something deeper and universal, a perspective rooted in a sacred attitude toward life. Staring out the window at the cloud-studded sky, I felt an aliveness of presence, as if the shimmering soul of humanity was expectant, waiting to be awakened.

A few days later, inland from the Northern California coastal town of Eureka on Highway 299, we drove for fifty miles without seeing a sign of commerce into the Trinity Wilderness. Endless stands of Douglas fir were bursting with energy, vibrant against the cobalt-blue sky. The old-growth forest awed me.

Logging trucks slowly threaded their way along the steep embankments. Strapped to trailers with thick steel chain, six-foot diameter fir trees were stacked precariously on top of each other. Whole hillsides suffered scars. Red dirt roads roughly cut into the forest marred the land-scape, lofty trees felled in their prime. The best specimens were carted off to mills on the coast and shipped to Japan, while saplings and imperfect limbs rotted in place, charred from recent fires.

Turning north, we followed the Trinity River along Highway 96 twelve miles to the village of Hupa, and our jobs at Hupa Valley Elementary. A designated Wild River, the Trinity was so pure and clear, schools of salmon could be seen swimming upstream. I loved that river. When the Army Corps of Engineers considered a plan to damn the Hupa Valley and make the river run backward, I wept. Thankfully, it never happened.

THIS WAS MY first experience living among Indian people, and I was welcomed into their homes with warmth and generosity. I listened with sadness, and anger, to stories of parents and grandparents forced to attend boarding schools away from the tribe, beaten for speaking their native language. "We're just 'dumb Indians' to them," one parent said. "White people who have no understanding of our culture or the challenges we face run the district and just figure if our kid can't read, it's not the school's fault." Before long, my desk was brimming with apples, cookies, and homemade brownies pulled from lunchboxes or gym bags.

I asked an elder everyone called Grandma Netta to teach me how to weave traditional baskets, which required a year of gathering native plants. "Every spring," she instructed, "when the Trinity floods its banks and then recedes, I gather willow roots for the weft." Used for ceremonial purposes and for cooking, basketry was a sacred art tied to the rising of the waters in spring, and summer lightning strikes in the alpine meadows. I was painstakingly slow but Netta was proud of my finished basket woven in contrasting colors of black maidenhair fern stems against silvery white bear grass.

Perhaps it was Netta and the Hupa people, or the wild landscape teeming with life, which gained entrance to my still-shattered heart. Sitting by the Trinity, feet dipped in its rushing waters, watching pink-tinted waves of salmon or osprey hovering, then diving straight down into the river, I was healing the pain. The earth gripped me with motherliness, as if it knew my loss. It wove me into its mysterious affinity; to the tender light of belonging I had felt in the woods near my childhood home.

Attuned to the songs of wind and bird and river, I discovered the pure language of prayer. While I didn't formally know how to meditate, I experimented with the use of breath to learn the nature of my spirit.

The power of the natural world was transforming my consciousness as the Creator took a little medicine from each plant and used it to instruct my soul.

Sometimes, even, when the air was still I heard Dear God whispering: *Go to the place where everything is undone. Let me pour in.*

Now TWENTY-ONE, my school contract and Kevin's were renewed, this time to teach at the two-room schoolhouse in Orleans, an area so isolated that food and construction materials were floated up the Klamath River in barges. Instead, we decided to return to Mexico, having saved half our joint income, six thousand dollars.

* 4 *

Freedom from the Known

I WAS RUMMAGING THROUGH the titles at a San Diego bookstore, attracted to a thin, unassuming book in the religion section. *Freedom from the Known* displayed a photo of J. Krishnamurti on a black and gray cover. Turning over to the jacket back, I was intrigued by the promise that Krishnamurti showed how to free oneself from the "tyranny of the expected." I purchased the slim volume. The first pages read as if Krishnamurti saw inside my soul and knew my pain: "For centuries we have been spoon-fed by our teachers, by our authorities, by our books, our saints.... We are second-hand people."[1]

It was clear that Krishnamurti had no patience for intellectual exercise. His wisdom, born from practice, from intimate knowledge of what he taught, exhorted me to trust that I, and I alone, could find a way out of the veils of illusion that cloaked everything like dense fog. Viscerally, I *felt* and *knew* what he said was true, but I had no idea how to get there. My underlined sentences and marginal notes began to crowd the text. I read and reread passages, as if by burning my energy into the page I could transfer his self-realization to my consciousness by force. "To be alone you must die to the past.... The man who is completely alone in this way is innocent and it is this innocency that frees the mind from sorrow."[2] I clung to the edge of a precipice just a hair's breadth from illumination, but that hair's breadth was an infinite chasm of unknowing away.

Before crossing the border into Mexico, Kevin stopped at a roadside gas station/restaurant-bar to fuel the van, while I went inside to get change for the phone. Entering the dark, smoke-filled bar, I was gripped by the usual knot in my stomach. Five or so men were drinking beer or swilling down whiskey. A few others were playing pool, cigarettes dangling from their mouths. Timidly, I asked the bartender if he could make change for five dollars. His mouth said yes, but his eyes registered lust. Kevin was outside in the van, but the men in here didn't know that. I was being purposely intimidated. But in tiny, imperceptible increments I was dismantling my fear. After a few whistles and lewd remarks, I noted heat radiating out from my solar plexus. Like a bubble bursting open, my instincts were attuned as never before as they registered that I, too, had power. Glaring at him from under my cap, I snatched the change and slammed the door.

On reflection, a good portion of my twenties involved mucking around in male-female inequality, trying it on for size, and feeling in my bones that it was not for me. I had to play out the obedient girlfriend, quiet helpmate, slightly less intelligent thinker or artist or writer, and swallow my power and wisdom. Unable to break out of a kind of passivity I simply assumed was my lot, I retreated into self-effacement and self-blame so often that "sorry" was my normal pattern of speech.

Still, I was the one who choked down my anger when men patronized me. I was the one who shredded my emotions until I was mute. I alone accepted my place as lesser.

Who can say how my destiny and those of my future children would have been different had I stood up for myself then? At the time I didn't know how to break through the unsaying that silenced my grandmother and generations of women before her to finally claim I had nothing to lose by speaking truth. Yet, how difficult it would be to "say" all that remained unsaid!

* * *

ON the drive south, the van broke down with frustrating regularity. Kevin insisted on fixing it himself. I read. Sometimes a repair stranded us for days in a small fishing village while we waited for a new transmission or clutch. Sometimes Kevin parked off the road on a high desert mesa to fix an oil leak. His legs sticking out from under the chassis, he didn't need my help. I seized every situation as an opportunity for spiritual practice. During long stretches waiting for parts, I prayed. Regulating my breath, I emulated yoga postures or sitting meditations gleaned from the new stack of books in my suitcase.

I'd brought Carlos Castenada's *The Teachings of Don Juan: A Yaqui Way of Knowledge* with me, and Kevin and I got into heated arguments about him. I couldn't attest to the veracity of Castenada's claims about Don Juan, or whether his anthropological account was fact or fiction. But it didn't matter to me. I understood the possibility of alternative realities, of breaking through barriers that separated one domain of consciousness from another. What Kevin perceived as hyperbole and outright fraud on the author's part, I embraced as the Yaqui shaman's mysterious gift of wisdom.

Nor was it significant to me whether the truth Krishnamurti or Don Juan offered, in its totality, was my truth. I already knew I didn't subscribe to everything they taught, nor did I intend to pursue every one of their methods. Yet through them, a searchlight illumined faint footprints marking the way: it was possible to find meaning and love, to be enlightened, or at least awake, in this life. If I immersed myself in another person's wisdom, without judgment or critique, I didn't become a passive follower. Rather, each act of trust challenged and tested my thought, bringing to the surface an inner knowing. Whatever path I chose, I questioned the beliefs I now took for granted, and advanced with impunity into the unknown. Krishnamurti and Don Juan were passionately committed to the path Spirit had hallowed out within them. I yearned to be an authentic devotee of God's path for me.

I harvested long stretches for study and practice. I continued to practice meditative endurance and worked to subdue my emotional turmoil. Many nights, camping in remote places, nestled in a sleeping bag on the ground, I placed myself in divine trust, unafraid. It may have been pure folly, but I slept with such abandon that my dreams were weightless, filled with light. Years later I would look back on my travels in Mexico as marking a pilgrimage from spiritual ignorance to the edge of awareness.

To be sure, a releasing of false attachment was necessary to survive the *voice* that summoned during those nights, and the feelings that welled up and threatened to capsize my small boat. My only safe harbor was to admit the passion I felt for life, while I clung in desperation to my raft of nothingness. I prayed to remain steady, to advance beyond convention toward the distant shore of the immeasurable.

Yet I did not have foreknowledge of the magnitude of change initiated by the nocturnal call. Or that it would tear up everything I knew about myself, exposing a depth of being from which I would never again be free. It would demand a constant search for truth, in others and in the world, but mostly in a continuous examination of my motives and foibles, of the "poisons" or "deadly sins" that thwarted dedicating one's life to the Holy. And through all this I would be astonished: every deed plants a seed of virtue or iniquity.

AT THE TIME the word held no meaning, but if I'm honest with myself, it was faith that kept me going. It pulled me from the morass of my own making and rescued me from a woman's lot. Faith, not the kind that knew where it was going, but faith that had no way of knowing anything, saved me.

Like the watcher of a doe sipping water from a stream, I approached faith holding my breath lest I startled her wild presence. Strident voices portrayed faith as conventional, a matter of choice. But faith was not unbounded trust in something or someone. It was not striving for finalized things or naming names. Neither was faith self-congratulatory pride in having found truth or the absolute. In its pure state, faith was not about god or the name of god, but finding out for myself if there was anything outside my own mind. Faith required I take away props, shuck off comfort, and find out whether whatever I was seeking was real.

What I called faith was not limp or weak, not the suspension of reason or humor. It appeared through a suspension of doubt, which was just another way of saying: openness to the "not yet" and the "to come." Faith was an unfinished narrative, a text of becoming—a free fall into the flow of life. Everything I am and everything I have done has been possible only because I threw my whole self onto its pyre.

* *
*

AVOIDING disapproval, I didn't divulge my faith experiments to Kevin. Yet my inner journey and our travel exploits often collided, precipitating my daily stomachache. Since it was now November and colder in northern Mexico, we decided one evening over a meal of rice and beans to drive south to Oaxaca.

Nestled at the convergence of the eastern and southern Sierra Madre, Oaxaca vibrated with the sounds of European, English, and Indigenous voices. *Zapotec, Mixtec,* and *Trique* Indians mingled in the streets with descendants of Spanish conquistadors and visitors from around the globe. Markets of every imaginable type crowded the sidewalks as vendors vied with each other for the best spot, plying their wares to residents and tourists alike. Enchanted by the noise and robust mounds of fruit, cheese, and bread, I spent hours wandering the stalls. Zapotec women in brightly embroidered blouses of native cotton cloth displayed their handiwork alongside hanging slabs of meat covered by flies. The rowdy array of textiles, sandals, hammocks, rugs, and dresses piled on tables or spilling onto the dusty street made it difficult to decide what to buy. No purchase was final without bargaining, an art that required perseverance and humor, a skill I'd yet to master. One afternoon I chose a white cotton skirt with blue cornflowers, properly sized for the waist by securing excess material with a safety pin.

Purchase in hand, I heard a woman's voice calling me to an adjacent stall: "*Ven aca! Vea mis vestidos hermosos!*" (Come right here! See my beautiful dresses!) Fingering the embroidered bodice of delicate flowers and birds, I learned that the vendor, Marta, was the director of a cooperative that sewed and marketed native costumes in San Antonino, a village near Oaxaca. Despite our fractured talk, for she spoke mostly Zapotec and I, Spanish, Marta invited me to her village to learn more.

I appreciated the familiarity and kindness of the Indian women. I also noted a marked difference in how they comported themselves as women from the way my female friends and I did at home. They exuded an earthy sensuality that was natural, easy. Taught to value their difference as females, the Indian women revered family and motherhood. Even as I witnessed the inequality between men and women in this traditional society, the mystery of femaleness had not been robbed from them.

Despite our differences we were bound as women to the culture of *machismo* and its worst stereotypes. Later that week, I bore the sting of exclusion and shame as I was escorted from a home factory where yarn was dyed for fear that I would taint the batch. Superstition about a woman's powers for ill during menstruation was sufficient to shun me, as was the fact that I was left-handed. Mexican men eyed me as fair game. I watched them fondle *gringas* who frequented the market, or taunt them with sleazy remarks. Even so, I was surprised one afternoon while filling my basket with fruit to feel rough fingers reach up under my skirt. Spontaneously, without thinking, I slugged the groper in the face, which elicited great peals of laughter and hand clapping from the women minding their stalls.

My chance encounter with Marta set in motion the idea of importing Mexican clothing to the US. I spoke Spanish, sewed, and loved traditional dress. Kevin was a good businessman. To further explore the opportunity of a clothing import business, we drove south and east from Oaxaca to Mérida, the capital of the Yucatán. By now, out of funds, we asked a friend to wire us money, which took days to arrive. In the meantime, we were surviving on potato tacos, three pesos (about 25 cents) for five, and water.

To supplement income, I tried to sell a few of my knitted scarfs to tourists. While I was sitting on a wood crate in a corner across from the main *zocolo*, an unmistakably American man in cowboy boots and a large, Western hat grabbed the scarf out of my hand. "How much do you want?" he barked. Like many of my fellow Americans, he had made no attempt to speak Spanish, yet he clearly thought I was Mexican. Hungry, I responded, "*Cinco pesos.*" I observed my mind, noticing how small and beholden I was to this stranger who could decide whether or not I would eat. My hunger turned me against myself.

For a fleeting moment, I experienced the desperation that stalked the poor, robbed them of dignity, and often led to early death. And I identified as never before with the crippled and bent, with those who had been laid low by the powerful and corrupt, forsaken on the margins of society. Right then I knew that it was not money, but the attitudes money engendered—privilege, specialness—that was all wrong.

Across from where I sat, a grandmother wove complicated patterns from memory on a back strap loom, while nearby her daughter worked another masterpiece, oblivious to a toddler ripping open her blouse to nurse. Peering from under my straw hat at the family scenes playing out in this traditional Mayan culture, I chafed against conventional roles. I didn't want to be "daughter" or "wife." But as female, as woman, where could I go? There were only men then. That was the only way. The time would come for freedom but it would be a few years off. It taunted me, and I wanted it desperately.

* * *

THE following day, we were winding over a mountain pass between Oaxaca and Mexico City, barely wide enough for one car like so many of these mountain roads. We dodged buses overloaded with passengers clutching baskets of live chickens or restraining a bleating goat, weaving across unmarked lanes. It was midday and the sun was beating down on our windshield, expanding the crack in the dashboard and buckling the vinyl. Kevin was driving and I was reading The Three Pillars of Zen, hoping to learn more about self-realization. The sky was the blue-green of a Mexican autumn.

Suddenly we were on a desolate stretch of highway, climbing a steep hill around a curve. Ahead, sprawled across the road was a dark mound of brown, a tail. As we got closer, I saw that a mare had been hit, her pelvis crushed and right leg and hipped splayed out. The horse's magnificent head was turned, its eyes wild with fear. When I recall the scene now the horse fills the whole road, there is no sky or mountain or brush. Just her. Hit dead-on. It seems the vehicle never slowed down or tried to avoid the animal. There were no skid marks.

The head-on crash was not the result of the driver's miscalculation or even of casual disregard. No, this was his thrill. I envisioned a pickup truck speeding down the road, the driver shaking his fist out the window. Ignorant beast is in the way. Hit the fucking mare. Black and brown and white she is. Blood pools onto the road. I think of Picasso's Guernica. I see war, horses' heads thrown back in terror, their teeth unfurled above chiseled jaw. The dark swirling movement of spilled fluids on wet pavement stirred up nausea, and I shielded my eyes from her plight.

Steering the van onto the right shoulder, Kevin jumped out to check on the horse's condition. "Stay here," he signaled to me, slamming the door. I couldn't stop my tears. My heart was wildly fluttering. Like drops of rain ricocheting off a roof, I heard Buddha's central teaching: "All life is suffering, all life is suffering," trickling down my mind. The mantra, like the scene in front of me, sparked a question: If suffering is caused by ignorance, and the solution to ignorance is the eight-fold path, what is the answer to my soul-numbing grief?

I didn't understand why the driver had hit her. Why didn't he slow down or veer off the road? Meditation eased my agitation, but it didn't take away the hollow knot in my heart, the feeling that I'd let her down. Was her suffering redemptive? Could karma explain this? I didn't think so—not for me. The cruelty was an affront I could not dismiss; I would not dismiss.

I knew then: there is no end to suffering. I could not put a stop to senseless desecration. I couldn't even minimize her pain. Confronted by the limits of language and the failure of emotion, I was left with only one thing: to be in solidarity with the spirit of the horse abandoned on a desolate road, to not avert my face from her dying life. I carry her image with me now. I will carry her with me to my grave. In entering her pain, I vowed to neither trivialize nor erase my witness. If I allowed myself to assume suffering, to withstand it without complaint, then maybe someday, someday I would understand raw faith and have something to give back.

With nothing available to ease her torment and hours away from a town, Kevin drove away. Forgive us, I silently prayed.

IN THE DAYS that followed, it was no longer possible to ignore that I was wasting away pretending to function in a purely material realm, while beneath everything a radical change had taken hold of my personality. These seemingly carefree travels through Mexico were the catalyst for a growing spiritual commitment that would strengthen in the months and years ahead.

Yet, to my parents and those of their generation I was a wayward child, traveling around like a hobo with no goals, living in sin. Where was marriage or at least a career? In actuality, it was all very conventional. I was still living for the satisfaction of someone else's desires, following a hollow path of boy and girl, intent on physical pleasure or at least a modicum of comfort.

It would not do.

PART II

HIDDEN CALL
OF FAITH

* 5 *

Motherhood of Mercy

B Y THE TIME I was seven months pregnant, I was so huge that strangers on the street offered to drive me to the hospital. My stomach lurched straight in front of me like a giant water balloon, while my spindly arms and legs seemed strangely detached from my body. Looking at me from behind, it was impossible to tell I was pregnant, let alone having twins. Finally back in California, I stayed with friends in Napa to find a house to rent while Kevin flew to Mexico on a three-week buying trip for our growing import business. I located a weathered cottage off a dirt road surrounded by fruit orchards. It had a homey, lived-in feel, even if an area of roof above the kitchen was punched in and the windows lacked sufficient caulk. It was not a van or a moldy bed in a fifteen-dollar-a-night motel room. By early June, the Sonoma hills were already parched brown from the heat.

Two months prior, I was unnerved when the doctor measured my stomach and announced: "You have either miscalculated, are having a ten-pound baby, or you're having twins!" Except for an unsubstantiated story about my great-grandmother's sister's twins, there was no record of multiple births in our family. Lacking two of everything, I sewed a second baby blanket and added it to the other clothes I kept in a flowered, cardboard trunk. After months of constant nausea, I felt terrific now. My skin glowed. As the babies developed within me, I soundlessly, furtively awakened from deep slumber.

When I found out I was pregnant, my parents astonished me by coming to California for the marriage ceremony, presided over by a defrocked priest in a friend's apartment. Afterward, they blithely climbed into the blue Chevy van, the four of us on a road trip across the country. Our mutual pleasure was short lived. My mother constantly mouthed, "cheap," shaking her head when Kevin didn't pay for every meal. In hotels, terrified of germs, she crop-dusted doorknobs, toilet seats, bedspreads, and each piece of furniture with the can of Lysol spray she kept in her makeup bag. Back on the road, Kevin grimly drove, Mom kvetched in the back seat, while Pop, who could not carry a tune, and I sang.

* * *

A MONTH before the twins were born, a political scandal shattered the national conscience. Evening news anchors and daily editorials were rife with stories about Daniel Ellsberg's leak of the Pentagon Papers. The first excerpts, published by the New York Times, documented widespread political-military involvement in Vietnam, revealing that four administrations, beginning with Truman, had deliberately expanded the war and misled the public regarding their intentions. Ranging from Kennedy's plan to overthrow South Vietnamese leader Ngo Dinh Diem, to Johnson's secret intention to bomb North Vietnam, even while claiming "no wider war" during his 1964 presidential campaign, the documents demonstrated unconstitutional behavior by a succession of presidents.

Glued to the television, these revelations, coupled with the ongoing cover-up of the My Lai massacre, the US invasion of Cambodia, and the killing of four student protesters at Kent State University the year before, led me to despair that our government had lost all accountability. What happened to the soul of our country? As street protests erupted in cities across the nation antiwar sentiment, previously tainted as anti-American, became instead the moral responsibility of a democratic citizenry.

My feelings were intense. Here I was pouring all my energies into protecting the development of two innocent lives while across the world my country was destroying the future of a people who loved their homeland and their families as fiercely as I did. When would conflict and destruction end? Many mornings, while the sun was just appearing on the horizon, I walked the fields behind our rented cottage and prayed for peace. When will there be peace?

* *
* *

BECOMING aware can be dangerous, particularly if your life is built upon the safety of denial. However, I was twenty-three years old and it was time—past time—for me to confront my choices. Unfortunately, or perhaps providentially, my awakening occurred while in labor. In the middle of the night, I roused Kevin, who had returned from Mexico only a week earlier, to drive me to the hospital an hour from our home. Due to the added stress of a twin pregnancy, my contractions were erratic, yet my doctor wanted me to deliver the babies, even though I was three weeks from my due date. It was 1971 and women's demand for natural childbirth in hospitals had yet to be fully implemented.

Although we were fortunate to have attended a crash course in Lamaze, it was not terribly helpful once I was given Pitocin, a hormone to induce labor. In the span of about fifteen minutes, the intensity of contractions had escalated from a sensation so mild that I'd dozed through the last five hours to a gripping, involuntary convulsion more than pain. My body was thrust into the machinations of a biological imperative, negating any notion that I was in control. Fixing my eyes on the second hands of the large wall clock across from my hospital bed, I counted breaths.

There was no way out. Like death, birth was inexorable. Even if I wanted to run away, even if I were to scream, "Make this stop!" the birth process was relentless, enigmatic. The only way to survive was to surrender. I could not prevent the babies from coming out of my body—I couldn't turn the clock back now—yet I didn't see a way forward, the intensity of the unknown, of relinquishing self-control, unthinkable. As I bundled my emotions in a tight knot, I felt connected to an ancient rite shared by women around the world squatting in rice paddies, clenching bark between teeth in savannas, or surrounded by midwives in gilded beds who sacrificed their lives, bodily health, and sometimes sanity to blind trust.

While Kevin coached me, I gritted my teeth, counting breaths and blowing them out in short bursts: hee, hee, hoo. Just as I reached the limit of endurance, my robust, self-congratulating physician bent his neatly combed blond head next to my face (which was now pressed against the bars of the hospital bed) and cheerfully boomed, "We're going to wheel you into delivery!" Next I was lying on the sterile table, feet in stirrups, nurse holding one hand, covered by sheets, and my doctor was at my feet, urging, "Push now, push!" like a cheerleader at a football rally. I was beyond embarrassment. Added to this indignity, the delivery room was crowded with residents, physicians, and nurses who wanted to observe a multiple birth. So much for the tender privacy I had planned.

As our two glorious daughters were whisked away to incubators, the staff cheered the doctor's success. All my energy dissipated, I was a crumpled, exhausted bundle of tears. Back in the maternity ward, the nurses were brusque and chided me for wanting to breastfeed, refusing to bring "Baby A and Baby B" to me. Dr. M checked on my progress the next day, reversed the nurses' decision, and allowed us to go home.

MAYA AND GINA were so tiny that the smallest disposable diaper ballooned around their little bowed legs. I was able to tell them apart because Gina was bald; Maya had hair. Overwhelmed by the prospect of feedings and diaper changes for two infants, and barely able to sit due to my stitches, I begged Kevin to cancel his previously planned flight to Mexico the next morning.

"I can't," he argued, "I have to finalize an import order."

The sugar water forced into the twins while in the hospital nursery gave Maya and Gina colic, and there was nothing for me to do but hold them, breastfeed, and pray that their screaming stopped. I didn't know how I was going to get through the week—or was it ten days?—alone. Each cry punched a hole in my gut.

The turmoil I felt over Kevin's absence was palpable. I wanted him to be with us, I wanted him to love us. At the same time I didn't ever want to see him again. Many nights I lay awake in bed fantasizing that he wouldn't return. After another night of nursing one baby and then another, I was exhausted by the time they both fell asleep at the same time, a rare occurrence. It was now 5 a.m.

I was unable to sleep—there were just too many thoughts. Lately little prayers scratched the surface of my activities, *please make me worthy; help me be a good mother.* I needed these unclaimed moments.

Wandering into the living room, sunlight streaming across the wood floors, I leaned against the wall to look out the window. Thinking about the girls, their sweet, warm faces, an understanding jolted me from grogginess. I knew with utter certainty that responsibility for my daughters' lives was sacred and forever. I saw through my charade and, perhaps, that of my generation. Freedom from social constraints, maintained by a delusion that I was not really present in my own life, was not the same as true liberation.

It came to me then that no one and nothing can destroy the soul's freedom. Circumstances don't matter. Freedom comes when it's supposed to come: in a prison camp; saddled with ten kids; wielding a weapon in some godforsaken hellhole; struggling to buy a crumb of bread. Freedom comes—no one can take it away and no one can prevent you from having it.

After nursing and changing diapers and putting the girls down for a nap, I returned to a book I was reading on the prison letters of Dietrich Bonhoeffer, a German theologian jailed and eventually executed by the Nazis for participating in a plan to assassinate Hitler. But while physically imprisoned, Bonhoeffer found inner freedom. "It's as if, in solitude," he wrote, "the soul develops organs of which we're hardly aware in everyday life. So I haven't for an instant felt lonely and forlorn.... I live in a great, unseen realm of whose real existence I'm in no doubt."[1]

I, too, was afforded a time of enclosure, able to nurture the "great, unseen realm" through a discipleship to my children. The seriousness of motherhood was not the curtailment of creativity and self-identity that I'd feared, but rather my chance at happiness. Maya and Gina's unconditional trust, their tender vulnerability, released me. I experienced love I'd never felt before. There was no defense, no barrier between us. Fully myself, no one curtailed or demeaned the pulse of my devotion. I glimpsed God's wish for me: to love unbounded, without fear or shame.

Pregnancy and birth opened a mysterious understanding of incarnation: a theology of bodily knowing. Every aspect of physical life contained a sacramental, even mystical counterpart if only we had the courage to bear our sacred origins. This was my goal: to see in everything the divine imprint, its luminous geography waiting to be mapped.

* * *

I STAGGERED into the kitchen from another sleepless night to survey columns of black ants pouring over the table onto the floorboards. They had marched in through a slot between the window glass and frame, each shiny mouth gripping a white crumb. I reached for ant poison under the sink, praying the babies wouldn't wake up. I doubted it was going to stem the tide, but it was all I could think of, each waking moment occupied with breast-feeding, changing diapers, and grabbing a few moments of rest. It had been three months since I last left the house.

When Kevin, back from Mexico weeks ago, roused me from a dreamless sleep to nurse the other twin, I protested, "I just fed the baby!" I couldn't make it to the bathroom to brush my teeth until three in the afternoon. I was starving all the time, wolfing down three-egg omelets, along with toast and butter, fruit, and a quart of milk. I was a feeding machine. Willing to try anything that increased a mother's stamina and milk production, I followed a friend's advice and sipped the occasional German beer, with no additives.

Nothing prepared me for the intensity of motherhood. Once the soundest of sleepers, I now bolted awake at the slightest noise. If the girls got a fever or were not gaining weight, I was stricken with dread. I watched each morsel of food that went into my mouth, concerned about protecting their immature intestines from colic and pain. My sense of responsibility for their well-being was all consuming. The possibility of something taking away their fragile, angelic lives constantly kept me on the alert. Holding a tiny hand in my own, I looked down at the sweet face nestled against my breast. They were barely the weight of full-term newborns, and I was still able to hold each of them in the bend of an arm.

Seated in the rocking chair with one twin on each side, a bond of intimacy stretched between us as if the umbilicus that once joined us physically was now spiritual, even more resilient and strong. We needed no words to understand each other. By love, we were bound together for life. An aura of tenderness enclosed us. As Maya and Gina grew from infants to smiling toddlers I, too, underwent a metamorphosis.

I was drawn to you, Dear God, then. I saw your divine seed in my daughters. You entrusted them to me. How could I not give everything of myself? How could I justify withholding my love, my hope? I could not. There was no choice. I would protect their Light, the Light you gave them.

At once through your Motherhood I knew in my heart that all creatures were my children. You alone showed me how we deny your infinite mercy, damaging the holy spark and severing our children from the sacred circle of life. It was your Motherhood that cried out in me against injustice, destruction, and war, your Motherhood that protested in me the defilement of the innocent ones. Through you I committed my motherhood to the alleviation of suffering and to the protection of creation. You, Holy Mother, tenderly set fire to my soul.

I knew then that when I left home you went with me, keeping me safe even as I was felled by my own desire and failure. It was you who gave me the strength to seek truth and not abandon the way.

Looking over at Kevin reading at the dining table, I was crushed by a remembrance from the twins' birth. I was absolutely clear, lying on that hospital bed in labor pains, that I didn't know him or why we were together. I suspected he shared similar thoughts, since he was hardly around anymore. I was forced to bear another kind of pain: the grieving that comes from wounding the innocent. Before Maya and Gina were born into the world, the loving family I had hoped to provide them was the product of careless love on my part. My suffering was doubly intense, for their beauty was the first I knew of happiness.

* 6 *

Love's Benediction

T HE GIRLS WERE fourteen months old and we were still traveling to Mexico, importing clothes and selling them out of the van to boutiques. In a rare moment of clarity, I demanded that we stop living like itinerant salesmen and find a permanent home. With money saved from the import business, we purchased an old Victorian in downtown Eureka. We sanded floors, scraped paint, and reattached window cords. Yet I was reaching a breaking point in our relationship. The years I lived with Kevin in fear, denial, and suppression of my deep self, none of this could I do any longer.

Perhaps to repent that I didn't have the courage to end our increasingly tense marriage, I became a vegetarian, a decision that marked my first consistent spiritual discipline. I stopped eating fish, beef, chicken, and any other kind of meat. I was not prepared for how much my identity was connected to food choices. But I'd made a vow. Having committed myself, I pursued vegetarianism with sober zeal, which was not the easiest diet to follow in the early 1970s. Health food stores and natural food restaurants were a rarity. Frequently, dinner at a roadside truck stop or mom-and-pop café consisted of tomato soup, a salad of iceberg lettuce, and grilled cheese on doughy, white bread. Every meal required re-commitment to my diet, dismantling with each mouthful the social construction of self.

In the midst of my turmoil, we had planned to meet friends in San Francisco for traditional seated baths and massage at the Japanese Cultural Center. To my dismay, I was assigned a male masseuse. Soaking in a chest-high concrete tub, bathing suit primly tied, I nervously waited. "Clothes off, massage table," he said, "I go out." Body and mind limp from the heat, I felt as if I were floating above the room by the time he returned. What happened next is hard to explain, but as he kneaded muscles and smoothed knots, energy flowed between us that was pure gentleness. As if I counted in his universe, cherished and safe. While sensual, our bonding was intimate without being sexual, strangers yet lovers of a universal desire.

After years of confusion, wrong choices, and stubborn resistance to speaking my truth, as if Kevin had been a stand-in for my mother and all that I feared, this hour of happiness was everything. From my first breath, when my mother, ashamed of having another girl, covered my face with her sheet, I had been hidden, wordless. Now I knew: I would have to speak.

The disjuncture between our two objectives and ways of life came to a head when we located acreage north of Petrolia, an isolated area of coast fifty miles south of Eureka. On the drive to the property, I was a jumble of thoughts and aching gut. I didn't want to buy land or do any-thing that sealed our futures. As the time approached to sign the legal documents, the chatter in my head became frenzied. Two sides of my soul were fighting for control. *I don't want to hurt him. I don't want to hurt the girls. I'm selfish, only thinking about myself.* As much as I wanted to believe that I could remain the quiet helpmate, as intensely as I argued with myself that I should endure for everyone's sake, a force of conviction greater than cowardice or pain tipped the scales. I couldn't go ahead with this large purchase and future life commitment. I couldn't live this lie.

Leaving the girls to play with a neighbor, Kevin and I went to lunch. Seated at a table outside, I was pushing salad around my plate. Kevin was staring at me, and finally asked, "Are you all right?" Steeling against my own resistance, nauseous, I said, "No. I can't do this. There's too much strife between us. I want a separation."

As the words flew out of my mouth, I was shaking and crying at the same time. I was so tense, so afraid I would be judged or punished or worse, cause pain, that I was paralyzed. But these sentiments were not noble or even benign. I *was* the cause of suffering, ignorant of my motives. Even as I practiced mindfulness and strove for greater honesty, I had no idea how to sustain a marriage, much less end one.

I did discover something about myself, though. I'd been frozen by fear and now I was thawing.

* * *

T HE girls and I moved an hour and a half south of Eureka, to a small cabin owned by a theatre professor from Humboldt State University, with no telephone, scant electric service, and gravity-flow water from a cistern perched on a hill. It was perfect. Not beholden to anyone, I planted vegetables in the garden, observed storm clouds gathering above the fog, and was charmed by dancing, lilting trees. Maya and Gina, now eighteen months, loved to run everywhere, pulling their little wagons around the yard. Keeping an eye on them from the front stoop, on good days I could see clear to the sea.

This respite from arguments anchored my decision. I needed time alone. I needed to find my center of being. A fierce desire for freedom grew in me: conscripted by someone else's agenda, I became agitated, sorrowful, despairing, frustrated. I was affronted by attempts to invade my space, to own or possess me. I was unsuited for commitments other people made, unfit for formal religious life. Along with the whole of humanity I wanted to be set free of anxieties and inhibitions, caught by obligation to remain with my spouse and knowing inside it couldn't be done.

At night, while the girls slept, I perused the ever-present stack of books on my bed and read. Our beloved Husky, Kai, nestled by my side, I studied the teachings of Krishamurti and Zen, as well as *The Fourth Way* by Ouspensky and *Life and Teaching of the Masters of the Far East*. Diving into a stream of esoteric consciousness, I was intrigued by the idea of immortal Himalayan masters who brought Light, guiding the destiny of humankind from afar. I identified with Krishnamurti's radical deliverance from a scripted life of worn-out thoughts and beliefs, as I did with Buddhist teachings on emptiness.

All the same, something was missing.

In the early hours of the morning before the girls were awake, I climbed the hill behind our cabin to meditate. My fervent prayer was to know divine love. What was unconditional love? I longed to experience a moment of unequivocal communion. My whole being now pulsed with a steady plea: *Please show me Love; please show me Love.* Every waking moment I prayed, my prayer urgent, all consuming. How much longer did I have to wait? An acute striving propelled me forward. At a precipice, inebriated by desire, I was unaware I could leap.

I'd been reading about the 1922 experience that changed Krishnamurti's life. Like other spiritual pioneers, Krishnamurti's periods of desolation and torment were juxtaposed with esoteric states of awareness. Nightly, for nearly forty years, intense physical pain in his head and spine preceded consciousness of the "otherness" and "immensity." I wondered if my anguish over life choices—and the choices themselves—were not catalysts for profound transformation. Still groping in semi-darkness, I dreamt of Krishnamurti standing in my room, his presence so real I could touch him. With his somber, dark eyes and bird-like nose, he looked directly at me. "You're on the right path," he predicted.

ON MY WEEKLY drive to Eureka, I stocked up on supplies. Afterward, I dropped the girls off with Kevin for the weekend, stopping on my way home at a food co-op. Interested in everything that reflected on one's spirit, especially the relationship of food and the energetic virtues of a raw diet, I was reading *Love Your Body: Live Food Recipes* by Viktoras Kulvinskas. However, my decision to be vegetarian was not something to impose on my children. Daily I cooked whatever they liked to eat.

I thought about the twins, how well they were doing, about separating from Kevin. I was not resolved about it, but I was happier than ever. My in-laws viewed my attitude as cavalier, even deceptive. But I saw it the other way around. This may have been the first time as woman and mother I'd made a decision that was mine alone. Not by default, not by coercion, not out of fear or denial or self-pity, but a clear-eyed, straight-on, sober choice.

While driving home I was mesmerized by the soft, moist wind rustling through the redwoods. Without warning, I felt my consciousness expand beyond the confines of my body. Lifted above myself, like a bird soaring on air currents, Love, pure Love surged through me, suffusing me with the sweet sensation of total, unconditional acceptance.

I pulled into a turnout and left the car. As I settled my gaze on the grove of ancient redwoods, I felt as if they were whispering: *Love is the force that rules the world. See how trees offer a glimpse of love's grandeur, mountains of its endurance, seas of its expanse, rivers of its flow, birds of its freedom, birth of its awe, and death of its mystery. All creation is permeated with Love's perfume, coursing through the heart of the world, inhaled with every breath.*

I had to sit down. I thought about how all my life I'd hidden that I loved God; that I was devoted; that I wanted to be a monk. Like peace, spiritual love was a threat to common sensibilities, which in large measure depended on the failure of love to disturb convention. For wasn't Love the greatest threat? Infinite Love that is made manifest in our finitude; Infinite Love that has given us everything there is to give and to whom we offer so little, so very little.

Sometimes passion was socially acceptable in artists or writers, kept within the parameters of a secular enterprise. Sometimes, even the worship of devotees was proclaimed on ordered days and inside the walls of temple, mosque, or church, not excessive. But to admit whole-out that you so loved the world and the creator who made you that you would give your entire life to see the Holy One face-to-face? It was this that had caused me to feel shame.

No longer would I deny Love had claimed me.

* * *

OVER time, the silence of the earth and the shimmering light playing in the redwoods healed me. I thrived on stillness, on the clarity of nature in this remote wilderness hours away from civilization, attuned to subtle energies, an experience I hadn't had since childhood. Looking across to a grove of eucalyptus swaying in the breeze, vibrant, pulsating energies radiating out in concentric bands from limbs and leaves captivated me.

This new freedom was contagious, exhilarating. I loved solitude. I loved to watch Maya and Gina play in the stream or follow a ladybug's progress across a leaf. I loved the way they hugged Kai and planted kisses on his nose. Each day they grew stronger and more joyful. Squatting down, Gina, radiant, intently studied a few blades of grass, breaking into squeals. She pointed to the tiniest flower, turning her dancing green eyes in my direction. Nearby, Maya was poking the dirt with a stick, her adorable, serious demeanor reminding me of a little professor. The days passed quickly as we healed in the calm of the earth and the simple pleasure of being outdoors.

As my studies deepened, I noticed a particular trait shared by others whose contemplative nature had been awakened: an intense need for silence and solitude, which could be said to form the center of the personality. Through this I recognized that my need for freedom was a form of active spiritual protest in which I was practicing how to be a fierce protector of and advocate for my aloneness with God. If I didn't accomplish this, I would never make it in the world of relationships, because my longing for solitude would always tear me. "If you love truth, be a lover of silence," wrote St. Isaac of Nineveh, a seventh-century hermit monk. "Silence like the sunlight will illuminate you in God."[1]

* *
*

I HAD two sets of neighbors. The couple about a half-mile away was a study in contrasts. Marvin, a retired logger, was quiet and thoughtful. Most days he sat in his rocker studying American history. Dottie was no-nonsense and brass. She kept chickens, goats, ducks, rabbits, and a donkey. I liked them both. Without children of their own, they'd adopted us and often stopped by with a dozen eggs or a handful of flowers.

My other neighbors drove a dilapidated pickup truck across the dirt road in front of our house. They weren't friendly. I was curious because each time a pickup truck passed our window, a different combination of men and women alone, or with children, was inside the cab. Dottie said they owned land about two miles below me and warned, "They're hippies living together in a commune and are up to no good."

A few months after we had moved in, a strange man with a beard and worn jeans came to the door and introduced himself as my neighbor. Kai was backing up and snarling but I quieted him and invited Carl in. Over tea, I learned that his family and four other families had formed a collective, making a living hauling produce and firewood into town. He seemed pleasant enough. But when I stood up to check a pot on the stove, he pressed himself against me and tried to kiss me. Disgusted, I ordered him to leave. I was now more wary of these people and watched them furtively whenever they drove by.

Several evenings later, walking to my bedroom to read, I spontaneously turned around and locked the front and back doors. In the months we'd lived in the cabin I had never locked the house. Meditating cross-legged on my bed, I heard the faint sound of tires rumbling over the gravel in the front yard. The vehicle's lights must have been off because I had no curtains on the windows but still didn't see anything. Suddenly, Kai was barking ferociously, lunging at the front door, clawing the glass, teeth bared. Rushing into the room, I saw a hand try to turn the doorknob. Terrified, I demanded, "Go away, Carl! You're not coming in!!" Kai was still throwing his body against the door, growling and barking. I watched Carl's steely eyes weigh his options: did he want to risk the dog? Rattling the doorknob one more time, he smirked at me and sauntered back to his truck.

I was trembling. Crouching down below the window ledge in case he hadn't actually left, I crawled to the closet to gather blankets, which I tacked across all the windows so no one could see in. With no phone, I couldn't call Dottie and Marv for help, who no doubt would have come over with their shotguns. Agitated and disgusted, I realized I couldn't live here alone with the girls anymore. Carl and his cronies were not going to give up, his stealthy approach grim evidence of malicious intent. The next day, all our possessions in the van, Maya, Gina, and Kai climbed in. I drove over to Dottie and Marv to say goodbye and hastened down the mountain.

* 7 *

Pure Mind

PRETTY TORN UP about having to leave our country house, I flew with the girls to Florida to spend a week with my parents. Soon after our arrival, my mother suggested we take a trip to Cassadaga, the historic spiritualist community thirty-five miles from Orlando. I was leery about seeing a psychic, but Mom convinced me it would be a good diversion.

A dilapidated sign welcomed us to "Cassadaga Spiritualist Camp." A hodgepodge of notices stuck into lawns at random angles advertised various services: Certified Medium, Spiritual Counselor, Medical Intuitive. Shaded from the Florida sun by a dense canopy of magnolia trees, the town was trapped in a 1940s black-and-white movie set.

A brochure in the visitor's center said George Colby had founded the Cassadaga Spiritualist Camp in 1894. Not based on a particular savior, spiritualism promoted an individual's personal experience of God. Many of the residents were old-time mediums, not the more showy psychics that one sometimes encountered at fairs, in movies, or on TV. Nor did they promote palm readings, Ouija boards, or tarot cards. Instead, certified mediums offered readings or spiritual counseling that brought mental energy from the higher plane of Spirit to the person.

I asked the receptionist if we needed reservations. "You don't need an appointment, honey. Just walk around and find a person's name or house that you like and see if the resident is in. Enjoy." (I've never understood the salutation, *enjoy*. Did it mean the person was doing you a favor? Was I supposed to have a good time? Be grateful?)

Mom and I meandered past overgrown yards dotted with plastic gnomes, concrete saints, and the occasional statue of Mary. Tired of walking, I took a blue jay landing on a palm tree as a favorable sign and knocked on the nearby door. A grandmotherly woman invited us into her aging wallpapered parlor, a bouquet of blue plastic flowers resting on a corner table.

My mother waited as I followed Rev. Hazel into a small room. "The reading," she said, "will last no more than fifty minutes. I'll speak about what Spirit allows me to see and know. At the end you can ask questions, OK?" I mumbled agreement. She lit a votive candle, closed her eyes, and said a prayer. I recall little of what she told me except for a short paragraph recorded in my journal.

"For a long time now you've been in the wrong boat with the wrong people. It's essential that you find the right path for yourself, the way that leads to truth. You are psychically and spiritually gifted and if you don't get control over these energies, they're going to control you. You must learn about your gifts and use them for good."

Hazel's sincerity, along with the little chills that ran up my spine—my inner sign of truth—made a deep impression on me. With an hour to my-self before my mother finished her reading, I explored the camp. Tattered gates and missing shutters no longer seemed neglectful. They were just right. Looking up at bearded moss hanging in clumps on the live oaks, I felt less burdened. A deep reservoir of knowing had been awakened, like a pebble tossed into a stream. I mulled over Hazel's reading. What did it mean? What were these gifts? How would I know what to do with them?

* * *

BACK home, the girls and I had moved to the Inner Richmond District of San Francisco, around the corner from Clement Street and the clamor of Russian cafés and Korean grocers. Recently divorced, I supple-mented child support of $100 a month by selling plants at weekend swap meets and farmer's markets. Across the street from our second-floor bay window, men from Larraburu Brothers, the once-famed San Francisco sourdough bakery, loaded racks of bread into trucks. I hadn't realized that the bakers noticed me trudging up and down the stairs with a double baby carriage or armfuls of groceries. But at Christmas time one of them knocked on our door and handed me, "the plant lady," a special loaf of sourdough bread almost as tall as I, wrapped in cellophane with a ribbon on top.

A few days later I was reading in bed when a radio ad, for what I'll call the Center for Meditative Studies, attracted my attention. I immediately jotted down the number and called for an appointment. Leaving Maya and Gina with a babysitter, I drove across the Golden Gate Bridge with a bit of trepidation. Welcomed into CMS offices by Ruby, the program director, a delicate woman with short white hair, I was asked if I would like to have a psychic reading. I followed her into a wood-paneled room, directed to sit in a chair facing eight people. On either side of Ruby were three student observers and behind them a woman artist, who drew my aura.

Ruby closed her eyes and entered into a meditative state. Around everyone's head I saw colored bands of energy: Ruby, green and gold, the student to her left, yellow, mauve, and blue. After an interminable period of quiet, Ruby turned to the student to her right and whispered,

"There's so much purple in her aura I don't know how she's remaining on earth and hasn't returned to spirit."

Although her pronouncement didn't make rational sense, I intuitively knew what she meant. Could this be the reason I never felt I belonged anywhere? The reading continued with extensive discussion about each chakra and its unique energies. I was told that I must probe the deep self and awaken my spiritual gifts. For the second time in a month, someone spoke to my soul. When I opened my eyes, I was handed a beautiful chalk drawing. Radiating out from my body in a wide arc were concentric circles of rich purples of varying hue. From my forehead gold beams of energy flowed, my heart and lower chakras vibrating green, which I was told signified "spiritual growth." For years I carried the drawing with me. Later that day, I enrolled in the Center's yearlong course.

CLASSES BEGAN WITH exercises on how to meditate, how to harness intuitive potential, how to transform consciousness. Seated in a circle, students introduced themselves: John's interest in altered states of consciousness; Hiroshi's years of living off the land in Maui, studying with a shaman. Sharon told about suppressing her psychic abilities with drugs, and how much she wanted to claim her true self. Others shared stories of self-betrayal, of denying one's sensitivity and one's divine call to fit in with family, friends, or work. I would come to appreciate all of these people and, in some cases, discover new friendships. John and Hiroshi, in particular, would have a significant impact on my journey.

We practiced every day, often for hours and with repetitive visualization exercises. I learned to control my energies and to develop a mature and detached level of awareness, serving as a conduit for divine sight. Like an oracle in a Delphic cave, I was blinded in order to open my third eye, to see, trained to meditate with eyes closed, feet on the floor, gently breathing and drawing earth and spirit energies into my body. Stanley, our teacher, said sitting on the floor was correct for Asian people but not for Westerners. I didn't know whether this was true, but sitting upright in a chair was easier than the Lotus posture I'd been practicing on my own.

During my first experiment in formal group meditation, the entire left side of my body was an energetic network of broken synapses. Energy smoothly rose up my right leg, but struggled to ascend up my left. Removing my shoes, I concentrated on energy flowing up through my feet and down through my head, breathing deeply from my solar plexus. Trying to balance the energetic patterns on right and left sides, I meditated at home and at school two and sometimes more hours per day.

We were exhorted to visualize everything with our mind's eye. With rapid-fire commands Stan instructed, "Visualize a shiny red apple, with a green stem. Now, erase the apple from your mind's eye. Visualize a shiny red apple again. Erase it. Visualize it again. Erase it." At first, I didn't understand the purpose of this exercise. I wasn't sure I visualized anything. Did he mean I was supposed to see an apple in my mind as real as the one in my lunch box? No. Seeing was not only for clairvoyants, for those people who visualized images clearly, it also was for those who know, whose creative imagination painted pictures in the space prior to the formation of image. Rapidly, now, I was able to distinguish between knowing and seeing, being and doing. I surrendered, allowing divine intuition to take over.

Other days Stan had us practice compassion. "Visualize a beam of love radiating from your heart to everyone in this room, then expanding out to all of Marin County, the state of California, the United States, the entire planet, and into the cosmos." Or, he conducted a guided meditation.

"Close your eyes and breathe deeply. Draw gold light into your crown chakra. Visualize your body standing in a sacred meadow, morning light streaming across your face. The sky is blue with soft white clouds. An earthen path meanders through the grasses. You place your feet on the path and start to walk. If people other than you are standing on your path, move them away. Now, ask your deep self, 'What is my intention? How far do I want to go spiritually in this life?'"

Immediately, spontaneously walking toward me from the farthest horizon of the landscape I saw in meditation was Jesus, then Buddha, then St. Francis. This was all I wanted: Enlightenment, God.

Part of my training was to be a student reader. Elevating my energy until I reached an empty, meditative state, I sat across from mentees, their thoughts bombarding my aura: *This is crazy! What does this woman know?* Momentarily, their doubt clouded my vision as I sought the gold light, spirit within. By drawing into my center, into the still point, I was able to intuit soul traumas and hidden struggles. Words flew out of my mouth before I could edit what I knew, confirming that the creative imagination, the Spirit's wisdom, was more immediate and more wise than my intellect. I was amazed at the divine capacity within to receive insight into another person. But I was cautious. How did I know I was not making all this up?

My three-times-a-week schedule at the Center, in which I might see eight or nine people, strengthened my resolve. Invariably when a reading was over, mentees were blowing their noses or reaching over to give me a hearty hug, grateful for entrusting me with their souls. A sacred bond grew between us. Forty years later I still keep a box of tissues by my side during such sessions.

At the time, if I had thought about it, I would have said my own journey was singularly unmoored to historical precedent. But in retrospect, I was undergoing spiritual initiation, a common occurrence across the world's cultures and religious traditions. Some type of deep, intense training, the kind designed to disrupt one's sense of self and perception of reality, was a prerequisite for more advanced states of consciousness. The shaman traveling to the upper world to retrieve a soul, the ecstatic sequestered to receive visions, or the Tibetan acolyte on a three-year retreat each practiced unlearning conventional modes of perception, cognition, and training.

Breathing techniques, visualization practices, and soul readings were not ends in themselves but ancient tools designed to deepen the body-spirit integration essential to establishing transcendent awareness or union with one's divine source. Through these otherworldly languages and contemplative methods, I was being drawn to a path already encoded in the deep self.

T HE girls were growing, laughing, enjoying preschool. They gave me so much joy. But it was a sad day when I had to send our beloved dog, Kai, to live with friends on their farm. Struggling to manage care of the twins barely two years old, selling plants for extra income, attending CMS, and walking a dog that had never been on a leash and lunged at people was more than I could handle. Before I put Kai in the dog carrier, I kissed his warm, black nose, hugged him tight, told him "I love you!" and said a prayer. Leaving him at the airport, his confused face peering through the bars, I broke down. I already missed his steady heart and generous spirit.

A few evenings later, at a friend's party in San Francisco, a man asked me to dance. Moving to Marvin Gaye's "Let's Get It On," across from this stranger, I had a chilling realization that the thoughts I was thinking didn't belong to me. I was thinking his sexual feelings about my body. Much of what I considered to be *my* thoughts, *my* feelings were not. I was reminded of a phrase I heard at CMS, "Ninety percent of your emotions don't belong to you." I got it. Spiritually unbounded, I energetically merged with everything around me, viscerally inhabiting another person's reality. The Cassadaga medium's prediction was starkly real: if I didn't harness my own energies, they were going to control me. The atmosphere in the room was charged with a silent, wild language I couldn't speak.

Gradually I developed proficiency in reading souls, diagnosing auras, and protecting my body, mind, and spirit from the intrusion of external energies. Raised to be sensitive to other people's emotions and needs, I lacked awareness of which feelings and thoughts were authentically mine. How did I recognize my vibration from those of others? What did "me" feel like?

I palpated symptoms and charted sensations. When I was afraid to say what I knew or was intimidated by cruel remarks, my fifth chakra, an area slightly below the midline of the throat, choked up, as if I'd swallowed a dry crust of bread. The sensation was slightly different if, instead, I empathized with someone's grief. If I were in a group meeting and a person in the room reacted with fear or lies, my solar plexus would spasm. I learned to recognize the difference between what the mouth proclaimed and the mind harbored. A friend might say, "You look nice today," but think *I'm so jealous of her outfit.* Energetically the discrepancy registered, generating emotional dissonance.

I observed nonverbal cues, which appeared as "pictures" to my mind's eye, traded between couples arguing in the park or singles flirting at bars. I was especially attuned now to sexual innuendo. I asked: Is my nauseated sensation the result of that guy staring at me in the grocery store? What does fear of hidden motives elicit in me? How do I transform my reaction? Every thought, good or bad, oscillated the intricate web of energies, affecting my consciousness and that of the planet.

I was also prudent and sensitive to the rights of others, stopping myself from interpreting auras while standing in a line at the bank or in other situations where I didn't have expressed permission. Persons who believed their psychic gifts entitled them to violate another person's privacy and dispense "truth" inflicted too much harm. Mentees revealed outrageous stories of gurus who effectively brainwashed their devotees, or healers who insisted with authoritative zeal that a patient's heart problem was the result of karmic debt. The most egregious was the time a mentee told me her practitioner attributed her multiple sclerosis to a "past life as a murderer who had a wanton disregard for life." Whether or not past lives were relevant to healing, I firmly believed no one was wise enough to impose causality.

DAILY EXERCISE of intuitive powers enhanced my dreamtime: Chinese sages instructed me in the hidden practices of The Secret of the Golden Flower, an ancient Taoist text I'd been studying. A quorum of prophets, dressed in gilded robes, presented me with the book of my life, saying, "You are ready."

One night a shimmering ball of electric blue energy hovering over my bed awakened me. As invisible beams of tender joy rolled over me, I was left with a sensual feeling of well-being. Perhaps most ethereal was the multi-dimensional, stereophonic music that engulfed my body-spirit senses one evening while praying by candlelight. It was as if heavenly choirs were singing a constant hymn of praise to their maker, anointing my soul with fragrant garlands.

Two powerful dreams of bodily transformation marked a turning point in my growth. In one, I was standing dressed in a white Grecian-type robe in a circular temple room with a high, pitched ceiling. A voice said, "Your mother's energy possesses the left side of your body and has taken over its function." The voice told me to lie on the floor facing east, then said, "We're going to perform a healing ritual on you." My body was spun around by a centrifugal force, rotating faster and faster until I lost conscious control. Like a centrifuge separating out dense particles, the acceleration escalated, expelling my mother's energy from delicate energy fields. Clawing at me, trying to prevent the rotation from throwing her off, she couldn't hang on and was spun out of my orbit.

Another afternoon, while meditating, my desire to sleep was so intense, I barely caught myself from falling out of the chair and onto the floor. Dragging myself to bed, I fell into a dream-like state. I was back in my crib, a few months old, my mother wielding a magazine, hitting me over and over, and yelling, "*Go to sleep! Go to sleep!*" Reliving through my psyche and in my cells the violence inflicted on my infant body, for the first time I realized I had been abused. I plunged deep into my memories, and this pain, too, eventually was healed by transcendent consciousness, riding the wave of my determination to be free.

* *
*

OTHER, more disturbing events intruded on my learning at the Institute. I was saddened and angry to discover that Stan exploited his spiritual gifts, used psychic energies as tools of power or deception, and disguised inappropriate sexual desire behind a façade of spiritual intimacy. As petty rivalries erupted among the faculty, I was increasingly alarmed by attempts to instill fear into anyone who didn't subscribe to the Institute's philosophy and although I learned many valuable techniques that assisted my spiritual growth, I was not a follower. Weekly I was on the verge of quitting.

No longer timid, I confronted Stan and questioned his motives. Why was he taking this path? Didn't he realize what he was doing to all the students? Typically, he brushed away my concerns. "You're not relevant," he said.

That night I had a terrible dream, suspended on a cloud-like surface, lying face up. Stan swooped down from the right side of the sky disguised as a large bird of prey. Letting out a piercing scream, he dove straight at me, attacking my throat, choking me. The sensation was so real I momentarily woke up gasping for air. Plunged back into the dream, I feared I wouldn't survive. At the last moment, I marshaled my strength, rising up to my full height. I was immensely tall and wielded all my powers (this was a dream, after all). With a flick of my hand, I cast Stan away, watching him tumble backward through the air like a fly.

"TRUTH IS A pathless land. Man cannot come to it through any organization, through any creed, through any dogma, priest or ritual, not through any philosophical knowledge or psychological technique."[1]

Such was Krishnamurti's teaching in 1929. At the Center, I practiced meditative techniques and studied spiritual texts. But every outside authority ultimately must be tested by experience. It was not for me to accept without question another's truth. My soul learning had to be verified by the divine within. Only God, Spirit could transform my life. Through both the challenge and grace of my time at the Center I learned that psychic energy in and of itself was no more or less honorable or dishonorable than any other form of consciousness. Knowledge, visions, meant nothing if the flame of Divine Love did not purify my heart.

*
 * *

TOWARD the end of my year's study, John, another student at CMS, and I had begun a relationship and were out for dinner, comparing stories about the Center. I had no recollection of the specifics of our mutual dismay, not that night. Seated in a tucked-away restaurant in the Mission District, a candle in a red globe flickered on the table casting shadows across our faces. Sounds of the street reverberated through the glass pane next to my chair. It must have been October, because dusk darkened the sky with a jaunty gray-blue mist, the air scented by burning leaves. Something about the light fading turned me inward. My mind wandered to images from the nightly news of soldiers killed in Vietnam, mayhem in the jungle.

I was staring into the space above the restaurant's bar when, without warning, my visual senses were engulfed by a living scene taking place across the globe, in a village somewhere in Vietnam or Cambodia. Like a hand tearing paper tissue from my eyes, I was spiritually transported to another world, hovering inside a squalid tent. Below me a mother was mourning the child dying in her arms. Nearby were broken earthen pots and overturned plates. Not a static scene torn from *National Geographic*, this was live testimony as I watched the mother claw at her blouse, clasp the baby to her breast, and muffle a plaintive cry.

I still see mother and child now in an amber circle, their glowing faces illuminated with supernatural light. I am there, in that village, in that tent, gripped by the futility of war and the horror of a world gone mad.

I, too, am mother.

In my witness to a mother's pain and the tragedy of war, John must have noticed my eyes swollen with tears, because he put a hand on mine.

"Are you OK?"

I nodded. Then a wave of grace overcame me, as if even in the midst of suffering I would remember: *Goodness is all there is. Humanity's attack on goodness is reprehensible, beyond pain. All that matters: Love now and in the end.*

* 8 *

Ray of Sublime Light

OCCASIONALLY IT IS possible to look back over a period in your life and see an inner transformation was taking place that you did not recognize at the time. In the future, I would identify two years between the ages of twenty-seven and twenty-nine as marking a fundamental shift in my perception of reality from active study to the dark faith of unknowing, and to a critical moment of surrender. This movement, which was not self-willed but instead arose from an action of the divine in my soul, would initiate a series of life-altering events and establish my inner self on a new foundation of universal consciousness.

If I had realized anything, it was that our beings were stamped with a pattern of spiritual growth in which each soul on its journey toward liberation underwent a process of purification and spiritual death. Beneath the surface of everyday events, I was moving forward by an exercise of deconstruction designed to take away the attachments, limitations, concepts, images, and memories that prevented me from giving my life to the Holy.

But at the time, I was unaware of what would soon transpire to shatter my world and contented myself with reading accounts of soul transformation in shamans, lamas, and other religious personalities. Particularly helpful was this passage from Sri Aurobindo:

In that tremendous silence lone and lost
Of a deciding hour in the world's fate,
In her soul's climbing beyond mortal time
When she stands sole with Death or sole with God
Apart upon a silent desperate brink,
Alone with her self and death and destiny
As on some verge between Time and Timelessness
When being must end or life rebuild its base,
Alone she must conquer or alone must fall.[1]

* * *

SEVERAL years after I departed from CMS, John and I moved from San Francisco to a log cabin at Lake Tahoe. In winter, I'd never seen so much snow, plowed in tunnels along the streets ten to twelve feet high. I bundled the twins, now four years old, off to preschool, went back inside, and propped my feet up against a windowsill to soak in a sliver of sun. The normal stack of books on Buddhism, Krishnamurti, vegetarianism, and spirituality rested on the windowsill, alongside new interests: *Zen Mind, Beginner's Mind, The Golden Notebook, Siddhartha, Black Elk Speaks, The Secret Life of Plants*. I also was reading *Autobiography of a Yogi* and *Seth Speaks: The Eternal Validity of the Soul*, a collection of spiritual insights channeled through Jane Roberts by a disembodied spirit who described himself as an "energy personality essence no longer focused in physical reality."

Four months pregnant, I struggled to haul myself out from under the covers in the morning bent over with nausea. The smell of food made me ill; only cola quieted my rolling stomach. As the weeks dragged on, John wondered if something was wrong. My physician considered me a marvel of health, but I had no energy, as if all my chakras stopped whirling, collapsing in on themselves and sucking my life into a void. It was painful to be upright, every one of my nerve endings frayed. The bones and cells that held me felt stretched, kneaded, as if a giant were shaking me, and everything within me, loose.

Every evening, from around midnight until 3 a.m., my energy returned and the pain subsided. My body, which felt dense and opaque most of the day, became light and translucent. Bubbles of merriment erupted in what the Taoist philosophers call the *dan tien*, an energy center behind the navel. Like Cinderella, wary of the stroke of midnight when magic went away, I crammed my notebook before the bewitching hours ended. Awakening from a kind of cultural amnesia, my thoughts turned to the suffering of women, and to the rise of a new female voice. I didn't, as yet, associate these musings with myself. But that would come.

"For thousands of years," I wrote, "in all corners of the world, where sages meditated and prayed, bowed down to their gods, and lifted their voices in praise and lament, few offered a cry for the plight of women. Rarified contemplative states did not compel yogis and biktus and lamas and abbas and roshis and rabbis and shamans to break the historical silence. Even fewer lifted themselves off their mats to ponder the subjugation of more than half the human race."

Despite my lack of medical training, I was aware that the daily juxtaposition of energy depletion and nightly illumination was not purely an emotional or psychological condition. It was not physical in the ordinary sense. Unlike the gradual mining of memories I associated with psychotherapy, in which the patient traces life experiences and traumatic events back to underlying causes, I neither initiated nor willed the process of my healing. From the center of my being outward, a divine fire burned away whatever impeded remembrance of the deep self. As a soul pain worked its way out of my body, a soul expansion routed the limits on love. It was not my will that sorted and dissembled, but the divine will that caused the collapse of ignorance and resistance. A fiery arrow of love purified my attachments, taking away false identity and belief. When pain receded, joy flooded in.

BUT IT WAS not easy to track the workings of the soul, of the inner light that moves us often against our own will toward greater awareness and love. In search of understanding, I discovered that medieval Christian theologians depicted the soul as an immaterial, indivisible substance conceptually divided into two parts or activities, the sensory and the spiritual, each with its own powers and faculties.

While the lower soul turned toward the world and was susceptible to human pain and sin, the higher soul, eternally pure and holy, was always in communion with God. Medievalists considered the lower soul to be "active," insofar as it speaks of what is achievable through human effort and the ordinary help of grace. In contrast, the higher soul functioned through supernatural grace and was "passive": its operations could not be self-willed, but were initiated by God alone.

Because soul and body formed a continuum, earthly sufferings were felt on one level of consciousness, but another, greater suffering existed that was not in the body but felt in the most intimate part of the soul. It was this particular teaching that our souls suffered the violation and oppression of the spirit in the world that resonated most deeply. For I realized how sensitive, how profound, how precious were our souls! How I felt in my own body every hurt my children received, physical and psychological and spiritual, because I loved them with such intensity. And thus I knew that at a magnitude beyond my understanding the Holy One felt our suffering and shared in our anguish and sin.

This meditation on divine pathos necessitated that I turn away from worldviews undergirded by dichotomies: good and evil, spirit and matter, intuition and rationality, purity and sin, upperworlds and underworlds. I was grateful for the esoteric philosophers, healers, and shamans I'd studied, for each contributed to the cosmic rhythm. Nor did I deny their wisdom or relegate their cosmologies to the region of the nonexistent, the illusory. In fact, I contained a remnant of each worldview within me. But these paths were not my ultimate goal or final state of consciousness. I sought a reality *beyond* psychic and esoteric, *beyond* good and evil. I wanted to find the root, the source behind the cosmic dance of opposites.

However subtle or overt, an element of fear tainted most spiritual teachings, the language of religions infected with violence. Archaic stories re-inscribed the tenuousness of the human heart and warned against angering the gods. Through cultural ethos, I, too, was implicated in tales of sin and retribution, disobedience and despair. Yet, beyond whatever paradox we humans created I yearned to know truth, whole and indivisible. Seeing God face-to-face, Oneness, was my sole desire. If I succumbed to the allure of a worldview in which the balance between good and evil was continually in flux, I would be trapped, forever living out an old story.

Later, when I studied the life of Julian of Norwich, the celebrated fourteenth-century Christian anchoress, I recognized a universal pattern of mystical transformation:

"I felt that there was no ease or comfort for me except hope, faith and love, and truly I felt very little of this. And then presently God gave me again comfort and rest for my soul, delight and security so blessed and so powerful that there was no fear, no sorrow, no pain, physical or spiritual, that one could suffer which might have disturbed me. And then again I felt the pain, and then afterwards the joy and the delight, now the one and now the other, again and again, I suppose about twenty times....

This vision was shown to me to teach me to understand that every man needs to experience this, to be comforted at one time, and at another to fail and to be left to himself. God wishes us to know that he keeps us safe all the time, in joy and in sorrow, and that he loves us as much in sorrow as in joy...For it is God's will that we do all in our power to preserve our consolation, for bliss lasts forevermore, and pain is passing and will be reduced to nothing...."[2]

*   *   *

SOON my realization of non-duality was tested. Since leaving CMS, I was being courted by the director to teach a class and become more involved in its mission. One morning, sorting through a pile of mail on the kitchen table, I opened a letter from the Chair of the Board, designed to persuade me that I was invaluable to the Center, but also to warn me I would be off my path if I withdrew and didn't adhere to their teachings.

For a week I worried, not able to trust my feelings: *What if I'm wrong? What if I really am going off my path? What if these people and this truth were the way God had chosen for me?* My thoughts were colliding. One night, after a rough day taking care of the kids and wrestling with these questions, I sat in a folding chair on the deck for hours under the stars.

By the next morning, I had reached a decision: I would strike out on my own. These spiritual threats were false. Love was never coercive. If I pursued Truth, I could never be off my path. Fear was not an attribute of the Divine.

In the future when I met people who were accused of betraying their religion or persuasive spiritual leader due to being drawn by the light of God in another direction, I would remember to share this important lesson.

*   *   *

IT could have been the baby forming in my belly or it could have been a natural progression of spiritual growth. But I was turning away from whatever was palatable and convenient. What I had been was rapidly peeling away.

Walking along the edge of Lake Tahoe, I counted my breaths and prayed: *Let my false self die so I may live.* As my consciousness expanded, a depth of spiritual fervor overwhelmed me. I could hardly contain myself: *I wanted to see God face-to-face.* I wanted to belong to the community of all beings, drawn into the center of the Divine Heart, resting in my true home. Many gifts I had been given, yet I wanted more. I was desperate to experience the edges and boundaries of reality, the meaning behind everything, the hope for which we were all born.

A few nights later, I had a dream of my body lain out on a pallet, covered with a transparent pale gray cloth. I was dead. Standing at a slight distance from where my corpse lay was another me: I was a tall, glowing, translucent Body of Light. My hair billowed, sparkling green and gold, waves of energy radiated from my heart.

Observing the scene, I realized that my old self had died, transfigured into new life. Flooded with remembrances of ancient cultures I'd lived and landscapes I'd walked, I shed history. However I had defined myself, challenged. Whatever identity I had assumed, dismantled. Whatever falsehoods infected my consciousness, repudiated. Religious history and theology were undone.

I was not a perishable chunk of flesh or a worthless being. I was not conscripted to a particular worldview or confined by salvation stories. I was not born in sin. I was not a lowly woman or a heretic. I was not the shamed teenager branded for disobedience, forced to live her fate. I was not lazy or naïve, stupid or stubborn. I was not someone's sexual fantasy. I was not mother or wife or daughter or sister. I accepted no name, no role, no anchor. My deep self was untouchable. I could not be bought or sold.

In the months ahead, I was taught spiritually how to die without dying; how to open the aperture of the soul to divine light; how to be free and detached without being unloving; how to become receptive to direct experience, allowing Spirit to transform and reform my nature. Painful and unresolved aspects of my personality were uncovered, as everything that I depended on was taken away and I was left having to lean on a dark faith, when even my deepest beliefs and God itself were exposed as *neti, neti* (Sanskrit: "not this, not this").[3]

The most painful, however, were not my errors and compunctions, but whatever prevented me from accepting the gift of being loved by God. While the conscious mind may become fixated on sins and be blinded by its incapacity to comprehend, this was not the process going on deeper and more hidden in my soul. Rather, I was being instructed by Love, by a reality more profound than can be known, willed, or remembered. I had to suffer the disjuncture between what I was not yet and hoped to become.

A great Light pressed into me, breaking down fears and attachments, burning away the dross. *Seek nothing*, I was told. *Wait for truth to find you. The important thing: Live each day with total awareness, detached. Then God must enter.*

* * *

I N mid-June our family moved from a rental in Lake Tahoe to an A-frame we purchased in Grass Valley, a town nestled in the foothills of the Sierra. Off the electric grid, we managed with a gas refrigerator and wood-burning stove. At night the house sparkled from the flicker of kerosene lamps, the starry skies still. Now seven and a half months pregnant, my bedridden state was over. Even better, I was fully awake each day—a triumph! Maya and Gina were endearing, chattering constantly to each other in a secret, invented language. Unable to crack their code, I imagined they were speaking a rare Italian dialect because every word ended in a vowel. They also called each other by the same name: Ni Ni (pronounced nee-nee).

Kevin, back in California from a year abroad, came to pick the girls up one Saturday a month. The shift from one household to another, even on the occasional weekend basis, upset everyone. As if blindfolded, Kevin and I groped unsteadily for a common vantage point from which to relate. More and more we lived in two distinct worlds, worlds so far apart that we literally saw different things when we looked from the same point in the same direction.

The fear I had suppressed of our ability to hurt each other surfaced. Sadly, I would learn how fear could cause me to act against my better judgment and could lead me to commit acts I would later regret. I would learn that despite my desire to be open and loving, I, too, was capable of being the enemy. Out of my suffering, I knew the only way forward was to be a presence for peace, but I still had much to learn in order to feel in my heart that I was united with the whole of humanity, that, like Thich Nhat Hahn, "I [also] am the twelve-year-old girl, refugee on a small boat who throws herself into the ocean after being raped by the sea pirate. And I am the pirate, my heart not yet capable of seeing and loving."[4]

AT MY CHECKUP the following Wednesday, Dr. M said he was leaving on vacation in two days and if I wanted him to deliver this baby, he would admit me to the hospital tomorrow and induce labor. I wasn't keen on the idea, but neither did I want to risk a fiasco in the delivery room with a physician I'd never met.

Next day, in the birthing room, the contractions were so intense I couldn't stop shaking. The nurse suggested a cervical block. Sometimes modern medicine had its perks. Numbed, I observed with curiosity my full-body trembling, but felt no pain. Squeezing my hand, John urged me on, soon to be rewarded with a hearty cry.

"You have a beautiful baby boy!" Dr. M shouted (Why do obstetricians think women in labor are hearing impaired?), gently resting Tobin on my chest.

I counted fingers and toes. Tears pooled in the corners of my eyes. Taking in the symmetry of forehead, eyes, and nose, I was especially struck by how long his fingers were, by the serene look on his face. I wanted to dance and sing. As the nurse swaddled Tobin in a blanket, I leapt off the delivery table, flung open the door, and walked out of the birthing room. Indulging this infraction of hospital rules, Dr. M called after me: "We'll bring your baby boy to you shortly, after we clean him up."

Resting in a little cradle beside my bed, Tobin's whole presence was deeply quiet, as if his spirit rose from a great depth. His eyes, still dark infant blue, were inscrutable wells of mist. I wondered what he saw. Soon Dr. M came strolling up to my bed, hospital gown askew, offering hearty congratulations. "Good job, Bev!" Then warming up his stethoscope to check Tobin's vital signs, he mused, "My, he's in bliss, isn't he?"

Two hearts, one beating inside the other, now pumped independently, tracing the unique rhythm laid down by the confluence of genes, cells, and spirit. Courage was necessary. After months of sharing a mystical symbiosis, all other expressions of closeness paled by comparison. *Your body grew inside me? Your heart beat inside my womb? Nutrients in my blood fed your soul?* Wow. Was gestation and birth not an unfathomable mystery of spirit and body?

BACK HOME, OUR new bundle of love was enchanting his sisters. Rocking his bassinette or cranking up his wind-up cradle, Maya and Gina thought he was the best toy in the house. As the months passed, it was more and more difficult to think of Tobin as a baby. He was so much a person. Often, when he looked at me, he smiled and laughed heartily.

When Tobin was about thirteen months old, I found him in his crib, sitting like a monk, legs crossed, back straight, eyes closed. He must have detected my presence because he opened his eyes, looked at me, and said, "I love you." He didn't speak another full sentence for a year.

Looking back on this time I can see how I was being prepared for a monastic spirituality that was earthy and embodied, not ascetic in the usual manner. Spirit was showing me another way of leading a contemplative life through the practice of motherhood, in which pregnancy and birth were mysteriously involved with the deconstruction and reconstruction of my personality. As I grew in the spirit, I was incarnating in my soul and through my body the union of spirit and matter, divine and human. I cannot explain why this was so, except perhaps I was participating in the divinization of female bodies, when there would no longer be doubt about women's capacity for revelation and prophesy.

*
* *

STRETCHED out on the green sofa, I was daydreaming. Sun was filtering in through the skylights, painting the walls golden. For weeks, since cutting ties with CMS, I had been puzzling over where my spiritual life was going. John had taken the kids out for ice cream; I was alone.

Quiet, I silently meditated. Time passed. I felt a shift in the room's vibration. When I opened my eyes, ten enormous Illuminated Beings, their bodies transparent and glowing, radiated waves of white light. I thought: *They are like the Special One that visited me as a child.*

Absorbing a wordless message transmitted from their hearts to mine, I consciously couldn't explain what I knew. But interior to my mind, I questioned: Why does our world lack understanding of the spiritual life? Is there anyone to share my intense search for God? How am I to help with suffering and anguish?

Suspended in the air, wings quivering, the Illuminated Beings transmitted a sober, compelling answer to my mind:

"If you don't like the way the world is, change it. Whatever you have not been given, whatever you fear is not available, you can make new."

Change the way the world is.

Later, at 2 a.m., light from the half-full moon shining on my face woke me. Unable to go back to sleep, I replayed the earlier event. The message: There were no victims in the Divine. No matter what I had suffered, or how alienated I felt from mainstream culture, I had the power of healing, of newness granted to me from the beginning. I could help sufferers; find others who shared my vision of a holy life. I could leave behind the past and help create a new, sacred future. *May I have the strength of character and openness of heart to change.*

The presence of the Illuminated Ones astounded me. Clearly, the eruption of alternate realities into my daily life belied the distinction between ordinary and non-ordinary reality. The two were intertwined, dwelling next to and within each other. More of late the veil between realities was effaced. In every action, every breath, every thought was holiness. Divinity was concealed within ordinary, everyday things.

Did invisible Beings guide my individual journey? Were our human lives integral to the workings of the divine realm, of the cosmos?

One thing I did know: I was slowly peeling away the false self, letting go of destructive beliefs and social conventions that prevented me from being whole.

YOU SHOWED ME *too much, my God, you gave me too much, and I don't know how to be normal. It hurts too much. For everyone's sake I wish I could be different, but you've made me this way and I don't know any other way. You alone. That's it.*

* * *

NOT long after this event, I was confronted once again with a heart-wrenching choice. Like others before me who left family and community to seek truth, I was driven away from my life with John, and everything society considered proper and acceptable behavior. What was this "everything" God demanded? Why was the path so profoundly wrenching? What did Siddhartha Gautama experience abandoning his wife and son for enlightenment? Did the Buddha suffer deep sorrow or compunction; did he apologize to them? Someday I would repent for having caused suffering to those who trusted me, even as I now know my choice could not have been different.

Is it ever possible to explain why one leaves a relationship? I couldn't explain it to myself. I only knew that I had to leave, compelled by a superior wisdom. And it was only after I left that I found out why: God was waiting for me on the other side of my longing. God was waiting every single day for me to take that step. Oh, it was painful. But I did it.

And then in a flash You came, Holy One.

PART III

GRACE POURS IN

* 9 *

Days of Awe

October 5, 1976

CHECKING THE MAP one last time, I located the corner into Hiroshi's driveway and saw ahead a rustic cabin on a slight rise shrouded in thick ocean fog. An acrid smell of eucalyptus shocked my senses awake. The drive from Grass Valley had taken four hours and by now the kids and I were hungry and needed to get out of the car. Running in three directions, Maya, Gina, and Tobin raced up and down the path. An old friend from the Center for Meditative Studies, Hiroshi had invited us to stay with him temporarily as I sorted out my recent separation from John.

Inside, Hiroshi was drinking coffee. Reaching for a hug, I said, "What a beautiful place! How did you find it?"

"The two acres and cabin were listed in the paper. Isn't it amazing? You must see the garden I've planted. Come this way."

Following Hiroshi to the side of the house, I marveled at orange flowers and yellow melons and tomatoes bursting full from vines. I had never seen a garden like this. Columbines and marigolds, interspersed among zucchini, Japanese eggplant, Swiss chard, and every imaginable herb, rose up in full dignity from the ground. Undulating in curved rows, the garden appeared uncultivated by human hands, as each round and succulent plant radiated its own light. As I breathed in the salty ocean dew, the fragrant light of Sebastopol filled my vision. I did not know that God had brought me here to break open my heart and claim me for Her own.

The kids and I spent part of the day picking tomatoes, which I chopped and sautéed in olive oil with crushed red pepper and handfuls of basil. I'd brought my orange Le Creuset pot with me, my oldest possession, knowing that its thick walls blackened to a shiny patina nurtured the best sauce. If I had had time I would have pondered why this beat up, crusty pot had survived numerous moves and went with me everywhere. The Moody Blues' "Nights in White Satin" played on the turntable and the aroma of fresh ingredients was all we needed to be home.

THE NEXT MORNING I walked through the garden, admiring its lush beauty, and pulled weeds. While my hands worked, I thought of John. If I tried to conjure what I felt, no words came. I couldn't make sense of the piercing pain in my heart. Turning toward the cabin, I was so consumed by trying to untangle my muddled thoughts that I hardly noticed my steps crossing the porch. But the lingering aroma of coffee brought me back to the present and to the sound of the kids laughing outside.

Edith, a mutual friend, greeted me at the door with a hug. We hadn't seen each other in months and she'd come by to spend the day. Barely inside the threshold, I was transfixed by a tremulous awareness. For a brief, excruciating moment my heart felt what my soul knew. I saw how daily John and I deflected each other from loving for fear of being unloved. We were unable to fully love; we could not give ourselves to love. I felt the pain of our "no," a pain that pierced right into the depth of my being. I knew something about fear; I had felt it before. It breathed upon my neck, skirting every attempt at evasion. It came right at me. In an instant, I knew why we fear love.

I turned to walk into the living room, feeling the warmth of the late-morning sun streaming across the wooden floorboards. All at once, right in front of me the wall dividing the living room from the kitchen dissolved away, revealing an endless expanse of palpable light. The Light, more brilliant and dense than earthly light, advanced with such intensity that I fell to my knees and then to the ground, legs weak, no longer able to hold my weight. I lay down on my side on the warm wooden floor and my body began to tremble. Looking up at the white curtains gently framing the window above my head, I remembered thinking how harmonious, how wise, everything is.

Responding to Edith's cry, Hiroshi rushed from the back room and cradled my head in his lap while Edith kneeled next to me, holding both of my hands. As Light beyond Light pressed into me with greater force, I started to vibrate until my whole being was stretched to an edge of emotional endurance. Every sense was heightened. My body could barely hold the magnitude of awe, of being consumed by a higher order of passion and wisdom. If my mind were capable of forming a thought, I would have marveled at how immediate, how profound, how benevolent the universe was. I would have been able to describe the feeling of being enraptured by love, as if every atom, every cell within me were a hymn of praise. But I had no words. Ceding myself to the soft wood and blazing light, tears filled my eyes.

Now an intense suffering racked my body. Acute pains were crushing my heart, choked, stabbing sobs in my throat. My wounded heart became everyone's wound, and the agony of this suffering broke open The Suffering. In wave after wave, suffering flowed into me. So intense was the pain that my heart broke open to become a host upon which the suffering world fed. In waves of anguish, I was shown the cause of suffering and the nature of suffering. No, I was the cause and the nature of suffering, perpetrator and victim, violator and violated. Every suffering was my suffering: I was the stricken, emaciated child in Ethiopia; the mother in El Salvador whose infant had no food; the Jew marched to a gas chamber in Auschwitz or Treblinka; and the battered woman in Somalia. Every person who cried, every soldier who killed in war, every tree sacrificed, every abuser of innocents, every father who mourned, and every torturer's nightmare was my suffering.

As the hours passed, the suffering became more intense until my breath was its breath, and my heartbeat the measure of its pulse. Tossed in the whirlwind of human violence, pain continued to rack my heart and my throat as the fire of suffering turned my illusions to ash. I was God suffering. The Holy One suffered; God suffered the suffering. The suffering annihilated me and left me vulnerable, spent. I died in the suffering. I died suffering. There was no me.

The pain of seeing the Suffering God, the Divine who suffers, was almost more than my heart could bear. The pain of experiencing that Holy Mystery suffered and that we do nothing to alleviate suffering killed me. Forever stamped and wedded to Her plight, I had seen the wounded heart of the Divine.

* *
 *

AFTERNOON ceded to night. The suffering itself, its explosive power forever changing who and what I am, became the catalytic force of entrance into a new world. The whole room shimmered with lights. The air, thick with angelic figures and great, expansive wings, quivered with sound. Around Hiroshi's head were delicate layers of visible energy, pulsating and radiating in multiple colors. I was exquisitely tender, as if the boundary between every one of my limbs and the world had dissolved, allowing me to see with the eyes of my soul and hear with the ears of my spirit. The tree outside the window, the couch at the edge of my foot, and my own eye looking upon them were joined in an invisible communion.

Still on the floor, my head in Hiroshi's lap, I used this moment of respite to ask, "Where are the kids? Have they eaten?"

"Edith took them out for dinner and is caring for them."

Silence now descended upon me, its great gravitational pull causing the waves of pain to recede. Impressed into my soul and the cells of my body was a Presence so comprehensive and a Love so intense that they were concrete, more real than Hiroshi sitting before me, more substantial than the giant redwood tree outside the door. I was pinned to the floor. The heavy, condensed weight of these divine energies turned its illuminative force upon me, restructuring the cells of my body and the memories of my soul. My awareness ascended until divine realms cradled in radiating folds of light surrounded me. At the distant reaches of my innermost sight, a regal figure stood guard before the portal of an infinite majesty I later named Most Holy and Unnamable Presence. Like the tide rushing back to the shore, from the mysterious depths came a torrent of love so total, so complete, that my heart could barely contain its joy.

Perhaps I was now on a couch or maybe still on the floor. But I sat up and it felt as if I had been suspended on a raised platform. I turned my face upward, fully attentive with every fiber of my being to words without sound, to Wisdom pouring into the top of my head. More than vision or illumination, this was an inflow of Divine Truth, a comprehensiveness only to be grasped whole, indivisible. As if the collective storehouse of mystery were revealed all at once, implanted into my soul and opened by love, the key that unlocked everything.

But despite the lack of mental tracking, I did know and understand in a depth of awareness beyond thought. As I write, I can still take myself back to that night as luminous records of wisdom and knowledge populated my consciousness, transfiguring my reality away from the past and into the future, nourishing my being not from the waters of Christianity or Judaism or any named tradition, but from the fountain of unplumbed truth.

And there and then I was a disciple of this new Way, and all that I would ever do and be in this life was established in my being.

Surrounded by beauty, I understood the purpose of life, which solely existed as a tribute to the Divine. I watched the world's sorrow and pain coalesce in a band of fog, a superficial covering over the splendor that lay beneath. Concealed was a unifying force raising everything up to its own incandescence. I swam in an ocean of surrender. There was neither past nor future. No error had been committed. We were all untouched by history or fate, washed clean of any misdeeds.

Annihilated, compelled by this radiant splendor too beautiful for words, all suffering was anointed and bathed in an immense joy. Stamped into whatever it is we name "I am" was a vast openness, a Heart concealed within a Heart, the fiery flame of another way. This was the site of our sin-less-ness; this was the Source from which all blessing flowed. In the luminescent darkness, silence defied and exceeded any truth yet spoken and knew with an unknowing every word uttered. As the watch of the night passed, a new Revealing took form. Impressed into me were ancient truths and future truths yet to be born. I knew by whom I am known and understood by the force of understanding itself.

Yet I cannot say that what was revealed was love or light or wisdom, or every word ever spoken or every thought in the mind of the world. Or even whether it was every hidden mystery, every sublime affirmation of love, or every tree of glory, because the beat of my heart, my life, was bound to its flow. Everything I needed to know was given. Everything I ever yearned for and prayed for was offered. This love, this generosity, broke my heart.

Weak and fragile, I opened my eyes to find that the wheel of night had turned to dawn. I lifted myself up from the mat Hiroshi must have slipped under me and looked around. In one fatal span, time and history were changed. Everywhere there was nothing but the divine imprint. Brought to the brink of death, the sheer passion of the Holy had invaded my separateness and claimed me for its own.

* *
*

You came to me in pain and you taught me what is real
    and what is on the other side of every pain.
You showed me love and the meaning of love
    and the measure of all measures — you alone.
You pierced my whole being with an intensity of longing
    and a consuming sorrow for the world's sufferings.
You broke me open, annihilated me
    and made me your own.
You came to me and offered me everything,
    and you filled me with everything, I had no self.
You gave me everything that is,
    and there was nothing that is you did not give me.
You impressed into my soul a new truth
    and you entrusted me with its care.
I've thrown myself upon your wisdom and guarded your solitude,
    while I've squandered my youth and given away my aloneness.
I've been committed to you from the beginning
    and I will do it over and again.
You have given me my whole life
    and I can only give you everything in return.

* 10 *

Secret Teachings of Love

NOW TWENTY-THREE DAYS since the October revelations, the door between unseen and seen worlds was still open. I was barely functioning in a numinous realm inhabited by figures that reminded me of a Sulamith Wolfing painting. Even during mundane daily activities—washing laundry, unbagging groceries, reading a text—enormous feathered angels with gentle faces surrounded me. Muted colors of gold and blue and purple. Pink wings. I wasn't the same person I had been several weeks before. Even if I had wanted to go back to my old ways, it wasn't possible. Everything had changed.

My core reality had been rewired with new equations. Time and space were malleable, past and future merged, the rules of causation did not hold. I was peaceful; a blanketing calm permeated everything. If I went against the flow of sacred time, the tremulous, roundness of reality splintered, disturbing my connection to the hidden depth, setting off waves of confusion and indecision. But more than anything tangible was the freedom from self-will, that thread of "I" that had distanced me from God. Previously inscrutable phrases—*samsara* is *nirvana*, *Tvat Tam Asi*—were suddenly clarified: my personality, my foibles created consequences in the world of materiality, yet did not disturb the eternal, dynamic *suchness*.

One evening Hiroshi confessed that during the twenty-four hours of my mystical transport, he and Edith were afraid I was physically dying. There were moments when they had been so worried they ran outside to discuss what to do. What would they tell my parents if I died? What would they do with my children? Should they call an ambulance? Luckily, Hiroshi was a spiritual practitioner who had many years' experience with shamans and altered states of consciousness, and recognized that what I was experiencing was more than physical. He felt the Presence and knew I was undergoing a profound transformation. For this I would be always grateful.

In a few years when I became a student of theology, I read in William James' *Varieties of Religious Experience* that a singular indicator of the aftereffects of mysticism was that the recipient had certainty that one's experience was from an otherworldly source. Yes. Transcendence—God, Suchness, Mystery, Holiness—broke into my world. I have never known why.

*
* *

SEVERAL days later I had dropped off the kids at a play date and was taking a break before driving home with provisions for dinner. I rested my groceries on a shiny park bench, which afforded the anonymity I needed to write. I took out my notebook. Observing leaves drift lazily onto the sidewalk or a toddler wobble unsteadily on the grass, I knew that a fundamental shift in my relationship to self, divinity, and cosmos had occurred.

If I were to summarize in one phrase, I would have said: All life is pregnant with intimacy. We swim in the cosmic amniotic sea; we are connected through an umbilicus to Source, to Mystery that never withdraws. Bending down to embrace our broken, swollen hearts, Divine Mercy leads us to a palace of forgiveness. Holy Benevolence quickens us from within, enticing us to shed ancient stories of retribution, fear, and sin. An inescapable cosmic unity invades stars and heavens, subatomic realms, and every living form. "God" was the name we applied to an intimacy and tenderness beyond comprehension, to a divine bearing of creation in all its beauty, messiness, and glory.

More than anything my experience of holy passion set the stage for a new practice of spiritual transformation. Instead of probing my nature to rout out sin and dispel the devil within as I was taught, I now understood that the true method of inner growth was predicated on inner goodness, in which every genuine impulse of the human heart came from the divine and desired to be holy. Thus whatever impeded the heart's purity was an aberration of one's original nature. Many religions considered this aberration to be ontological, the taint of sin that in a sense defined "human."

By viewing my life through the lens of divine pathos, I suddenly realized that human error was the result or effect of a prior wound to a soul's divine integrity. Only by a willingness to suffer, by an expression of one's own pathos that was God's pathos in the soul would our wounds be uncovered and transformed. Renunciation, repentance, and other ascetic practices had their place, insofar as they peeled away layers of social consensus and habitual untruths, but they were not sufficient to bring about healing. It was our identification with the suffering inflicted on divine tenderness—both in God and in us—that opened our hearts to love and strengthened our capacity for grace.

Yet the usual descriptions of spiritual events hardly convey what happened to my soul in mystical rapture. The overwhelming impact of divine suffering upon my mind and heart completely gripped my personality as if I had assimilated the divine pathos into my own emotional life and it had become the focal point of my relationship with the world.

During the midnight grace of my transformation, when stars stood still and stones were soft, I was given an injunction: Do not privilege one religion over another. The claim of absolute truth or exclusive salvation violated the secret teachings of love, tearing a hole in the fabric of creation and wounding the universal heart. Here was something else astir in that command: The unimaginable and universal mercy of God was not to exclude anyone, believer or unbeliever. So powerful was this commandment that I vowed to uphold it. The Divine not only was the source of religious diversity and dialogue, the foundation of nonviolence and peace, the fount of benevolence and mercy, but God also suffered—with us and for us—our possessive and narrow hearts.

In my night wandering, I didn't meet Jesus or Buddha or Rumi. It was not the God of the Hebrew Bible I saw. On the other side of Suffering was neither Moses' vision of YHVH, the Christian Jesus, the Hindu Ishvara, Zen sunyata (Absolute Nothingness), Great Spirit of the American Indian, nor the Muslims' Allah. Perhaps it was a kind of all-encompassing or generalized revelatory vision that called upon the structure of spiritual consciousness without itself being a religion.

I was not given to speak of God by name. I did not know how to speak of an intimacy so total that no words were formed in its flow. Nor how to pay homage to a generosity so vast that all gifts paled in comparison. How could I offer adoration to an ultimate reality that encompassed all beings and was the living vein of consciousness itself? The God of my heart who preferred namelessness taught me unsaying. The God of my darkness showed the way of undoing and unbeing. To say that I was lifted up in reverence only illuminates the inadequacy of speech.

Untethered from tradition, a living path of faith had been imprinted in my soul. Complete and whole unto itself, this sacred way of being affected everything: how I prayed, the meaning of life, the divine. I was a pilgrim, a devotee, of this *way* now forged into my nature. I would learn that my ardor did not shield me from mistakes or reign in my personality quirks, which would be tackled in the usual way. But the quiet stillness, the absolute peace, remained.

Later, as a student of the world's religions, I would recognize my experience as a breakthrough into new sacred territory that was, at the same time, bound to the spiritual traditions that had come before. It was certainly true that the moment I read Meister Eckhart's description of the God beyond God—the God who frees us from God—I felt an immediate kinship. I was being drawn into the great river of silence from which the many streams of religious thought flow. Its central message, the unity of Divine Love, its primary command, no one and nothing excluded.

I envisioned it thus: Alongside the ancient wells generated by the revelatory consciousness of our spiritual forbearers—Rig Vedic seers, Lao Tzu, Buddha, Zoroaster, Hebrew prophets, Jesus, Mohammed—the thrust of divine energies into my being created a new well deeper into the substratum of sacred ground, striking the ancient river that nourished every religious insight and bringing forth a vision of reality previously unknown and unspoken. Whether this new well was initiated in my case or was previously plumbed by others before or contemporary with me, I could not say. But the fact that a new expression of the sacred *happened* and was *revealed* indicated my co-participation in a creative unfolding. Although this knowledge eluded my mental awareness at the time, even then I knew without words I had entered a new revelatory consciousness, and this knowing remained foremost in my mind.

A number of years later I asked Rabbi J, an academic colleague, if she could locate the date of my revelations on the Jewish calendar. I was not surprised to learn in 1976, October 5 began the Days of Radiance, immediately following the period known as the Days of Awe. In a ten-day span—marked on one side by the Jewish New Year of Roshashana and on the other by Yom Kippur, the most solemn Day of Atonement—God, Blessed Be He say the Jews, opened the gates of heaven and became ever more present. This was the holy space given to repent, to make amends for the sins we humans committed against the hidden glory.

Jewish mystics claimed that the *Shekhinah*, the feminine presence of God, was particularly immediate and strongly felt during the Days of Awe. Choosing to remain with humanity after the expulsion from Eden, She voluntarily suffered exile until all creation was redeemed. Belonging to both heavenly and earthly worlds, She was the Divine Heart who felt the tragedy of the human condition, as well as Wisdom who led the way back to our creator. Perhaps because She had been hidden for too long and was co-opted by dominant religious cultures, I refused to name Her. I preferred my *Shekhinah* to remain a smoldering ember burning up my heart.[1]

It would take more than twenty years before I was able to develop concepts to express the poetic quality of my God-experience. In retrospect, part of the challenge before me, both personal and theological, was to travel the pathway of spiritual integration as woman, as female. Godliness, enlightenment, could no longer remain gender exclusive. I was bringing transcendent awareness into my body and mind, constantly reminded that spiritual maturation was a lifelong and eternal process of growing closer to the Infinite One. Everything I have done or become can be traced back to the Days of Awe when the Divine united with my soul.

*
* *

SOON thereafter, standing at the washing machine with a bottle of detergent in my hand, I suffered a stabbing pain at the base of my spine. Hobbling into bed, I covered my head with blankets and immediately fell asleep. When I woke up several hours later the sun was setting behind the trees, casting a golden glow across the Dharma wheel poster hanging on the wall. My head was pounding, my eyes puffy. In my sleep, I had been wrestling with a life decision taking place below my conscious awareness: Would I continue on the path of truth, even if the journey was steep and risky, even if I were maligned, threatened, or ridiculed? Or would I return to a conventional way of life, hoarding what I'd been given as a treasured, but ultimately unrealistic and transient memory? I had free will to refuse, but already knew I could choose no differently than the narrow path.

Spirit had chosen me but I must consent by a deep interior decision. If I did not accept the invitation with full consciousness I would not be a renunciate who devoted one's life to God. The mystical revelations I received a mere three weeks ago had permanently centered me in the Divine Center, around which my entire life now revolved. My soul was wedded to solitude, which was nothing less than everyone's birthright: to be in perpetual communion with Mystery. Having fallen into pure silence in the midst of a mother's busy life, my task was to realize in myself a universal consciousness. Seized by intense longing, this inflow of superior benevolence cancelled my debts, wiping away my tears, and all the old pain and sin.

Transported beyond the psychic and the esoteric to the mystical realm that preceded religions and philosophies, an archive of wisdom, a secret teaching of love, poured into my soul memory that I was now bound to preserve and to share. It was as if a cosmic mind had been imprinted into my being such that if I were to teach or write for the rest of my life I could not exhaust the spiritual understanding I possessed. Yet, despite what I learned and in what I now placed my faith, I was sober. Life would test the veracity of my experience. Only time would tell if my spiritual awakening held meaning for anyone else. I would not proselytize or proclaim.

I would have cried with tears of joy or been overwhelmed by duty, but I was too astounded. I no longer viewed the world through my eyes. The shift in my awareness was more than personal and final; it was cosmic, universal, religious. I saw everything from the perspective of universal love such that all things were included within it. All creation was a child of the radiant orb of divinity. Reality was neither religious nor against religion; it was just that the sacred was already contained within everything; there was no need to demarcate its presence. How could I possibly contain this vantage point?

If I ventured a description, I would have said that the breaking in of the Divine opened up in me the structure of the religious, a reality so comprehensive and total that evidence of it was everywhere while it in itself was nowhere. This curious fact allowed me to embrace my parents' and thus my own Catholic heritage and to find in it and in every other spiritual path an irreducible beauty. I was a visitor who found truth in great mother wisdoms and valiant father theologies. I could dwell in any religion, but I was not of it. And what I was shown or understood or perhaps remembered was this: We are so loved and embraced by the One without name that the spark of divinity in our very finite and small self is infinitely greater than any religion. No religion can contain us; every religion is subsumed under the mystical point of unity in our own Divine center.[2]

I was no longer my own. I'd fallen into Your ocean of compassion. What was most real was that I *am not*.

* *
*

THE shift in my consciousness was exorbitant but also fragile. Normally alert, my awareness was now even more sensitive and attuned. I had trouble balancing the spiritual and physical worlds—ascribing mystical meaning to everyday emotions or events (when, in retrospect, no evidence existed) and dismissing social convention or common sense as unnecessary and limited. I must have been so immersed in universal consciousness that, lacking a spiritual mentor to guide me, I was unable to reconcile human inhibitions with the divine love I experienced. My inability to integrate these two truths created more difficulty in my life; but just as I had not initiated the revelations, I now had no power to turn them off. Soaring far above Earth, I balanced atop the Spirit's crest until it leveled out.

Hiroshi's landlord threatened to evict him for inviting a family to stay and gave two weeks to rectify the living arrangements. Desperate to find our own place, I scoured newspapers and billboards in local health food and grocery stores. Between the demands for housing and the required security deposit and first and last months' rent, money I didn't have, I was doubtful I'd be able to find a suitable rental quickly. The situation appeared bleak, yet within a few days a little miracle happened: I'd found a house on five acres surrounded by vineyards, only required to pay the first month's rent. It had three large bedrooms, spacious living-dining room, and a fabulous yard for the kids.

The months from October to January were a blur. I recall driving Maya and Gina to kindergarten and spending afternoons with Tobin in the park, eating lunch at a picnic table, or pulling him in his red wagon. Halloween, the girls were dressed in matching outfits, Gina was a red fairy, Maya, blue, Tobin, a swarthy pirate. As I followed behind them down the street—Tobin sandwiched between the girls—my heart fluttered with joy. The three of them were so cute! Knocking on doors, they squealed, "Trick or Treat!" Afterward, neighbors gathered to inspect the candy, alert for dangerous items in the haul, and treated the kids to an apple-bobbing extravaganza.

When I tell my story to friends today, they wonder how I was able to raise children and have time for my intense spiritual path. Their question seems to imply that these two moral imperatives should be opposed, when in fact they were intertwined and inseparable. But it was the advent of the October revelations that permanently centered me in the divine heart and, supported by my years of meditation practice, led me to develop what Teresa of Avila once called "*muy determinada determinación*"—"a great and very determined determination to persevere until reaching the end, come what may, happen what may, whatever work is involved, whatever criticism arises, whether [I] arrive or whether [I] die on the road."[3]

Raising children and devotion to a spiritual life rose from the same place: total commitment of self. Of course, on a practical level, my journey was assisted by the cost of living in 1976, which was so affordable that our lovely Irish neighbor babysat my children in her home for five dollars a day.

OVER THE INTERVENING weeks, Hiroshi and I had grown very close and in December I discovered I was pregnant. Still absorbed in the divine realm, even in physical intimacy the heart of matter was alive with sacred, incandescent energy. Overwhelmed by the intensity of divine presence, I thought this was a shared experience but would soon learn I was wrong.

One afternoon Hiroshi returned from a visit to his parents' home in the Bay Area. I was in the garden, raking leaves. Normally gentle and easy-going, Hiroshi appeared sullen and agitated.

"What's going on? How was your visit?" I asked.

"Not too good. I told them about our dilemma, and Dad gave me the standard parent's lecture."

"Well, what did he say? Do you want to talk about it?"

"Dad's convinced me I'm not fit to have a child—I'm too absorbed in myself. I'm not ready."

"Oh."

"Let's just be friends," Hiroshi said, extending his hand to shake mine.

Late autumn light filtering through a canopy of oaks cast shadows across my eyes. How different was this conversation from the exalted communion we had shared a few weeks ago. It was such a shock, that I still wonder if my memory of events was muddled. Because Hiroshi was so attentive, so loving, during the most radical change in my life, I had assumed that he, too, experienced the otherworldly light. But now he admitted while he certainly witnessed the spiritual transformation in me, he did not experience anything superordinary himself. How could I not have known that he would, rightfully, have questions and concerns? Not yet able to reconcile practical considerations with the inflow of overwhelming grace, I was blind to what was directly in front of me. I don't know if it was due to shock or pain, but I didn't feel the heartbreak until later. One of my most difficult lessons would be to put everything in its proper place, to recognize and honor the two truths—social and divine—and not mix them up too much.

I prayed long and hard about my predicament. How would I support another child? Would my already unorthodox life subject our family to further scrutiny and ridicule? I spent hours by the ocean meditating and many nights I lay awake in deep reflection. But finally I had my answer: I was bound to this new life; I was meant to have this child; I would raise four children alone.

Jolting my thoughts back to the notebook in my hand, I noticed an older couple walking together. My eyes fixed on the lovely pair. Both had white hair, he a head taller than she. I could tell by the way their bodies swayed in unison, his red flannel jacket sliding against her gray wool coat, that they shared a familiar grace. As if privy to their thoughts, I imagined the cycle of memories they had lived. But then my thoughts were abruptly curtailed by an aching thought: *I will never have such a relationship. I will never grow old with another person.* What had previously been intimations of my difference, my aloneness, I now assumed was a definite fact: God had called me to a solitary path.

Years earlier I remembered being fearful that I was doomed to be unmarried. In my day, marriage was the supposed final outcome and highest achievement of a woman's life. I'd come a long way from these early misconceptions, but the imprint had been set and it would take heroic efforts to dispel it. While ruminating over these thoughts, pen poised over my notebook, I heard the familiar interior voice: *Until you let go of the illusion of romantic love and the compulsion toward marriage, you won't have a genuine, equal relationship. Only when you know that you are whole and complete in yourself, will you be able to live with another.*

I understood, I truly did, but many years would pass before I untangled the cryptic message.

*
* *

CLOSING my eyes, I silently prayed for strength to shepherd the October revelations into the world. Surely it was not bravery on my part, but God's bravery in me that gave me the courage to assent. The past stripped away, I would follow wherever the Holy One led. Then I took up my pen and wrote:

"Oh should I be able to write this life, to convey beauty to others, to gather ardent lovers of you my dearest Love, to liberate you from the confines of our hearts, to spring open the hidden places where you have been wounded and dwell. O fiery love that sears my soul: may I be worthy of Your Life.

"Solitude is my tabernacle; silence my prayer. Infinite Mercy has made me without country or home that I may possess nothing, even though she has given me untold riches. She has taught me that the heart cannot be owned or the spirit tamed, and that God is not a name that can be bought or sold. I travel with her and she with me in regions of intimacy, where my longing is divine longing and love is all there is. Her gentleness is so powerful all sins redeemed, her openness so immense nothing withheld. From her benevolent embrace we are never separate, and in her compassionate heart all truth is known.

"Every moment is sacrament."

* 11 *

Leap of Faith

I DREAMED ABOUT A MAP of the United States. A light was shining on a town named Bloomington in the middle of the country but I couldn't tell from the dream which state it was in. *This is where you must move.* Once awake, I dragged an old atlas out of the closet; there was a Bloomington, Illinois and, a Bloomington, Indiana. I felt certain the light pointed to Indiana.

Still heartbroken over Hiroshi and estranged from my other relationships, I fled California without telling anyone where I was going. I gave away or sold most of my possessions, packed up the car with what was left, and drove east with my three children. It was winter and Interstate 80 across Utah and Montana was treacherously icy. Our day began before dawn but the old midnight blue Fiat station wagon I was driving was not accustomed to below-zero temperature and each morning I had to implore a different stranger to help jump-start my car. My plan was to arrive at the next stop along our route in time for Maya, Gina, and Tobin to swim in the motel's heated pool before dinner and a night's rest.

We arrived in Bloomington on January 25, to an unusually cold and snowy winter. Temporarily settled at a hotel, I looked for a house to purchase with the small amount of funds I'd saved from the proceeds of property

John and I had sold. Leafing through a local real estate flyer I picked up in the lobby, I was drawn to the photo of a two-story farmhouse in Ellettsville, a village about eight miles from town, on an acre, list price $21,000. At the real estate office I was introduced to June, the listing agent and opening the flyer to the marked page, told her, "I'd like to buy this house."

Back at the hotel, I spent a few hours wondering if I was not certifiably crazy. I was in a new town with three children under six years old, pregnant, no job, and only enough money to last five months. What was I going to do for a living? I submitted my resume to the University of Indiana for a position as a lab technician in one of the science departments. But realistically, I hadn't done lab research in over ten years, and there was nothing on my current resume to support an appointment. One day not long after, June asked me what I really did, and I told her about my healing work and spiritual readings. She immediately wanted one and introduced me to the go-to person in Bloomington for all things spiritual. Before long, I had more students and mentees than I could handle. At night, after the children were asleep, I scheduled private sessions. I also offered weekend workshops on deepening one's spiritual life. The wisdom pressed into me in the October revelations was pouring out. I hardly knew how I knew, but I was what I taught.

Friends I still am close to today were among my first students in Bloomington. It was a seminal time that required a radical leap of faith. I learned to trust the gifts Mystery had given me and to be grateful to support my family doing spiritual work I loved. I didn't have much money, but even better, I had hope. The people I met were gentle and supportive. My neighbors, retired farmers, no doubt thought of me as a wanton woman (three kids, pregnant, no husband), but they were so kind. Sadie stopped by with a loaf of fresh bread or her husband, Kurt, offered to mow the lawn. Tobin, particularly curious about them, would toddle around the low hedge between our yards, step onto the back porch where Sadie and Kurt were rocking in unison, and climb onto a lap. Not given to many words, he gently patted Kurt's hand or threw a chubby arm around Sadie's neck.

Life was simple. Maya and Gina, golden ringlets framing their faces, bounced down the steps to wait for the bus with a friend from across the street. While they were at school, Tobin and I often ate lunch at Wendy's, one of the few restaurants in Ellettsville. Now almost two years old, he comported himself with dignity, sitting in the food-stained high chair dressed in his favorite green flannel shirt. Farmers and truckers stopped at our table to say hi and, lifting Tobin up, pointed out their latest semi, backhoe, or front loader in the parking lot. Summers, we spent swimming in lakes or in the cold, clear water of the quarries. The three kids shared a silent bond. While Maya and Gina splashed around in rubber tubes, Tobin stood at the shore, arms folded over his chest and surveyed the scene. He suffered no fools and thought of himself as his sisters' protector even though they were a head taller than he.

* *
*

M Y belly was finally growing. Still a vegetarian, I'd only gained eighteen pounds. "Every pregnant woman should have low blood pressure, no swelling, and low birth weight," my doctor said. I suspected my supposed healthy lifestyle was the result of enormous stress and the amount of physical labor I exerted each day taking care of three other children. Despite seeing an ob-gyn for checkups, I was having a home birth with Hilda, a midwife.

My due date was July 8, but a week earlier I was on a long walk in the fields behind our house when my water broke. Distant thunder rumbled behind an ominous ceiling of black cumulus clouds. Scrambling back to the porch, I made a frantic call to Hilda, only to discover she was stranded in another part of the county assisting a woman in labor. The bridge she needed to cross to reach me was flooded but if the mother she was tending delivered soon, she assured me she'd find another route to my house.

My sister Carol had flown in to help with the kids and had just returned from the grocery store. It was early evening, Tobin was already asleep in his crib; we decided not to disturb him. While Carol helped Maya and Gina pack an overnight bag, I called my good friends Judy and Ari, who earlier had offered their guest room. Ari would be leaving work shortly and promised to stop by my house on the way home. Soon after I hung up, Hilda phoned to say she'd be by my side in ninety minutes. Confident she'd arrive on time, Carol left with the girls before the storm got worse.

Before long, there was a knock. Opening the door, I was greeted by blue eyes dancing under a crown of curly black hair as Ari bounded into the living room. "Should I boil water? What are we going to do if Hilda doesn't get here?" he said while pacing, a perfect imitation of his Jewish mother. Calm, as if I'd delivered babies at home my whole life, I guided Ari to a chair. My contractions were getting stronger, and Hilda still hadn't arrived. Now the phone wasn't working either. Just when Ari and I were on the verge of packing up for the hospital, we heard the unmistakable grind of Hilda's Volkswagen station wagon. By some miracle, she managed to cross the rising waters. Relieved, Ari gave me a hug, reminding me to call when the baby was born. "We'll be praying," he said.

By now it was 8:30 and my contractions were insistent. Perhaps because I was in my home, I was especially attuned to the events taking place. Bent with pain, I was oddly able to experience labor from a detached vantage point, in touch with the spiritual process of birth at the same time that I was physically giving birth. United with the stars and shielded by the light of the moon, I was held within an ageless rhythm without beginning or end, the entire cosmos breathing my every breath.

If I fully surrendered to the respite of stillness between contractions, I found that the moment of rest, more powerful and more real than the moment of pain, gave me the strength to push on. I saw Carol, Ari, Judy, Maya, Gina, and Tobin in a circle above my bed cheering me on, as real as if they were standing in front of me. The room was crowded with angels, and tall, stately beings of light. All of us—midwife, my family, my body, my soul, and the infant to be born—were participants in a sacred mystery: life birthing itself. I was psychically alert as never before. "The baby is going to be born on the full moon," I announced, trying to get up to pace the wood floors.

"Stay put," Hilda insisted. "Let me check you. Eight centimeters dilated, two left to go." It was now 10 p.m. Hilda was trying to be supportive but clearly thought I was way off base with my prediction.

Abruptly I was gripped by the strongest urge to push. My entire focus was on one thing: Push the baby out! I'm *never* doing this again!

"You're not ready yet," Hilda responded with calm. "Less than twenty minutes ago you were at eight."

"No! No! I have to push!!" throwing myself on the bed with an exasperated cry.

"OK! I'll check you again.

"Oh, wow," she said. "I'm so sorry. I didn't realize you had transitioned so quickly. Push, now, PUSH!"

In no time at all, I was holding in my arms a darling girl with black hair and dark chocolate eyes. She smiled. It was 10:24 p.m. Shana was born on the minute of the full moon. Nestling her in my arms, I was awestruck. O my goodness, she was so beautiful! I knew then, stroking her angelic face, that she was born of spirit, a child of grace, dwelling in eternal light, a child of wisdom, incarnating some hidden depth. How tender and gentle did love flow between us, my heart overcome with gratitude.

The next morning, Tobin climbed out of his crib and came downstairs. Hair tousled and pajamas rumpled, he rushed to my side and gave me a kiss. Pointing to the bassinette, he said, "Baby?" flashing me a knowing grin.

Each of my children came into our world with distinctive soul wisdom, a knowing born from hidden depths. They heightened my consciousness; drew me closer to truth. We shared a bond no one could dispel.

* * *

MY appointment book was filled with people scheduled for spiritual guidance. I saw mentees five or six times a week, often two or three a day from all walks of life and religious or nonreligious persuasions. I served as a soul healer, a friend in spirit who helped to uncover the root causes of spiritual disease and the inviolability of the heart. While I relied on my training, I was not conducting a psychic reading or predicting a person's future. Instead, I used meditative techniques as a springboard to mystical interpretation, much as a composer selected keys on a piano to construct an entire melody. Since the October revelations, the difference in my practice was marked. I was concerned with the soul or deep self and its relationship to one's divine source, however defined or named. A mentee's prayer life and meditation, or lack thereof, was of interest. Experiences of non-ordinary reality or spiritual awakening were noted. I asked, What is your relationship to your God or Great Spirit? Do you have a spiritual practice? Tell me about the first time you felt awe.

Diagnosis and treatment were based on a mystical rather than a psychological or a social understanding of the person. My job was to focus a magnifying lens on soul wounds, a misunderstood and seldom-addressed aspect of spiritual growth. I heard painful stories of sexual abuse, betrayal by spouses and families, and shunning or rejection by lovers, religious communities, and friends. I welcomed those who had been laid low, who could not lift themselves up to the world's idea of success, who had exhausted every other attempt to assuage loneliness or despair.

Sometimes I diagnosed directly from studying a person's aura. Sometimes I was called to extricate a mentee from an unhealthy relationship with a spiritual teacher or counselor. I also was a consultant for psychiatric patients suffering from schizophrenia and other mental ills. When I placed my hands above someone's head and prayed, I often chanted. I had no idea where the chanting came from; I had never been taught to chant. It sounded American Indian but I was certain it was no known Indigenous language. Alternately plaintive, commanding, joyful, when the session was over, I was in awe of the changes in a person's facial expression and well-being.

There were times when I saw mentees' visages change: they were old, they were infants, they were in fourteenth-century costumes, they were Indian maidens and Taoist sages, they were Hasidic masters and street urchins, prostitutes, kings. What did I make of these things? Were past lives real, these various faces and stories instructive to the present life or were they digressive, a diversion? Always, always, I returned to the Divine within. It didn't matter how many props one used, or what kind of images one received, there was only one essential thing: What did Spirit want? What was the deep self telling me? Where did the person need to be mended? It was easy to fall into the trap of being special, holy, or chosen. But then one was not a true healer. Daily I prayed to empty myself of name and identity, to be nothing, so that more and more Divine Love flowed. That was all that mattered.

At the time, I had not heard of the term "spiritual direction," but later discovered that, in large measure, this was my practice. While some form of spiritual guidance was found in every religion, the term "spiritual direction" traced its roots to the desert fathers and mothers of early Christian monasticism. Soul guidance was concerned with the inner life, that dimension of existence that deals with the interior landscape of the heart, with its own rules and properties, ways of knowing, and ways of seeing in order to awaken the individual to the action of the Divine within. The work of the director is not to give spiritual direction but, wrote St. John of the Cross, "to prepare the soul, and God's office, as the Wise Man says, is to direct its path ... toward supernatural goods, through the modes and ways understandable to neither you nor the soul."[1]

Since spiritual direction always involved an effort to heal the person, medical terminology was often used in the traditional literature. This usage was already rooted in Greek philosophy, where healing occurred through the sage who guided the person into the inner life. Thus, Socrates saw himself as an *iatros tes psyches*, or soul healer. In the Christian writings of the desert elders, the spiritual director was described as a "spiritual physician," *iatros pneumatikos* in Greek.

A spiritual director persuaded through tenderness and mercy that it was safe to rediscover the meaning of one's life, and to observe how deep feelings, frequently suppressed or ignored, were clues to the Spirit's call within. One of the key factors that distinguished spiritual elders more advanced on the path from beginners was the ability to see the core of another's soul with love and compassion; to see truth without judgment, condemnation, cruelty, piousness, or the desire to inflict suffering.

"Love takes one's neighbour as one's other self," wrote Thomas Merton, "and loves him with all the immense humility and discretion and reserve and reverence without which no one can presume to enter into the sanctuary of another's subjectivity. From such love all authoritarian brutality, all exploitation, domineering and condescension must necessarily be absent.... The saints of the desert... renounced everything that savoured of punishment and revenge, however hidden it might be."[2]

But as profound as spiritual direction was, before my stay in Bloomington was over I began to feel that I'd been tending casualties in a war zone of wounded souls strewn across a spiritual battlefield. Since I treated in the unseen, mystical realms, I had no one with whom to share my grief and pain. The responsibility of one who took on the role of soul healer was sacred: only prudence, humility, and gratitude were adequate responses.

* * *

GRET was about forty, solidly built, her skin puffy like that of the older women I saw at the check-out counter, fingers swelled around rings, keepsakes of their vows. She had squandered her love on boyfriends and booze, and on a smoking habit that left her lungs longing for air. She came for spiritual guidance out of desperation; she came because she was too far-gone to get better on her own. Ravaged in her way by life, poor choices, and even poorer self-esteem, she clung tenaciously, like a sailor overboard at sea, to the life raft of her spirit. How she had survived was a miracle of its own, how love overcame suffering and betrayal a testament to something true and holy and precious.

She threw herself in the chair and pulled out a notebook. "I tried the meditation you told me about, you know the one to get at my buried feelings?" I nodded. "And something important happened. I'm going to read it to you, OK?

"I'm walking in a dry stream bed. There are sheer rock walls on either side. I have a heavy pack on my back and my head is down. My clothes are torn and gray. I have sandals on my feet. I'm dusty. I walk straight ahead and drag my legs, barely lifting them along."

"How did you interpret this visualization?"

"Me, I mean, I have no hope. I don't believe I can change my life. I have no options. No matter what I do, it will make no difference. I'm damaged goods, tainted."

Gret and I had been working together for about five months. Diagnosed with an advanced stage of uterine cancer, she previously had received radiation and chemotherapy treatments. Afterward, disoriented and unwilling to express her emotions, a nurse referred Gret to me. At our first meeting I listened to her intently for what wasn't being said and for what her deep self was trying to reveal. At one point I gently suggested that I felt that a trauma had divided her inner self as a child. She then divulged that a trusted and beloved male relative had raped her when she was five years old. Soon after the rape she became mute. Her parents had sent her for an extended period of therapy to combat her silence, but until now she had not correlated her earlier body trauma with her current illness.

For months Gret had been exploring how her cancer was another form of body-terror that mirrored and reignited the trauma of her original physical rape and soul suffering. While she continued with her medical treatments, the realization of how her body-soul sustained profound wounds became her lifeline to a kind of miraculous transformation.

"Is there anything else you'd like to share from the experience?" I asked.

"Well, I think I've had a death wish for years."

"What do you mean?"

"I don't know, really. It's something I feel. What do you think?"

"It's not uncommon for a patient to hear a diagnosis of cancer as a death sentence. But perhaps in your case it may repeat an earlier wish to die that you've carried for years."

"Yes!! That's it!! I did want to die when I was raped. I've hidden a death wish all my life. That's why I'm trapped with no way out. Is this why I feel despair? Is this possible?"

I loved "soul recognitions," when someone had an intuitive grasp that short-circuited the intellect. These "aha" moments fueled the forward movement into feelings obscured by lifelong denials of pain. "Buried under the outer conventions of your life, you've struggled against guilt and pain, and a belief that your life is over. Remember our last discussion? Your conviction that you would never reconnect to your soul?"

I grabbed paper and diagrammed the soul, using a conceptualization I'd adapted from several mystical texts of a circle with seven concentric rings. "Take a look at this, Gret. If you think of yourself as a spiritual whole, it sometimes helps to visualize the soul as having a lower or outer consciousness that turns toward the world and is susceptible to injury and sin, and a higher or inner soul that is free and untouched, always turned toward God. See, I've drawn rays of light to indicate God bathing your soul in love.

"The violence inflicted on you as a child damaged the soul's integrity, cutting off your conscious connection between the lower soul and God within. Thus, you may feel separated from God, but in actuality the inner light of the divine in your soul can never be destroyed. Soul healing is possible because the universal field of silent intelligence within is always available to mend the fragmented self, radiating love to the entire body, mind, and spirit. Does this make sense to you?"

Reaching for a tissue to blow her nose and wipe away tears, Gret sat silently for a long while.

"Are you saying that I have a chance?"

"Yes. No one can take away your belonging to the Holy."

"I've never thought of it this way. Do you think when I got cancer that my old wish to die surfaced?"

"Yes, but I'm not making a causative association: Because you suffered childhood trauma, you now have cancer. Rather, when two different but related sufferings coincide, the original scar is given the chance to heal. It's like infected tissue that must be painfully scraped away and exposed to air before it can regenerate. So too, the soul's suffering cannot be remedied by applying bandages on top of buried trauma. Cancer was the trigger that helped you see into your life wounds. It has helped you become aware, to marshal your passion for life."

"I don't want to die. I'm going to fight for myself. I'm going to take back my innocence. I'm not to be discarded."

On a return visit, Gret shared with me her efforts to heal since we'd last met. First she had to combat her guilt, pain, and anger over the realization that her cancer raised a previously unacknowledged death wish. As these feelings were confronted and the debris cleared, guilt turned to sorrow over how she had abused her body. For a while, she also was consumed by anger and disgust at God. Yet slowly she worked through the pain and accepted her paradoxical situation. She was healing, physically and spirituality, but she might still die before her expected time. Standing in the chasm of not knowing, she ceded her heart to the great surrender.

＊
＊ ＊

M Y students and spiritual direction mentees were not the only ones
who survived by moving forward without stopping to feel loss or
pain. When I think back on this period, I was functioning on one level in
a state of heightened spiritual awareness, deeply happy and bursting with
energy. At the same time, on another track of personality, I was working
out fundamental issues of the lone traveler. I always had felt different,
perhaps no different than everyone feels at one time or another. But
my sense of isolation was intensified by the October revelations, which
placed me further outside mainstream culture. Identified by others
as a spiritual teacher or healer or guide, and lacking the social context
accorded established religious authorities—shamans, roshis, priests, or
lamas—loneliness resurfaced. This, coupled with the painful departure
from Hiroshi had crippled my heart, which I knew needed to remain open.

Content to be alone, I nonetheless grieved lost and fractured
relationships. I would lie awake at night not understanding why my
spiritual journey was so threatening to the men I'd known, why in the
aftermath of the October revelations it seemed that the very fact that I had
been called by God made me suspect, dangerous. Male participants in my
classes often said I was not a "normal woman," which I was supposed to
take as a compliment.

All of these relationships, including an important one I had established while in Bloomington, were lost. Sometimes at night feelings of
anguish would rise up in me. One evening in the throes of this deep pain,
an angel appeared above my bed, extended a hand into my chest, and
drawing out my sorrow, cauterized my wound. *You think you need another's
love more than you do* the angel spoke inwardly. *You think you are incomplete,
but you are not!*

The next morning, instead of suppressing my feeling, I demanded to see
its face: "What is loneliness?" I offered the question to prayer, concentrating
with my whole being: *Please show me what loneliness is. What is loneliness?*

Suddenly, loneliness appeared in the guise of an enormous maw, eating into my being, trying to consume me. It was a collective illusion that
clamored to occupy my soul and to obstruct my eternal union with the
beloved, which was already and always *fact.*

Then I understood that while I might feel isolated at times from
humanity, I never felt lonely in nature or in the deep self or with God. I

must claim my right to be spiritually out of the mainstream, to not shred myself for being called away from the daily clamor into solitude, where I was most comfortable and never alone.

I was not separate from the world; I was not lonely. The Creator had given me life and sent me into the world. I would establish myself in society, sink down roots, because I, too, belonged on Earth.

**
* *

ON a dry summer evening several months later my telephone rang. Picking up the receiver, I listened while one of my students asked if I would be willing to conduct a healing and prayer session with her friend Daniel, who had suffered a near-fatal accident and was paralyzed from the chest down. I didn't know what I could do but was willing to help. She offered to stay with my children overnight while I made the five-hour drive.

When I entered the hospital waiting room and introduced myself, Daniel's parents were skeptical and not pleased to see me. After all, not only was I only thirty years old and female, I also was not a minister or other type of recognizable religious professional. But since their son was insistent on seeing me and he was medically unstable, they agreed.

Opening the door to his private hospital room, I was taken in by an aura of serenity. Daniel was lying on his back, unable to move his body, with limited mobility in his hands. I learned that his fever had recently spiked to 103 degrees, the doctors watching him closely because pneumonia could be a potentially fatal complication. I remember Daniel as a young man of about twenty-two, long and lean, with sandy blond hair and intense blue-gray eyes. Approaching his bed, I was greeted with a big smile as he gently placed his fingers on my wrist.

"Hi, Daniel. I'm Beverly. Thank you for inviting me to visit with you. How are you feeling today? Janice tells me you'd like me to pray with you and to ask for healing. Is this what you would like?"

"Hi, Bev. I'm so happy you're here. Yes, if we could pray together, it would help me so much. Thank you so much for coming."

I SAT IN A metal chair next to his bed, closed my eyes, and took Daniel's hand. I dispelled whatever outside energies might be intruding into the room, affecting Daniel and me, and breathed from my solar plexus. Practicing the meditation techniques I'd learned, I settled into a steady rhythm of breathe in, breathe out until I felt myself rise above ordinary reality to a higher, golden plane of light. I offered myself to Spirit and prayed for wisdom, neutrality, and faith, opening my heart to Divine Energies. Without thought, I heard an intonation I remembered from childhood, *Lamb of God who takes away the sins of the world*, in my mind. Next I stood over Daniel and placed my hands a distance above his head. Without touching his body, my hands moved rhythmically over his energetic field: head, front of face, neck, ears, throat, heart, solar plexus, trunk, base of spine, legs, feet, arms, and hands. I asked to be empty, to open myself to divine love and to be one in faith. I prayed that Daniel would heal not only in spirit, but also in body, so that he might be restored and walk again. The outcome was God's alone, and I prayed with an understanding that "Thy will, not my will" be done.

I continued moving my hands over Daniel's aura, praying fervently that God would heal him. He was such a gentle, trusting, and surrendered soul. *Please Dear God, please heal him so he will be whole again. Dear Holy Mother, please hold Daniel in your heart of mercy and heal him of these crippling wounds to body and soul. Please give him the strength to overcome the infection and to walk again. May my body and spirit be of benefit in his journey; may my love of you, Holy Ones, bring solace to him and to his family. May he rise up from this bed and laugh again. Amen. Amen.*

Continuing to pray, heat rose within me, building to a crescendo. Inside my eyes, I saw the room infused with rose light. The light grew brighter and more expansive until I was forced to open my eyes. The room was pulsating, glowing. Daniel felt it; I felt it. We held each other's hand and looked into each other's eyes. "May you be healed, Daniel. I love you with my whole heart."

"I love you, too," he said.

On my way out, his parents gave me big, round hugs. Maybe they, too, felt the room radiant with love. I had no contact with Daniel until eighteen months later when I received a letter from his parents. By the evening of his healing, Daniel's temperature had returned to normal for the first time in a week. Presently, he was in a rehab facility and doing well. Daniel had use of his arms and his parents hoped he would slowly gain leg strength with a walker. Convinced that his faith in the healing had helped him to survive, they thanked me for all I had done for their son.

I will never understand what transpired that day. But I do know, with God, every good is possible.

* 12 *

The Friends of God Suffer

I F ANYONE COULD help me understand my revelations and spiritual condition, their rebbe could, my friends Judy and Ari said.[1] Having already decided to leave Bloomington and move to the larger population centers of the East Coast, I rented the top two floors of a brownstone in Jenkintown, a Philadelphia suburb, in part to be closer to where Reb Zalman Schachter-Shalomi lived.

One afternoon I tiptoed up the stairs to gather the laundry. Shana was singing a little tune in her crib, and I didn't want to arouse her interest in getting up. I'd spent the last two weeks nursing all four kids back to health from the flu and would take whatever quiet I could get. Before I had a chance to put clothes into the washer, Maya and Gina were yelling, "Mom, come down, Tobin's hurt himself!" I dashed down the stairs two at a time to find him crashed on the floor, crying. "What happened, Tobe? Are you OK?" He told a garbled story of playing tag and tumbling headfirst into the radiator. He had a good-sized gash in the center of his forehead and it was going to need stitches.

Three hours later we were back home from the doctor's office. I barely made it up the two flights. On my hip I was clutching Shana, asleep in her car seat. Tobin had my other hand, and behind me the girls carried four little bags of treats as we trudged up to their rooms. I hadn't eaten all day and rushed into the kitchen to grab a piece of celery from the refrigerator. Before I got food into my mouth I slumped to the floor, racked with sobs. I didn't know how much longer I could go on like this. After paying the doctor's bill, I had $26.25 in my checking account.

STILL, THE LIFE-CHANGING mystical events had not gone away. In fact, they were more intense than ever. I negotiated my days around the onset of symptoms, which began with a sensation of joy or love so overwhelming that my body felt crushed by a pain of passion it couldn't sustain. I was often bedridden by the sheer magnitude of the revelations, which had developed a rhythm of their own.

Friends who lived in the vicinity and those I'd recently met through my classes offered to help when I was in these altered states. Kate, one of my students, and I must have had an intuitive connection because she frequently showed up when I was on the verge of collapse. More aware of the telltale signs, I monitored the escalation of symptoms while dashing around the apartment, broom in hand, to tidy up and make sure there was food for the kids. I prepared my bedroom as a sacred space, straightened the bed covers, lit candles, and placed an icon in view. It wouldn't be long before I'd have to lie down.

I didn't know how I looked when I was bedridden, but Kate told me my face was ashen; my eyes burning coals; and the circles beneath my eyes black. She said I looked "scary, like you're dying," but my whole aura and inner being were "luminous, radiating amazing light and love." Attuned to the slightest shift in energy around me, I was painfully aware of thoughts and emotions, positive and negative.

I curled on my side, every fiber of my being compressed by the flaming heart. The white plaster walls reflected the violet light of dusk. Prayers floated above my mind. It hurt to turn my head. I traveled interior spaces where the soul mapped what the eyes couldn't see. Suddenly I was in a scene. Huge blocks of marble rimmed a poured slab. Invisible hands wedged the massive cornerstone in place. *The foundation of the future is set,* the voice said.

Maya and Gina climbed on the bed to hug me. Such love passed between us, as if our hearts were one. Shana was too young, but Tobin in his nonverbal way seemed to know what was going on. He placed one of his hands on my head and one on his head, looked into my eyes, and kissed my forehead. I wrote in my journal, April 5, 1978: *Tears pour from my eyes. God is inside me. God is me. "Grateful" is such a small word for the magnitude of what I feel.*

* * *

In mystical dying, my consciousness was fluid, passing back and forth to practice the transfiguration of body to spirit, spirit to body. In these moments, I knew that the capacity to die was a sign of our divine origins. What I didn't know was that these spiritual events foreshadowed my father's impending health scare.

May 1978 Carol called to tell me Pop had been diagnosed with multiple myeloma, bone cancer. He was sixty-five. My breath was clutched in my throat; no words came. Was this a dream? "Dr. V says Pop's bones are like Swiss cheese," she said, her words a code I couldn't decipher. "He may only have six months to live. He's scheduled on Tuesday for a lung biopsy to figure out what kind of cancer he has. You should fly down here as soon as you can."

I banged around the house looking for my phone book. I dialed students and friends to find someone to babysit while I made the grim journey to Tampa. Thirty thousand feet above the earth, I was praying that Pop would be given a reprieve. He was our shining light. *Please, God, give him a chance.*

Pop was in intensive care, tubes sticking out of his mouth and nose, IVs in his arms. He looked so fragile and gray that I couldn't bear to see him like that. Surgeons had sawed through his ribs to gather a tissue sample. We now learned the test was ineffective in identifying Pop's type of cancer. Carol and I held his hands and prayed; what else could we do? Mom was outside the ICU accosting the attending surgeon.

"Doc, we believe in miracles, in *healing*. Tell me what you're doing. We'll pray, Doc, we'll pray."

"Mrs. Lanzetta, we're doing everything we can."

"Did you hear what I'm saying? You're not doing *everything* you can! He's still in PAIN."

"Um, look, Mrs. Lanzetta, I have another patient to attend to in Room 314."

High heels clicking on the linoleum, she followed the surgeon down the hall, her finger pointed in the air, determined to make him listen. If it weren't so sad, it would have been funny.

Months passed and contrary to predictions, Pop was responding to outpatient treatment. An advocate of alternative methods, Mom had Pop on an Edgar Cayce healing plan and Carol, the angel of baking, showered him with pignoli cookies, baba rums, and cannolis. My once-slender father now had a nice potbelly. Mom's unswerving belief in a miracle and our constant prayers provided as much or more benefit than his medical regimen. Pop would eventually outlive his prognosis by eight years. His oncologist didn't understand our tactics but even he knew medicine alone was not enough.

Whenever I could, I flew in to be with my family and drove Pop to medical appointments. Waiting for him to emerge from Radiology, I looked around the room. Red lines stenciled on shoulder or neck outlined the boundary of treatment as patients swapped stories, their worried faces and shaven heads speaking a language no words could hold.

With each weakening of his legs and each decrease in blood count, Pop's spirit grew stronger. His capacity to surrender with the same quiet equanimity to every treatment—chemotherapy, radiation, prayer, healing touch—amazed everyone. It was almost as though it had taken this confrontation with death to bring him to a deeper power where his real life flowed.

* * *

BACK home I scheduled my first appointment with Reb Zalman. When he opened the door, I tried not to stare at his face. Like a prophet from the Hebrew Scriptures, he had a long white beard, full head of wavy hair, and the demeanor of one who wrestled with ponderous thoughts. Ushering me into his book-lined study, he invited me to take a seat in a broken-down rocking chair across from a battered desk. His eyes darted about the haphazard room; books in various state of consumption piled everywhere, notes stuffed into the desk blotter. The atmosphere was charged, as if awaiting the whirlwind, when the rebbe would touch down on the plane of the merely human.

"So, what brings you here?" Reb Zalman asked with a charming Eastern European accent.

I shared as much as I remembered and could commit to words about the spiritual events over the last two years, as well as the growing number of people who asked me to teach and to heal. I particularly related my experiences of taking on the suffering of others and somehow knowing how to reach their souls.

Rebbe was nodding, his massive head bending toward his chest, eyes closed. Just as I began to wonder if he'd fallen asleep, he looked directly into my eyes. "Tell me more about your relationship to God. What is the aftermath of these events?"

"Each revelation, when it subsides, draws me closer to God. I am happier and more compassionate. Yet I struggle with tremendous bodily pain during these events. I also don't understand why I'm able to heal souls. Or how to handle the pain I take on from their suffering."

Reb Zalman raised his ample body from the chair to locate a slim volume, which he handed to me. The cover title, M'Shivath Nephesh (Restoring the Soul), was stained with coffee rings. Turning to the first page, I noted that the text was gathered from the sacred writings of the master and Tzaddik, Rabbi Nachman of Bratzlav.

"Do you know what a Tzaddik is?"

"No, I don't."

"The Tzaddikim are the 'righteous ones' who have mystical powers and are able to take the hand of a soul who is lost and walk by his side, guiding him through darkness into light. Only the Tzaddik is capable of descending into the depths of another's suffering to bear his burden and to heal his brokenness and sin. According to the Hasidic tradition, at all times there are said to be 36 Lamed-Vav Tzaddikim (hidden saints) on earth whose virtue and faith withhold God's judgment from destroying the world."

"That's amazing."

"In the old days, in my country, we would have said you have 'saints' disease,' and, if Christian, you would have been cloistered in a monastery. Or, if you were a Jewish male, you would be protected studying Torah in the back room of a shul. But you are woman, mother, and you will struggle. The path God has chosen for you is steep and arduous, because God has granted you the wisdom of a Tzaddik without the support of tradition to uphold you. But God, Blessed Be He, always knows the soul's capacity and depth and He doesn't make mistakes. There is a reason you have been blessed with this great gift."

"Thank you so much, Reb Zalman."

"Don't worry or despair. You are surrounded by love. Study M'Shivath Nephesh in depth and it will nourish your inner light."

* * *

Lying in bed that night, I listened hard to make sure the kids were asleep, but my mind wouldn't stop wrestling with Reb Zalman's words. This was the first time someone had used the word "mystical" to refer to my experience. In fact, I'd never spoken at length to anyone about the revelations. Knowing there were ancient, even hidden, traditions that described the spiritual work I did encouraged me. The Tzaddik must be an archetype, a model or form of divine-human cooperation, of transformative power on earth. Rebbe said my work was like that of the Tzaddik. I wondered if the title was earned or ordained. Was I born this way?

In M'Shivath Nephesh, I read: "They [the people] suppose that the holiness of Tzaddikim is due to their holy soul, which they had from their very youth, but the truth isn't so. Days and years he worked, he overcame and transcended himself at every turn, until he merited what he merited. Now, each person can be exactly like a Tzaddik, for a free choice is given to man."[2]

Padding to the kitchen, book in hand, I scooped out a bowl of brown rice and steamed veggies from a pot I kept in the refrigerator. The macrobiotic diet I was on had helped my stomach, and I tried hard to adhere to the advice of my Zen consultant who urged, no oil, no oil! *Tahini OK!*

My mind was churning. I absently poked rice in my mouth with chopsticks, thinking about the intuition I'd had the other day while ironing the twins' gym clothes. *The sensitive soul, the soul attuned to mystery, exceeds the limits of the individual self.* Like the Tzaddikim, my emotions were not always mine. They were more than me. Sometimes they were my mother's or a student's. They could be the nation's or the earth's or cosmic. My soul felt suffering and was unconsciously drawn to heal. When I struggled with what I assumed was a psychological issue, often I was tuned instead to the mystical depth.

There was that word again. Rebbe must mean that the soul of a Tzaddik was holy because it was mystical and universal. The mystic soul not only guided troubled souls, it also was a force that healed. It bound together what was distant from God, what was pained or estranged. It wasn't a static thing but the *activity of one-ing.* Like the lens of a camera redirected diverging rays of light back to one point to render a real image, the mystic soul condensed the divine light, thereby mending the fragmentation caused by suffering and creating a new, undivided image.

Turning the pages of the M'Shivath Nephesh, my eye was drawn to this sentence: "*Therefore, before one can create a world, one has to have the condensation* [contract oneself] *to make an empty space.*" I understood. When I was bedridden with a revelation, the imprint of divine love was painful because it created an empty space in my soul. Only by opening my soul and stripping it of reason, could I become a vessel for God's work. The intensity of the divine descent cleaved my heart to the divine heart. Then all my faculties of thought, memory, and emotion were absorbed, exceeding my body's stamina.

Years later, I found an anonymous fourteenth-century author who echoed my new insight: "My opinion is that he who is the true friend of God is never without suffering.... He always suffers.... He suffers in his actions, and he suffers in his will; a third suffering is in his spirit and a fourth in God. And each suffering fosters a particular joy."[3]

* *
*

Immaculate Conception Church, Jenkintown, April 13, 1979:

PRIESTS and altar boys dressed in Good Friday vestments emerged from the side door of the vestry. The organ sounded a dirge of lament. I stood in the back of the church, my gaze fixed on the blue-robed Madonna painted in a semi-circular arch behind the front altar. Gilded angels kneeling on pillars were covered with purple cloth. This was the season of mourning.

It was dark outside, and the procession slowly advanced along the side aisle. A priest chanted the Passion narrative from the Gospel of John. Behind him another priest carried a large wooden crucifix, stopping to allow worshippers to venerate the cross. By the time the procession reached the back of the church, my face was stained with tears. When they got to me the priests cast down their eyes. I didn't know if my tears troubled them, but I was not ashamed of my feelings. It didn't matter to me whether I was in a synagogue, ashram, cathedral, or kiva, I honored the ones who bore humanity's sins. I kissed my fingers and touched Christ's feet.

I hadn't been to a church service in over twenty years. But I had come this evening because a few weeks ago, while walking by Immaculate Conception, I felt drawn to grasp the handle of the large wooden door and enter. Kneeling on a padded riser in a back pew, I was offering silent words of gratitude when suddenly two angels floated into view. Approaching me on each side, they drew me out of myself to an otherworldly region. We descended to witness the suffering of those who were branded by their own form of hell. Pain governed the darkness. Conceit and despair ruled the hearts of these fated beings. Their damaged souls were tormented by combat and greed. My mind was reeling. Why must the sorrow be so great or the price so steep? If only we could tear down all the crucifixes, swastikas, and other emblems of our insufferable cruelty.

As quickly as my descent began, the twin angels wrapped their arms in mine and carried me aloft. I was facing a translucent wall of energy. People were suspended in a wall of limits, a consciousness of "I can't go any further" or "the end." A purgatory of neither here nor there, no one was touched and no one could touch anyone else. I focused on a person who looked familiar and realized that all the suspended people were crucified, arms outstretched, heads slightly bent. But their penance was illusory. It was nothing but thoughts. Out of fear, despair, loneliness or pain, they were trapped by their own negation.

Arm in arm, the angels and I floated through the wall. On the other side was a flowering meadow of never-ending beauty beyond beauty, and love, pure love. From all directions, radiant figures, angels and archangels, appeared. Three of them glided up to me. On my head they placed a crown of exquisite jewels and glistening light. Around my throat was fashioned a necklace of precious stones unseen on Earth. A gilded belt, meticulously carved, was tied around my waist to bring wisdom and strength. Then the middle illuminated figure anointed my forehead, "All that you do not receive on Earth, is given."

Wiping away my tears, I turned my attention back to the procession moving up the center aisle. The air glistened. My heart was full.

* * *

A WEEK or more after the Good Friday service, I dreamed night after night of nails pounding into me. I saw God's hands reaching out to me. Yet, I resisted. Why me, God? Why me? In one of the dreams, I said, I won't be a messenger. But for each "won't," I uttered, I was bombarded with a resounding YES. It was not even my yes, but YES. I cried out loud and furious NOs. How could I not accept where I was called? What must the total suffering be if my suffering seemed so great?

The roaring fire burning from inside woke me at night, parching my throat with the fury of its demand. How could I believe God was calling me? How could I let go of the place that was avoiding, that wouldn't give this gift? I must surrender my resistance and let go. Here, on the brink between realities, suffering was endless.

I toiled in my dream up the mountain of deception, scarring my feet along the way, to ascend to the summit of peace and contentment where only one light shined forth. I was still bleeding. Was there no one to extend a hand? There were millions and millions of hands.

For weeks I struggled to understand the meaning of these dreams and visions. In that second-story flat, where I moved to be near the rebbe, at age thirty-one, I was constantly questioning: Did the merciful God I experienced cause souls to suffer in hell? Why was I so affected by the crucifixion narrative? When the twins were at school and the little ones on a play date, I spent hours in meditation. I prostrated on the living room rug and prayed. Watching candles flicker on my home altar, I begged God not to abandon me in my quest.

Slowly I detected a thread uniting my Good Friday experience with my crucifixion dream and the journey through the lower and upper worlds. Attachment to self was the cause of suffering. No higher authority condemned souls. Even the torments of hell I witnessed were illusory, magnifications of self-will, replayed and made real by distorted minds. Divine Love was *All That Is*.

Subtle elements of self-will were also buried in my personality. I feared that if I fully embraced God's call, would I be accused of pride or worse, of delusion? Yet I could no longer deflect the gift I'd been given by holding out for conventional desires or saving a piece of myself for a partner. Even the shame I harbored of being "too much," too intense, too incisive, too committed to this path for my parents, for the men I knew and the women I befriended, unraveled.

Now I knew the crucifixion was deeply personal. I also understood it was not solely a Christian event. Like all profound religious manifestations, it was universal. One might approach its mystery through the life and death of Jesus of Nazareth. But as I experienced in the October revelations, it was possible to participate in the sacrificial offering directly. A state of total vulnerability, a complete releasing of self-will, Christ's physical sacrifice also represented a mystical death, when temporal and eternal, soul and Divine interpenetrated. A Zen *koan*, the Sufi's *fana* (annihilation of self), or the shaman's dismemberment each practiced the dissolution of separateness, a mystical re-enactment of the universe's primordial oneness.

When I allowed myself to be vulnerable, when I held sorrow as both ontological and empty, the promise of becoming divine-like in all my imperfection was real. Yet no one could sustain total openness. Only by the continual practice of letting go of my will did I draw closer to Mercy, weeping our salty tears.

13

Nine Jewels of Night

S NOW FELL OVERNIGHT, dusting the rocky shoreline with a glistening layer of white. I was dreamy, not quite awake, when I felt Your presence in the still dawn. Looking out the bay window, waves lapping against sand, I was filled with gratitude for everyday miracles.

Several months ago, we had moved from Philadelphia to a furnished Cape Cod in Southampton right on Long Island Sound, for the low off-season rent of $250 a month. Decorated in the typical manner of 1980s summer homes—wicker furniture, glass-top tables (which I immediately locked away), and lots of flowered cushions and drapes—the interior was an array of orange, pink, and beige. With an airy kitchen, large living room, and two bedrooms downstairs and two upstairs, there was ample space for our family.

I remembered the room arrangement precisely because the couch where I usually read at night was directly facing the hall connecting the girls' bedrooms. Almost every evening, I stifled laughter as an enormous pillow with two little legs sticking out scurried across the hall. It was Shana, sneaking into the twins' room to sleep at the foot of their king-size bed.

Through a mutual friend, I had met Selma, who offered teaching space out of her residence on the Upper West Side, where I was now heading on December 9. Typically, I spent Tuesdays and Wednesdays in Manhattan while my friend, Marjorie, stayed with the kids. During the day I scheduled mentees for spiritual direction and healing sessions; in the evening I taught a six-month course on the inner life and spiritual transformation. One weekend a month students came to Southampton for extended study.

I dropped the kids off at school and by 8:45 a.m. I was on the Long Island Expressway listening to WKCR when the announcer interrupted the music with continuing coverage on the death of John Lennon. At 10:50 the previous evening a lone person had shot Lennon in the back four times at the entrance to the Dakota. Selma's building was only a few blocks north of the Dakota on 72nd Street. Gripping the steering wheel, I visualized the crowd of mourners gathering outside Lennon's apartment, the makeshift memorial overflowing with flowers and cards. My thoughts drifted to his spirit, whether there was deeper meaning to the time and manner of his tragic death. All I could do was pray.

* * *

SELMA owned a penthouse overlooking Central Park West. Stepping off the elevator into a living room larger than the entire bottom floor of our Southampton rental, I greeted twenty or more people reading or engaged in light conversation. Judy, a 50ish former dancer, her flowered skirt splayed out on the floor, launched into questions before I sat down. "Can you explain what you meant by soul suffering in last week's talk? Doesn't the spirit transcend pain?" I suggested we suspend questions until after the opening meditation. Fifteen minutes later, the energy in the room had calmed down.

"Let's start with Judy's question about soul suffering. Last week I described the soul as having a lower and higher aspect of consciousness. The lower soul, turned toward the world, suffers violations of the body, mind, or spirit, creating tangible physical symptoms. But always the higher soul is one with its divine source and untouched by sin. It is in this way that a soul heals from within.

"Let me clarify with a quote from Teresa of Avila: 'It should be kept in mind here that the fount, the shining sun that is the center of the soul, does not lose its beauty and splendor; it is always present in the soul, and nothing can take away its loveliness.'[1] Thus, the soul or deep self can suffer, even as the pure light within transcends pain. Does this make sense to you, Judy?"

"Yes. I get it."

"Does anyone else have questions from last week, especially the emphasis I placed on how a materialistic worldview or dogmatic spirituality can violate a person's integrity?"

"I do. I've been trying to apply last week's lecture to my counseling practice," Jeremy said. "But I've noticed that often I either aggressively override a client's beliefs, thinking I possess a superior position, or am at a loss about what to say."

He told the story of Lucy (name changed, of course), a woman he was assisting who had a terminal illness. The last time he saw her she was distraught because she had been told by a psychic healer that her sickness was karmic, the result of some atrocity she'd committed in a previous life.

"I choked up and didn't know what to tell her. I wanted to say that her healer was an idiot and had no right to impose her beliefs. So I gave her my standard counseling spiel about loving oneself and looking for the positive in every situation. I felt fraudulent because I really didn't address her concerns. But, then, I would be imposing *my* beliefs, right?"

"In every healing situation," I said, "it is important to maintain humility and recognize when your interpretive system is inadequate. One way to evaluate is to question whether your approach is doing harm. When you offer only one type of causation in an atmosphere that by definition defies linearity, you will not contribute to healing. Because in truth, we don't know how healing occurs. What are its principles? Why does it work in one case and not another? All of these factors require an open mind.

"The way I would address the problem is by saying this: 'Karma is not a broad enough concept to evaluate Lucy's illness. Disease is more complex than any one philosophy; there are environmental factors, emotional factors, genetic predispositions.'"

"But what if she's right? What if her illness is a payback for some horror committed in another life?"

"How does knowing this help? Does it make her anguish easier?"

"I don't know! That's the problem. I didn't know what to do with her interpretation. What do you think about past lives and all that stuff?"

"I don't factor in karma as the only or final interpretation because the law of cause and effect does not account for innocent suffering, suffering without prior offense. In fact, I don't think humans ever know enough to pass final judgment. We can only approximate. More important are one's moral compass, the soul patterns present in one's life, and the spiritual desire to re-establish a state of inner harmony."

"Can you explain that again? What do you mean by soul patterns? Are you saying that karma is illusory or she didn't commit atrocities in another life?"

"I believe we carry certain soul predispositions, whether through some kind of spiritual genetics, energy intelligence, or other means, that may become gifts or challenges in a life. These patterns affect our thoughts, emotions, spirituality, and even our susceptibility and resilience to particular mindsets, behaviors, or diseases. Can these predispositions be traced to a concrete past life? At times such a perspective should be taken into consideration, but at no time have I found it sufficient in solving the complexity of the mind-body-spirit connection.

"Soul healing transcends cause and effect. Whatever identity you've assumed, whether through personality or soul, can be changed through love. Beyond every interpretation you hold is the eternal and mysterious quest for balance. I cannot absolutely know that someone's physical or soul health is affected by a karmic situation, but I can recognize suffering and do whatever is possible to alleviate it."

As a group we spent a good portion of the evening grappling with Jeremy's questions, as well as Lucy's confusion caused by her healer, and the ways in which a particular worldview influenced either the liberation or suppression of the deep self.

Packing up my notes, I thought, *I love teaching*. It was a privilege to devote time to preparing lectures and drawing on relevant spiritual texts for what was to this point the most comprehensive course I'd designed. But, mostly, I taught from experience. This was not an intellectual study about a spiritual way of life, but the transmission of that way of life, heart to heart and soul to soul. Because true contemplative learning was a participation in and transference of divine energies, our studies had catalytic effects on practitioners, transforming old habits and deepening awareness.

This positive expansion of self often generated cellular, even soul resistance. When a topic disturbed a belief held by one or more group members or threatened ego identities, the collective atmosphere trembled. Suppressed feelings and unspoken thoughts permeated the room as participants struggled with letting go of the false self. The intensity of collective anger and fear generated by a roomful of people desperate to hold the ego intact took a toll on my energies.

To maintain equanimity, I taught participants a contemplative practice that I later named the "inner monastery meditation." Centering consciousness in the heart, one breathed slowly and rhythmically, drawing energy up through the feet and down through the top of the head. With each breath, one's awareness was directed to the cave of the heart, to abandon cares and rest alone with the Divine.

At the end of the long evening, I felt complete. Work done. Yet I barely had the energy to get into my car and drive the ninety miles home.

* *
*

THE next Tuesday, eating lunch with Selma, I discovered by accident that a few of the attendees were coming to class high on cocaine or other drugs. I was stunned. Apparently, there was a prevailing sentiment among a certain contingent of students that if you didn't use drugs, you were pedestrian. Or that mystical experience was the likely outcome of substance-generated altered states. Ritualized drug usage certainly occurred in religious ceremonies throughout history, however, such practices were sacred and closely supervised within a cultural context.

I had limited knowledge of the subject. The few times I had experimented as an undergraduate with psilocybin, I had been yanked outside my normal frame of reference. But while time and space distorted and everyday reality expanded, I was not taken out of my *self*. In contrast, the October and subsequent contemplative events were ontological, freeing my whole being into a limitless expanse of meaning and love. I was profoundly certain that what I experienced was a *gift*; that it came from outside or above *me*, not subject to my volition.

I wondered if drug usage was the result of our American fascination with quick fixes. Perhaps our love of individual self-advancement was a hindrance on the path. We lacked healthy models of the sacrifice required to turn one's life around. The 1960s influx of disreputable spiritual teachers hadn't helped. Surrendering to a higher truth was accepted in theory as a noble goal, but in real life most people found vulnerability frightening.

Despite these unsettling realizations, a close spiritual bond formed among class participants. Coming together weekly to study and meditate, a distinctive energy signature permeated our gatherings. I glimpsed what it must have been like to belong to one of Buddha's sanghas or to an early Christian community. Central to our spiritual practice was the deconstruction of harmful religious beliefs and psychological habits that violated dignity or denied equality of persons. Students learned that emptying of self and longing for the divine invigorated an interior transformation guided by the secret teachings of love.

While prevailing wisdom taught that God consciousness, salvation, was tied exclusively to religion, I witnessed the organic unfolding of a mystical theology with global implications. If a person could profoundly, authentically grow in spirit without belonging to a named tradition, there was hope for other people fleeing from religion, abandoned or abused. This was more than a solitary path for me alone, coming to fruition along the marshlands of Long Island Sound. It was the breaking in of a new type of religiosity, which I would later learn was connected to other emerging spiritualities: interfaith, ecological, feminist.

This universal mysticism celebrated our differences of orientation—it was the embodiment of Gandhi's belief that "there are as many religions as there are people." By sinking into the vibrant overflow of love, there was no desire to proclaim, convert, or stereotype one's spiritual progress.

Nevertheless, I had great respect for religions and sacred texts, and for the important role religious communities exerted as repositories of humanity's shared spiritual heritage. I was standing on the shoulders of giants, indebted to centuries of wisdom, and to the radical, life-changing promises of sages, prophets, saviors, and monks.

When I look back, it was during this period that I first recognized that teaching and writing about emerging spiritualities and new monastic consciousness would be my life's work. Since I had not advertised classes or sought students, I can only suspect that spirit was at work drawing souls of like intention together. Grateful to serve other pilgrims on the path of inner realization, I was fortunate that many also would become close friends over time. We helped with children, supported each other during periods of turmoil. We became a spiritual family, one that is still together after thirty-five years.

* *

A ll week I had been grappling with questions: What did it take to be free from patterned behaviors and psychological traumas? Inner disturbances derailed the spiritual consolation that had sustained me over the last several years. I questioned God: Why, if I had experienced you so profoundly, had I thrown myself on scraps of love, even marriage, as thoughtlessly as going on a date? Intellectually, I could cite reasons: I was looking to replace the absence of a mother's love with men. I was operating from a teenager's moral compass in relationships that were not mutual or supportive.

A few nights later, writing in my journal, I almost knocked a cup of mint tea off my nightstand, overcome by a mental vision: cascades of nine precious jewels, set into interlocking gold spirals, floated above my head. Colored lights exploded from the spirals—pink, green, violet, yellow, blue—the beauty of the shimmering image stunning. Glancing out the window, the rising moon was a golden orb in the cloudless sky. Time and space were dream-like.

As the image grew more vivid, I was able to see that the entire spiral contained multiple factors of wisdom and multiple stages of soul development that were neither linear nor hierarchical. The nine jewels represented three divisions of three degrees of spiritual growth. Yet the number "nine" was not mathematically precise. Each jewel was a limitless mystery of divine-human possibility.

Suspended in the divine milieu, the glistening jewels were called "nights," their fiery light turning to ash our distorted habits and beliefs, plunging the soul in darkness. But these nights of surrender were also "jewels" because every degree of spiritual development guides us to a new future, to a more whole and embodied understanding of our place in the sacred web of life.

Titling the vision the "Nine Jewels of Night," I sketched into my notebook a diagram of three levels of contemplation: in the person; in the collective, which included the whole of humanity, the natural world, and the cosmic forces; and in the divine. If the first two divisions traced the soul's experience from the human side, in the third division, the soul participated in the radical openness of divinity, bearing suffering, sacrificing "I-hood," and plunging into Great Silence, where God images and religious languages were shed.

A directional beam of light shone on the second level of contemplation, in the collective. Informed that I had done considerable work in the personal and divine levels, the next stage of my journey involved unraveling social, cultural, and religious constructs. These included the norms and assumptions that identified and controlled what it means to be a bodily being: in my case, physically, as girl and woman; mentally, in women's ways of thinking and knowing; and spiritually, in categories of consciousness supportive or harmful to my person.

Here was the answer to my questions: I had to retrace my steps and descend from unearthly heights to accomplish the more arduous task of turning every wound into gift, of spiritualizing the body. In order to fulfill the task put before me I would need to understand the particular wounds and shadows that afflicted my embodiment as female, woman.

I wrote the words in my journal but little did I realize how many years would pass before I was able to reclaim the fullness of this truth. I'd been looking at the world and my self through divine eyes, but I had yet to see my self and the world through *my* eyes. At home in the mystical realm, in certain personal or social interactions I was sightless.

I realized then that my journey and that of many other people differed from classical categories of spiritual growth, which tended to focus on *personal* trials and sins, neglecting the social conditions that impinged on and violated a person's inner health. Over time I would learn how the details of everyday life was the medium of mystical transformation. A cartographer of my soul, I mapped the geography of liberation, noting whatever mindset prevented or obstructed integration of my divine-woman self. Yet, I not only had to pass through my sins, errors, and imperfections, but also institutional and social transgressions that harmed the dignity of persons and of creation. While critical self-reflection was necessary for spiritual development, the traditional culmination of the spiritual path—union with God, *nirvana, samadhi*—was not the highest achievement unless it consciously took into account and mystically bore the pain of *otherness* and the suffering mass of the world.

It was no longer sufficient for me to have experienced truth or God consciousness. I must *be* what I now knew. This was my deep desire: to offer myself for the divine experiment, to reciprocate this unimaginable, staggering gift of love.

* * *

MORE lately, suffering had become personal as I agonized over my father's illness. I believed sacrificial suffering was redemptive, but I didn't want Pop to go through it. I wanted to take away his pain, keep him with us for more years. But I was able to bear my sorrow because even when we were not physically together, Pop was spiritually with me.

One night in a dream Pop helped me to accept his prognosis: Sitting on the top of a small series of steps and pointing to a general area near the groin he said, "I have pain." Red irradiation lines covered his body; his legs were scarred from surgery. "*Where is the pain? Where, Pop?*" I grabbed my father's hand and started running, running through grassy fields, dotted with potted plants and flowers, tears streaming down my face, staining my shirt. Pop floated along like a balloon in the air. When we stopped to water a dying plant with a garden hose, Pop looked so frail and small. "I can't bear to see you in pain, Pop. I don't want you to hurt! I don't want you to hurt!"

Despite his frailty, Pop reached over and put his arms around me. He was radiating Light. We merged; became One. The experience of union was overpowering, the love between us palpable. His embrace was stronger and sweeter than my tears.

Awake, my thoughts turned to my mother. She was suffering as well. Her days were occupied with doctor's appointments; fear over whether Pop would survive; and devotion to his healing. While my heart was unshielded from my father, the love I had for my mother was constricted by something I couldn't name. Yet this distance was everything. Was it anger or pride or stubbornness on my part? Was it something my mother did not possess and could not give? What barrier was between us? I wanted to love her unreservedly, but instead this is what coursed through my soul: a Fire.

Compassion commanded more of me. I set about excavating buried layers of pain: my fractured relationship with my mother, its effect on Pop, my sister and her family, my children. Was my pain about the absence of love of mother for child? Was it my brother-in-law's contention years ago that Carol and I were abused children? Perhaps Mom's heart also was divided, too caught up in her mental distress to give herself to her children. I couldn't ignore this absence between us, as if we had blasphemed the Holy One Herself. It pained me to think these things. It pained me to be outraged.

As the sun rose in the morning sky, I prayed:

> May I be worthy to love and to be loved,
> May I be a source of forgiveness,
> May I be empty of desire, except yours alone.

* *

By now it was Christmas Eve. I was stringing lights on the tree; Maya and Gina were taking turns on a step stool hanging decorations, while Shana gingerly passed them the next ornament. I didn't see Tobin, who a short time before had been intently stapling a paper chain. Worried, I found him lying on the floor behind the couch with a flushed face and glassy eyes, hallucinating colored animals. I rushed for a thermometer. With a fever of 104, he was becoming disoriented. I quickly asked Marjorie if she could come over to stay with the girls, then bundled Tobin into the frost-covered station wagon. Only five years old, already he was too heavy for me to carry.

Back in June, right after school let out for the year, Tobin woke me one morning with a large red protrusion on the front of his neck. Over the last months, he'd seen five doctors who told me it was "nothing" or a "spider bite" and to give him Benedryl. Not to worry, they said. Yet the bump had never gone away.

In the emergency room at Southampton Hospital, the attending physician diagnosed a systemic infection. "If we can't keep the infection down, we'll have to admit your son to the hospital," he said. "But first I'm going to call an ear, nose, and throat specialist."

An hour later, Dr. C poked his cheery young face around the white curtain dividing the patient cubicles. "Well, what happened to you, my young man?" he asked, tousling Tobin's blond hair. I pointed out the red bump under his chin. He palpated, checked vitals, and shone a light in his eyes. "Let's talk outside," he told me.

Pressed against the gray-green wall, I heard the doctor say, "Your son needs surgery." Fluorescent lights cast a yellowish pallor across Dr. C's face. All I could muster was "Surgery?"

"He has a thyroglossal duct cyst and as soon as the infection comes down, we need to remove it. Haven't you taken him to doctors previously?"

"Yes! Over the last six months I've had him to five physicians. I was told it was nothing. Or it was a spider bite and to give him Benedryl. What's a thyro... whatever you said cyst?"

"No, this isn't a spider bite! In an embryo, thyroid cells migrate from the base of the tongue along the neck to above the breastbone. The tube-like path these cells take is supposed to close up. But in some cases, it doesn't and the space fills with a thick mucous-like sac called a thyroglossal duct cyst."

"Is it dangerous? Why does Tobin have a systemic infection?"

"Well, his body is no longer able to fight off the infection. But I wouldn't be overly concerned. It's a standard procedure, and I'll make sure I remove every bit of excess tissue."

Without health insurance, I dreaded the bill I was anticipating. But when I spoke to Dr. C's receptionist, I learned he had cut his normal fee by two-thirds and wanted me to arrange my own payment schedule. On the day of surgery, Marjorie stayed with the girls while I drove Tobin to the hospital. Anxiously awaiting the results, I was profoundly relieved to see Dr. C beaming as he came out of the operating room. "The surgery was a complete success," he said, taking my hand. Despite Tobin's sore neck and my cramped back from sleeping overnight in a chair, we were both smiling the next morning and giddy to go home.

By the time Tobin told the girls about his surgery and we had put our things away, my throat was on fire. Gasping for air and choking, no sound came out. If I ever doubted the raw connection between mother and child, this event dispelled that. I would NEVER again succumb to a professional diagnosis if it didn't ring true to my maternal instinct.

* * *

ALL the good things this year—living on the Sound, Dr. C's kindness, and the kids' great teachers—reminded me that Spirit was always at work for the good. Without a conscious effort to imbue my children with love, we swam together in its liquid atmosphere. What I was unable to do physically, about the world, about friends or adults who betrayed their trust, I tried to compensate for by instilling in them a steady dose of generosity. I wanted them to have integrity of heart and resilient souls. I wanted them to know that they were loved unconditionally even if and especially when they were troubled or in trouble. Like a conductor of their pure hearts' symphony, my job was to teach them to hear the divine harmony until they were able to tune their own souls. Perhaps the best I could do for my children was to strive for emotional honesty.

The contemplative life I'd been granted was not just for me or to pass onto students, it was the glue that held our family together. Without my children, without the five of us, I would have been nowhere. I cannot say what I would have done had I been born a man. But I know, as a woman, I have been blessed to offer myself to the formation of loving, respectful, and brave adults.

We laughed a lot. Cracked up at the silliest things. Sometimes when I picked them up at the bus stop, I'd say, "Hop in, we have a very important, mysterious errand."

"What is it, Mom?"

"Oh, I can't tell you that. I can't divulge anything until we're there." I drove back roads and across parking lots, taking a long, circuitous route to the local K-Mart or Target. The kids kept asking, "WHERE ARE WE

GOING?" "I don't know, I think I may be lost." Finally at our destination, I handed each of them the extra money I had made that week to buy a treat.

Sporadically throughout the school year, I gave out "hooky day" passes, taking one of the kids out of school for a special excursion together—a movie, a trip to the City, a Broadway show, a drive to the shore. Some of my adventures were well conceived, others not so much.

I still have flashes of standing at the kitchen counter, dipping bread in beaten eggs for French toast. Bacon's on the grill and a half-gallon of orange juice is on the table. *Get the sandwiches made and into lunch bags, remember to pick up more milk at the grocery store, get the kids into snow boots and jackets and to the bus stop, load dishes into the dishwasher.* Looking at my watch. 7 a.m. and we're on the move.

Even in the midst of family activities and everyday difficulties, the spiritual help was there.

THE SCHOOL YEAR over, I couldn't afford summertime rents in South-ampton. We moved to Bayside, Queens, to a less expensive apartment in a decent school district, and later to a nice house in upper Westchester. For the first time in years, I thought about returning to school. It was difficult to support a family on spiritual work. I needed to pursue an advanced degree if I ever hoped to get out of financial stress. Whatever visions guided me, or spiritual gifts I possessed, my future was to be tested in the "real world."

PART IV

LOVE OF THE WORLD

14

Night Vigil

JUMPING OUT OF THE CAB, I was rifling through graduate school applications in my briefcase, trying to find directions to the hermitage I'd been assigned. I had an appointment with Sister Mary Ann for spiritual direction at 11 a.m. and wanted to get settled in my room first. On a cliff overlooking the Hudson River, the retreat center exuded serenity and expansiveness, the stone buildings and 400 acres a haven two hours north of Manhattan.

I found my way to the small meditation room Sr. Mary Ann used for spiritual direction, invited to settle in a rocking chair across from her. Taking my hands, sister prayed for the Spirit's guidance during our soul sharing, asking that our time together be blessed with wisdom. After a brief review of my spiritual direction sessions, scheduled once a day for each of my four-day retreat, she turned her piercing gaze in my direction and asked, "What brings you here, dear Beverly?"

"Lately, I have been struggling with conflicting emotions and a deep remorse over my past." I then told her about my recent lack of interest in spiritual things and a strange inability to resolve my turmoil.

Her deep gray-blue eyes looked into me with compassion. "When did these feelings begin?"

"They've been building over the months, but recently the sense of disjuncture and lack of spiritual consolation has become more intense. I've been reading *The Confessions of St. Augustine* and identify with his distorted will...Wait, I have the quote here," I said, pulling the book from my bag. "'Thus did my two wills, the one old, the other new, the first carnal, and the second spiritual, contend with one another, and by their conflict they laid waste my soul.'[1] A similar conflict is taking over much of my spiritual time."

"Let me understand. You are saying that recently you have become disaffected with ways of life and even spiritual activities that were previously important to you. And you are at an impasse between two conflicting life directions. Is that correct?"

"Yes. It's as if there are two parts of myself that cannot be reconciled. I'm stuck."

"What do you attribute this to?"

"Well, I've given this question a lot of thought. And what comes to me immediately is that when I was a teenager, I was forced to marry a college boyfriend."

"How old were you?"

"I had just turned seventeen. You see, I went to college when I was fifteen." I told her most of the story about my parents' rejection, marriages, divorce, and raising four children as a single parent. I also shared the suffering-exaltation experience of the October revelations, subsequent mystical events, and teaching.

"From the moment of my God-experience, my spiritual intention has never wavered. But I realize that I still am running away, like the disgraced sixteen-year-old I had been, from shame and blame."

With silent attentiveness, she listened. When I had finished, she reached over to embrace me. "I am so sorry for your loss," she said.

Choking back tears, I was moved by her compassion.

"Tell me about your prayer life. Where is God in all this?"

"My prayers are heartfelt, although more silent, more interior, without words. I still feel the Divine Presence as intently as ever, but it's painful because I'm also caught in this troubling contradiction, unable to heal the fracture but not able to go forward, either. Of course, I've read John's description of the dark night of the soul. It fits my situation, especially because of the pain I feel over my poor choices and lack of clarity."

"I agree. John of the Cross has a perfect understanding of this period of impasse and turmoil, when the light of the divine shines on the soul's deepest wound, darkening one's faith and stranding the self in a netherworld of unknowing. Interiority, desire for solitude, and anguish over one's sins are marks of the dark night experience. What is most troubling for you?"

"I can't understand how to forgive myself. How could I have contributed to causing pain when I have been given the gift of Divine Love?"

"This is the paradox of the spiritual, is it not? That one's journey to God-consciousness and body-mind-spirit integration is lifelong and fraught with challenges.

"Yet the dark night is that interior contemplative process that leads to integration, to the reuniting of lover and beloved, as John so eloquently stated. It seems that the divine light is illuminating your wound, calling you to greater healing.

"For your reflection over the next several days, I suggest you get in touch with the loss you feel. But I want to give you specific instructions: you are not to think of solutions to your dilemma, rationalize what you feel, try to make it better, or strategize a future. Your task is simply to feel the loss. One way to do this is to be attentive to the ways you avoid feeling pain, and to redirect yourself away from rational distractions back to feeling."

AFTER THE SESSION, I followed the edge of a little stream flowing through the north side of the property, my mind a jumble of thoughts, my heart swirling with pain. *Feel my loss?* I had never let myself do that. I wasn't sure I knew how.

So, I began with what I knew. I wrote. Sitting on a bench overlooking the Hudson River, I took out my journal, wrote down the loss of a childhood, of a wedding with family, of acceptance and recognition, of true love. The loss of a life direction barely begun, derailed by a marriage I never wanted, denigrated, trussed, kicked. The loss of a stable family relationship, one in which two people shared raising children in a mutual, loving commitment. The loss of belonging, cast out as a migrant who did not fit in either my parents' world or in that of my partners because the self that was choosing was a false self.

I had wandered between realities, relentlessly pushing forward, never looking back or confronting my pain, in the mistaken belief that my survival depended on it.

Writing brought on hot sweats, chills. Trembling, I left the bench and unsteadily moved to a rock outcropping visible among the bushes.

Leaning my back against its cool surface, my heart overflowed with supplication: *Let this stain of my will perish in the fire of your love. Cauterize my wound by the power of your mercy.*

For the rest of the day and into the night I prayed and wrote. When I digressed to rationalize or judge or predict, I would stop that thought and write, WHAT DO YOU FEEL? Then I would begin again.

* * *

T HE next morning I rose before dawn to watch the sun rise over the river. Then, abandoning my perch, I meandered through the forest, leaves rippling in the shadows, to the streambed, water bugs skimming across rocks. I was ruminating over the previous days' events, creating eddies in the water with my hand, when a torrent of emotion assailed me with such explosive force that I fell on the ground, sobbing convulsively. As if my guts were twisted with pain. As if twenty years of pent-up grief and confusion and shame were being vomited up. I was reliving the horror of that August day in our kitchen on Old Barto Road, my mother screaming, threatening me, "You WILL get married, you brat! You ingrate, how DARE you do this to me?"

Doubled over with spasms, a voice rose from an unknown depth and cried: *It's not my fault! It's not my fault!*

Later, when the pain abated, I splayed out on the soft green moss, spring winds rustling over me. Everywhere was silence. Lulled by the still air, I felt as empty as pure light.

At 2 p.m. I was in the rocking chair sharing with Mary Ann my emotional breakdown. She wanted to know what I made of these events.

"I'm in shock over how many years I've hid in shame and guilt, unaware of my wounded soul. It's hard to believe that I never considered my parents' complicity or that I'd been set up to fail or was the object of intentional harm. I had been a vulnerable sixteen-year-old who was essentially orphaned, alone in the world without guidance.

"But, I have to say, the most shattering effect was the bodily experience of innocence, of radiant goodness, that was mine alone and yet greater than me, when I blurted out, 'It's not my fault.!' Even though I know that every pain, patiently confronted, unravels the causes that violate the purity of one's soul, I was still protecting my damaged self. I had never applied this method wholly to my trauma."

Mary Ann sent me away with new instructions. I was to spend time in prayer, asking what I most deeply wanted. And then to meditate on this: "God, who do you say I am?" I was to complete the prayer time by imagining myself in the gospel scene from Luke, Chapter 6, verses 6–11, where Jesus heals the man with a withered hand.

Leaving the meditation room I thought, if only I had the courage to abandon myself to darkness, when faith and mind no longer gave strength, when I was bereft of ever again being right or loved or whole, this was the answer to my prayers.

An hour later in the retreat library, I read this from Thomas Merton: "When we seem to be useless and worthy of all contempt, when we seem to have failed, when we seem to be destroyed and devoured, it is then that the deep and secret selfishness that is too close to us for us to identify is stripped away from our souls. It is in this darkness that we find true liberty."[2]

* * *

I RETURNED to my room and dropped like a stone into a pool of dreams. When I woke, it was dark outside, and I had to rush to the dining room to catch the evening meal. I ran into Sr. Mary Ann and Br. Joe at the buffet table, and over plates of spaghetti and salad I listened to stories about church politics and the declining enrollment in monastic orders.

The next day I was waiting for my appointment with Mary Ann, ruminating over the deep amnesia and frozen apathy that had stolen my resolve, smothered by life choices I falsely assumed were beyond my control. It was as if one part of me was moving at light speed toward divine love while the other part of me was shielding myself from blows. With greater clarity I understood the message of the Nine Jewels of Night: how a soul could be completely infused by Divine Grace yet not be free of a worldly wound.

It suddenly came to me that the moral conflict of my story, the difficulty I faced to simply admit, without anguish, regret, or shame that I gave birth to four children with three different men, had wrenched from my heart whatever superiority I may have carried. There was no justification or recompense. Forgiveness didn't figure into the equation. Even now that American society is awash in single parents, unmarried parents, children of multiple parents, children of LGBT parents, I had been unable to share my history with any but my closest friends. Yet it was the pain of being cast out as the rebellious and headstrong daughter that was the very thing that broke my heart, allowing God to flood in.

Looking through a window at the undulating waves of the Hudson River, I wondered what would have become of my journey without these challenges and failures. Thinking back, I realized my defeat as much as my success had been a gift. It humbled me and tore apart my narrow view of accomplishment. Breaching social convention aroused escape from the traditional family life I knew growing up; the pursuit of the unthinkable became my doorway to freedom.

Yet, in the midst of upheavals, I had difficulty remaining steady in ways that would have shielded my children from moving around the country, enrolling in new schools, and losing friends. Because of the spiritual demands on my soul, I was an inadequate breadwinner, struggling as a single mother to feed and clothe my children and still have a creative life, a life of meaning not ground down into a daily round of tasks.

In retrospect, I lamented my lack of clarity and my inability to overcome the fear that this man or that father might hurt me, take the kids away, or even in some deep recess of my soul, kill me. Certainly, later, upon first reading St. Teresa of Avila's stark analysis of women's lot in sixteenth-century Spain, I commiserated: "After [they become nuns], they do not realize the great favor that God has done to them by choosing them for Himself, and by rescuing them from being subject to a man in the outside world; a man who often kills their bodies, and God forbid, could also kill their souls."[3] These thoughts seem far-fetched to me now in the quiet of my writing studio, but they were all too real to the girl-woman running away from home.

Years ago when I was an undergraduate, I was intrigued by a novel about an American Indian woman who raised children outside the tribe. I wanted to be like her or I already knew I was like her, outside the familial circle and surviving by my own rules. I had no concept of social convention or perhaps simply ignored it. It didn't occur to me that a nontraditional family that wasn't the standard 1950s version (mother, father, kids) would be shunned or suffer prejudice by the dominant culture. Spiritually, the truth seemed so simple. Society could not dictate family. Biology did not dictate family. Bloodlines did not dictate family. We were a perfect family exactly the way we were.

I'd never found anything noble in the perceived advantage of lineal descendants from so-called "pure" bloodlines. Strictly speaking, no one had unmixed ancestry. In fact, obsessive concern with purity was simply another form of control that exacted its greatest toll on women and children, fueling cultural aggression and possessiveness. Even the language used to describe lineage or family dynamic was demeaning: out of wedlock, half-sister, stepbrother, bastard. Nonetheless, I no longer naïvely believed that systematic, structural prejudice against children of mixed blood or blended parentage didn't stigmatize those who, through love, fate, or happenstance, did not conform to local custom or etiquette.

This, too, I wanted to deconstruct.

By the time Mary Ann called me into her prayer room, I had made a leap in self-awareness. When I recounted these realizations, she agreed this was cause for celebration and for further reflection. She suggested I walk the recently completed Labyrinth, created with stones on a knoll overlooking the river.

"It's a circular journey, inward then outward," she said, "that follows an archetypal pattern of the three inner stages of the soul's progression through purgation, illumination, and union. I have a feeling if you walk the Labyrinth as a contemplative practice, you will shed these limiting self-views and establish a more complete union."

I did spend several hours in walking meditation. But that night, I was pacing around my hermitage, unable to get comfortable. I'd tried to meditate, but was plunged into hopelessness and grief. A deeper disjuncture was being routed out. It was one thing to be a naïve teenager forced into a life direction, but I still couldn't reconcile my mature self, the self who had experienced God, with my terrible choices and moral failings. How many people have I hurt, running away and blind to my actions and refusals? How have divorce, separation, and my pursuit of a spiritual path created further suffering for my children, my parents? The two realities lacked a common standard of comparison; they did not add up. What did this mean? Wasn't life made of innumerable injustices, betrayals, and contradictory truth claims? Had not some of the greatest saints started out as the greatest sinners? My heart torn to shreds, my two wills were in "mortal combat."

Please help me.

* *
*

SOMETIME after midnight, I jolted awake, drenched in sweat. Reaching for the glass of water on the nightstand, I looked up at the crucifix over my bed, lit by the full moon. I was staring at the bent body nailed to the wooden cross. For a moment, it seemed as if Jesus looked down upon me with the greatest compassion. What could be more contradictory than the Christian story of holy innocence dying on a cross?

I leaped from bed, throwing on a bathrobe, and knelt on the floor. With my whole heart, my whole being, I prayed: *May I suffer the pain I have caused, the sins I've committed. Dear God Please, break open my stubborn, prideful heart.* Until the early hours of the morning I prayed and wept and surrendered.

Just as light appeared on the horizon, I found my notebook, intent to record the night vigil when helpless and alone, with nothing of my own to rely on, I was made empty and pure. The thread woven through my life was that the incommensurability of elements in my story mirrored the incommensurability of reality itself. I learned through the struggles and sorrows of my life, including the pain of shattered relationships, single parenthood, and children with different fathers, of divine mercy. To suffer the anguish of what did not and never would add up was God's way of breaking me open to love and benevolence. But this was more than the standard theological insight that suffering was redemptive.

Incommensurability was not superficial or illusory; it had more ontological weight than that. It was the great mystic teaching, the high achievement of the human heart. Dissimilarity marked the surface of an infinite depth, a portal through which each squandered act of betrayal, abandonment, or failure served to transport me into another, more loving realm. I discovered through my deep regret and my pain over not having a tidy life the openness of God, and the priority of nonharm, most especially in the realm of spirit, religion. Against my stubborn refusal to let go of shame and guilt, I was forced to learn that each quandary I faced was the measure of my ability to withstand paradox and inconsistency and thus to invite compassion to take root in my soul.

The fact that I couldn't unravel my story, that my actions could not be explained away or understood, that I had to bear my own burden, sparked a fire in my heart and humbled me.

I was not released from responsibility. But the pain I had harbored these many years over ruptures in my social fabric, I now understood was God's action in me, guiding me to unimaginable freedom. Paradox, division, disunity, conflict became the catalyst of transformation and the impetus for self-analysis that finally allowed me to let go and forgive myself. Within every unthinkable act was the possibility of bearing the disparity of what could never be understood or made palatable, and to emerge unscathed by hate or revenge. My job was to uphold the elusive center, the unifying, deeper level of awareness that forged divine compassion from the disparate and fractured elements of my journey. It was because these paradoxes could not be resolved that I was shown a love beyond measure. Through brokenness and suffering, I was led to wholeness and strength.

And, again, not because my story is important. This *is* the Story.

Filled with inescapable joy, I danced around the hermitage. I no longer needed to deny the painful parts of my journey or hide the blessings I'd received from motherhood and family. I couldn't make amends for the harm I'd caused or the hearts I'd broken or the lamentable decisions I'd made. I couldn't change the past. I didn't want to change it. I didn't know how completely and actively (if subconsciously) I had rejected the standard female story. I had to admit, I must have wanted to raise children alone. I threw away a traditional family life.

The men in my life also were complicit. They, too, most likely didn't want to be husbands, tied down to unequal relations. They might not even have wanted to have children. I don't know. But if I looked at myself honestly, I chose them in part because of this fact. And, what if they chose me for the same reason? And because in the end I had no right to judge them, whatever private ranting or solitary anger I possessed over their actions or inactions or refusals, their stories were not mine to tell. Nonetheless the inability to parent together did not absolve us from the pain we caused our children, nor could it substitute for the benefit of a mutual, loving two-parent family.

All I was left with was inscrutability.

I offered no defense.

And then, from these low places, from the anguish of confronting my violence, my fear, my cruelty, grace poured in. My will began to crumble and, with it, pride. It didn't matter what had been done to me, I vowed to never again pass on the pain.

I couldn't honestly even write as the guilty party any more. Even guilt, a supposedly confessional emotion, was a sham, a diversion. Holy Wisdom led me away from every identity, every psychic prop or emotional crutch. When the pendulum ceased to swing, when the paradox yawned open its cavernous jaw, I stepped through into a timeless space, a hollow of nothingness. Liberation.

* * *

My final session with Mary Ann was a blessing of love, hugs, and prayers for continued healing. Leaving the meditation room, I gathered my suitcase and waited outside for my cab ride back to the train. Soon a fellow in a yellow minivan pulled up. As I stepped into the backseat, the driver asked, "Where r' you goin?" "To the Metro North station." "Oh, that's not far, it'll be $10." As I'd taken this same route prior, I knew that the flat rate was a rarity and a few dollars less than the usual fare. Directly in front of me was his identification card, which immediately attracted my attention because his name was Mahatma Das.

"Mahatma Das, that's a noble name," I said.

"Yes, I'm Indian. Do you know what it means? My name?"

"Yes, it means Great Soul, and it always reminds me of Gandhi."

"You've heard of Gandhi? What do you do?"

"I have read many things by Gandhi. He was a great soul, no doubt. I'm a student of religion," my catchall phrase that summarized an identity vague enough to be inclusive.

"Yes, yes. But do you know what means, 'great soul'?"

"Do you mean what does it mean in English, or to Americans, or what does 'great soul' mean spiritually?"

"What does Great Soul mean? What does it mean?" I now wondered if HE didn't know what it meant and wanted me to tell him—an odd request since this was his name. Or if was he testing me: did I know the meaning?

"Well, a mahatma is a person whose soul is venerated for his or her spirituality, for one's identification with a universal concern for all creation."

"Yes, yes. But that's not all, that's not all. A great soul is one who spends every moment, awake or asleep, focused on God. Their focus is only that. Always on God."

"That's a very good definition. I like it, Mahatma Das."

"I am a disciple of my sainted teacher. 'Das' means disciple, you see. He taught me everything I know. Can you see that I belong to a religious group? See the painted line on my forehead, down my nose? I am a Hare Krishna."

"Oh, yes, I can see that you are committed to a spiritual path."

"I am. My teacher tells me that what we all need is God-consciousness. Not material consciousness or mental consciousness. God-consciousness. This is what we need now."

* 15 *

No Hunting Except for Peace

ABOVE MY HEAD the TV was tuned to one of the morning talk shows. I was staring at the screen, but the sound of the drill pierced whatever break I'd taken from study. As I reclined in a comfortable dental chair protected from pain by Novocain and high-speed drills, around the world right now bodies were tortured, infants starved, soldiers died. A fragment of a poem by Reza Baraheni rattled my mind:

it takes only 3 hours to change a man

the delicate bloom of a student
    whose eyes shone with joy
    becomes a clubbed
    starved prostrate cur...

    when the door has opened and shut, the prisoner
    whispers, I haven't confessed yet, I
    haven't confessed...

    it takes only 3 hours to change a man[1]

"Are you all right?" the voice asked, jolting me back to the drill in my mouth.

"Yes, fine."

Walking the palm-lined quad to the Social Sciences building, I found it hard to believe I was in graduate school on a scholarship at the University of Arizona in Tucson. It had been more than fifteen years since the disastrous undergraduate events. Distracted by an iridescent green salamander wriggling its long tail under a bush, I wondered, Will I ever be fine? Last night I had been reading Terrence des Pres' study of survivors of the Holocaust. Des Pres raised a question that constantly had occupied my thoughts: When all we believe is fractured into shards, when atrocity is so heinous it is absolute like God, what kind of language makes silence speak? Only "a kind of archaic, quasi-religious vocabulary," he wrote, "…only a language of ultimate concern is adequate to facts such as these."[2]

I had submitted my master's thesis to the Sociology Department with a dedication to survivors and victims of genocide, but was told to remove it because it was "unprofessional." This by the same professor who threw a cup of coffee into his colleague's face at the last faculty-student brown bag lecture over a dispute about Foucault, the French sociologist. Truly there was no limit to the rash behavior of the person who has stabbed his own heart. Already approved to enter the doctoral program, I had decided to move on.

Not reconciled with the systems approach of sociology, which was never meant to penetrate the façade of conventional behaviors, or with the Marxist leanings of my cohorts, I failed to understand why macro social theories ignored the spiritual dimension of culture. Two semesters of theoretical statistics almost did me in, and I balked at forced scientific objectivity when my interests lay elsewhere: What was the relationship between speechlessness rendered by atrocity and the silence of God? How did damage to a people's dignity, such as occurred in colonialism and the resulting aftermath of social instability, affect the individual soul and by extension the soul of society or nation? Who or what spoke for the deep self?

Thirty-six years old, I was an outsider among younger graduate students, dressed in shifts and low heels, not the short shorts, tank tops, and flip-flops favored by the majority on campus. Between the time I spent in study, care of the kids, and household chores, I had little energy left for socializing. It had been years since I had written papers or taken tests, so it was difficult to shift into academic thinking, and the intense concentration caused me bodily pain. Yet, sociology was an important counterpoint to the spiritual worldview I inhabited, turning my focus to another dimension of analysis, the structural forces behind poverty, racism, sexism, and war.

I dropped my briefcase onto a table under the yellow canopy of a palo verde tree, spreading my papers out. In the fading light, the Catalina Mountains turned purple and orange, while a cactus wren, its speckled head bobbing up and down, gathered nectar from a wreath of white blooms atop a massive saguaro. Everywhere I looked the earth was illuminated.

Rifling through documents loaned from the National Library, I had lost count of the number of human beings killed worldwide through government-sanctioned exterminations. Not to mention the estimated 187 million persons lost in the numerous wars since 1914.[3] No theorist could explain this level of atrocity. It was outside reason, alone and unto itself. Reading accounts of mass murders by one citizenry over another, or the methods of torture used to dehumanize prisoners, many of whom were intellectuals caught in the machinations of a government's latest ideology, the demonic was no longer an abstraction. Yet while evil had reality, it was not the Real. Even in the depth of tragedy, we did not suffer alone. Like post-holocaust Jewish writers who searched for new notions of divine agency in the seeming absence of God, I also had discovered *Shekhinah* weeping with victims in an outpouring of divine limitlessness. I was surer than ever that the Holy One was not the author of human ruin. Whatever malignancy grew in the soul, it was an aberration of the will to power. *We* permitted atrocity to spread. *We* authorized and valorized cruelty.

I wondered if belief in God as a transcendent being who experienced no pain contributed to human callousness. What if we took to heart the equally strong scriptural tradition of a God who not only cared about human suffering, but suffered our suffering? In Jewish Scripture, Yahweh suffered with the enemy, and mourned and wept over the distress and destruction of his people; humans pled and argued with God. Likewise, Jesus entered into the brokenness of the world and "emptied himself, taking the form of a servant, being born in the likeness of men." (Phil 2:7) An Iranian friend introduced me to similar passages of divine pathos in the Qur'an: Allah is closer to a human being "than his jugular vein," he "careth for all" and listens "to the prayer of every supplicant." These holy books reminded me that love entails responsibility in the face of suffering, reordering the human ideal toward compassionate solidarity with our suffering earth and its inhabitants.

Over the last months, I despaired of completing my thesis on the genocidal massacres in Rwanda and Burundi within the confines of the statistical analysis required by the Sociology Department. Statistics could not account for individual turnings of heart, and the spiritual response, which saw into things with compassion. It did not further our moral responsibility, or our commitment to stand against all forms of violence and oppression. If not for my discovery of the social mystics, among them Abraham Joshua Heschel, Dorothy Day, Mahatma Gandhi, Howard Thurman, and Martin Luther King, Jr., I never would have found the courage to finish my degree.

Once again I would draw sustenance from great minds, individuals who sacrificed personal comfort and political threat to proclaim the Spirit's power over nihilism and fear. They, more than anything, helped me to reclaim my place in society by reconciling the prophetic world of justice and the mystical world of compassion, convinced that the true religious person was also prophet. "Prophecy," Heschel wrote, "is the voice that God has lent to the silent agony, a voice to the plundered poor, to the profaned riches of the world.... A religious man is a person who holds God and man in one thought at one time, at all times, who suffers in himself harms done to others, whose greatest passion is compassion, whose greatest strength is love and defiance of despair."[4]

In the years ahead, I would take to heart Rabbi Heschel's commitment to the dignity we owed survivors by retitling my Human Rights Seminar, "The State of World Suffering." It was important that students recognize that our approach would not exploit survivors' witness for personal gain, whether to assuage our guilt by becoming "concerned citizens," or by doing our duty as intellectuals. No, these events defied the pretense of clinical objectivity and demanded instead solidarity with sufferers. Only through a personal bearing of another's pain, in whatever small way, could we hope to find our deep humanity. Des Pres was right: "only a language of ultimate concern is adequate to facts such as these."

My studies helped to bridge my inner life with the academic world I hoped to enter. Yet daily I struggled with conflicted emotions about being in school and subjecting my children to a standard of living below most of their peers. In addition, I was increasingly pulled toward silence. In the emptiness that was a taking away of names, forms, and concepts, I sought solace in the desert, walking among majestic saguaro cacti, sentinels in an ocean of peace. I especially loved San Xavier del Bac Mission, its sparkling white dome rising above the desert floor. Often I drove south from Tucson to meditate in its Baroque splendor, allowing my heart to rest.

In the midst of these contrasting desires, friends from New York had arrived for a visit and offered to stay with the kids while I spent a few days at a nearby retreat. I needed time alone to work on my thesis and to renew my spirit.

*
* *

A FTER driving past the NO HUNTING EXCEPT FOR PEACE sign into the dirt lot, I climbed out of the car. A wobbly dog with a black-and-white face ambled over and licked my hand. To my left and behind a low-slung faded green building rose Safford Peak, revered by the ancient inhabitants as a holy mountain. I already felt the benefit of silence at this desert retreat northwest of downtown Tucson. The spiritual vibration was intense.

A robust hug from Sister Nancy welcomed me to Desert House of Prayer. "This is the main dining room," she said, opening sliding screens to a spacious room overlooking wavy hills of saguaro. A well-used wooden table and ten chairs paralleled the right wall. "We take breakfast and lunch in silence but come together for sharing at dinner. Of course, if you prefer, you may take all your meals in silence." Leaving, we walked along a dirt path to the Thomas Merton Library, which housed six thousand volumes including all of Merton's major works and associated writings. I was interested in the library since I had recently completed *Disputed Questions* by the late Trappist monk. His call to contemplation and to monastic solitude put words to the orientation of my entire life, and I was looking forward to further reading.

Afterward, we toured the simple elegance of Our Lady of Solitude, the retreat chapel. Directly behind the altar a floor-to-ceiling window framed a two hundred-year-old saguaro, arms outstretched.

Inside my hermitage I curled up on the bed and slept for an hour before being wakened by *tap, tap, tap* on the sliding glass door. Gently lowering myself onto the floor, I crawled over to the glass door, face-to-face with a roadrunner's yellow eyes, its crested head plume, black-and-white speckled feathers, and long tail unmistakable. We gawked at each other for some moments before it turned on blue legs, walking away with a clownish gait.

Up before dawn in the cool air, adult quail and a covey of babies the size of marbles scooted across my path. During my stay, I would see javelina (wild hogs known for their pungent odor), countless lizards, and coyotes mingling among chaparral and ocotillo. Bobcats and an occasional mountain lion roamed the property as well. I walked the Stations of the Cross set among prickly pear cacti, tracking the rising sun. I couldn't remember when I'd last had time to quietly reflect, alone. Did I ever? This was exactly what I needed. No radio, no television, no telephone, no talk.

Later that day, I was hiking back from viewing petroglyphs carved into high stone cliffs by the Hohokam, when I stopped to look at a dead roadrunner lying alongside the path. Rushing to keep my appointment with Father John Kane, founder of Desert House, I wondered if my new power animal had sent me a message: *Slow down before it's too late!* Fr. John must have heard my sandals on the gravel because he called out, "Come in, come in!" before I reached for the screen door handle. Seated behind a desk stacked with reading material, his eyes sparkled. What was most compelling was his simplicity, as if every extraneous desire had been distilled into one essence.

I trusted him.

"I am called more and more to silence, John. I like to be alone. Even in the midst of my busy life, I feel an unrelenting pull to solitude."

"As you know, John of the Cross said the ache for solitude is one sign of moving from spirituality into contemplation, from the active spiritual life into the mystical life proper. God is calling the person into a deeper, solitary relationship. Doesn't this sound like what's happening to you?"

"Yes, I think I'm a monk without a monastery."

WE SHARED AN admiration for Merton's writings on the spirit of monasticism. Merton understood that the monk was not a special type of person, but expressed the archetype of solitude in the deep self. Viscerally I identified with Merton's longing to live "in God's time," to empty myself of unrequited desires and ego struggles to discover "the freedom and peace of a wilderness existence, a return to the desert that is also a recovery of (inner) paradise."[5] When I confided in John how much Merton's quest for meaning in Zen, Sufism, Judaism, and other traditions mirrored my own, I detected neither judgment nor dismissal. He also had crossed over to a universal spiritual perspective and had come back transformed, committed to its singular way of life.

Walking together to lunch, I asked John if he would speak to my next spiritual group about contemplation. He refused. "If someone has a call to contemplation, I let the spirit guide him or her here. It is not for me to go out and promote the life. No. The heart drawn to silence seeks its own source. The one who has thirst must drink from the well."

* * *

THAT afternoon, returning to my hermitage to savor our discussion, I read Merton's critique about the materialism of the West and the "stupor of the collective mind," spurned by his lament that the West had shown the world its economic prowess, religious zealotry, and technological wizardry, but not its spiritual treasures and ancient wisdom. How many people had I met who were hostile to religion, but knew little of its mystical depth? Merton identified monkhood as a rejection of and protest against the crimes of war and political tyranny. "By my monastic life and vows I am saying NO to all the concentration camps, the aerial bombardments, the staged political trials, the judicial murders, the racial injustices, the economic tyrannies, and the whole socioeconomic apparatus which seems geared for nothing but global destruction."[6] He taught that deep social engagement was not only possible but also essential to monasticism. Prayer, silence, and solidarity with the oppressed were forms of activism empowered by the pure action of love.

Now eight years since the October revelations, I believed they had been granted solely to help others, to serve as a bridge-builder between spirit and soul. It hadn't occurred to me that I could hope to fulfill my longing for solitude, to be a monk outside religion. Yet more and more lately I turned inward. There was nothing left to prevent me from embracing the monastic call, not parenting, not fear of lost relationships, not my need to make a living, not graduate school demands. The traditional distinction between ordained and laity, vowed religious and lay religious was flawed. The monastic heart informed every circumstance. I would forge a new monastic way of living outside walls.

The moon midway in the sky illuminated my feet when several hours later I decided to take a walk in the desert. Leaning against a boulder, I took in the vast dome of stars suddenly aware of how small and insignificant life was in comparison to All That Is. Precisely because of the very smallness of things, I dared to glimpse the immensity, against which nothing anyone has ever done measured up. Only the wisest among us knew that freedom was on the other side of nothingness, of being released from our own insufficiency.

Exhilarated, for a moment every name was my name. No name could refute the immeasurable. Even when names were wielded to harm the holy excess, when they were meant to exclude, even then names could not offend me. To which name was I called? The One who bends down to kiss the brow of every disciple of peace; who anoints us with the elixir of uncreated light. Amen.

Having voiced what had been true all along, I needed to establish a new reference point. Ambition and accomplishment had their place, but this was not the way of the monk who strove to be useless on the world's terms and thus humble in the eyes of God. The monk rejected the mind's aggressive nature and abstained from the clamor of self, intent to possess, conscript, and claim for one's own. Traveling in a completely different direction, away from false individuality, the contemplative way opened the heart and emptied the false self. It was not a rejection of the individual will, but rather recognition that it was of little importance. "Complaining is nothing," Rilke wrote, "fame is nothing. Openness, patience, receptivity, solitude is everything."[7]

* * *

"SHANA, I'm home!" No answer. I put my book bag on the kitchen table and looked around the living room. Maya and Gina were doing homework at a friend's house. *Where is she?* She wasn't with Tobin; I had just dropped him off at Little League practice. "Shana?" I called out, turning the knob on her bedroom door.

"I'm here."

"Where?"

"Under the desk."

"Why are you hiding under your desk? Tell me what's wrong."

"I can't! No, I can't!"

Coaxing her onto my lap, I stroked her silky, black hair, holding her tight. "You can tell me anything, Shanita. What happened to you?"

Choking back sobs, her hands clenched. "Alison and Mark called me chink, slanty eyes, said Tobin's not my brother, that we don't look alike at all! I don't ever want to go back to school. I hate first grade."

Over the last months, I'd already had two meetings with the principal about Shana's reading progress, which had declined since she started school. Last week I learned the cause. Her teacher made her sit in the corner with a dunce hat for not tracing every word with her finger. My daughter, who could read before she started school, now stammered when he called on her. Livid, I had met with the school superintendent and demanded to have her moved to a different classroom with a more enlightened teacher. Now this.

Days like this gripped me with remorse. Wouldn't our family be better off if I just got a job so the kids could attend better schools? Wouldn't they be happier if I had money to buy the electronic toys their friends craved? Was I being terribly selfish to want to study? If it weren't for the emotional support of the faculty who reminded me I was Ph.D. material, I would have withdrawn from my master's program weeks ago. Every day challenged my resolve.

Later, the kids and I were sitting at the dining table, fooling around with cobs of corn when the phone rang. It was my mother, calling to make sure her grandchildren had good table manners, using their forks and knives correctly. Butter was dripping down my chin, while suppressed giggles filled the background.

Recently, I realized that I had been raised to be especially vulnerable to my mother. Unable to shield myself from her demands, impressed into the malleable transparency of my childhood psyche, I kept physical and emotional distance. But since my father's cancer diagnosis, we had become closer, spending time together and sharing more deeply. We still struggled, of course. I couldn't explain to her my spiritual commitment; she didn't approve of my "stubborn refusal" to give it up and move to Florida.

But, I didn't seek acceptance. With each passing week, the practice of being a monk in the world grew easier, especially when I set aside time each day to pray in solitude and to celebrate the sacred in our midst.

16

Blessed are the Poor in Spirit

Those who seek true knowledge and the essence of universal truth will come upon that realm of the Heart, wherein begins enlightened quest. This Heart, oh wondrous beauty, reflects the magnitude of Divine Presence. . . .

Despite fear, pain, ignorance, or other frailties, the Great Heart remains bonded to physical form and nourishes the body throughout life's journey. Here, among our sorrows and erroneous paths, and here, amidst desecration and travail awaits the answer to our prayers: the infinite Love that heals all wounds and teaches us compassion and humility.

THUS BEGAN WORDS that intruded into my waking hours, and demanding to be written, would eventually become my first book. Recently returned to the East Coast after completing my master's degree, I gratefully accepted the offer of a friend's guesthouse and let Path of the Heart write itself. Naïve about the literary world, I read books on publishing, mailing proposal, outline, and manuscript to various religious houses. If I had an idea that certain publishers were Catholic or Lutheran or Jewish presses, or favored particular types of spirituality, the rejection letters, especially one that accused me of being a false "mystagogue," would have dismayed me less. But more important things gripped me: my father's cancer had reached a terminal stage. Torn apart by his failing health, I wept at night when the kids were asleep.

During this period of confusion and uncertainty, a graduate catalog from Fordham University arrived in my mailbox. I threw it out. Shortly thereafter, I was speaking to a professor from Yale who recommended that if I wanted to study the mystics, I should contact Fordham. Digging the catalog out of the garbage, I leafed through the offerings and called the Theology Department. In response to my query about their Ph.D. program, the woman answering the phone asked which field of theology I intended to study: "Systematics, Biblical, or Historical?"

Uncertain what Systematics was, and not interested in Biblical Theology, I replied, "Historical."

"Wait a moment and I'll connect you with Professor Ewert Cousins."

Professor Cousins was genuinely interested in my desire to incorporate the study of mystics and religious experience into my doctoral program. I also mentioned the book I'd recently completed. We set up an appointment to meet the following Tuesday. The drive from Connecticut to the Bronx was relatively easy, and I soon found a parking space. The stately stone buildings and manicured lawns of the Fordham campus were an oasis of calm. It also felt strangely familiar, as if I had studied there before. Crossing the quad, I consulted the map to the Theology Department, increasingly excited with each step that I might find what I had been looking for. I was not disappointed.

Tall and dignified, Professor Cousins welcomed me into his office with enthusiasm. He reminded me of paintings I'd seen of Plato or St. Bonaventure. He had the gaze of an icon, light radiating off his face. Student papers were piled on his desk, manuscripts for book chapters scattered all over the room. Speaking in a gentle tone, he asked about my background, previous studies, current interests. I learned of his research in Franciscan spirituality, and his work as the editor of an ambitious project to publish the writings of Jewish, Islamic, and Christian mystics. His love and knowledge of spirituality were contagious. Whatever apprehension I may have had about telling my story fell away. Expressing my disappointment with graduate education, I told him I couldn't pursue a doctorate if it meant suppressing spiritual experience. Right then he said, "You have everything you already need. You come here and write what you *know*."

He asked to see my manuscript and read through the pages rapidly. "This is a mystical text; how did you come to write it?" The second time someone associated me with the word "mystical," I recounted my spiritual life and the October revelations. He took it all in, especially the part about the openness to all religions, and handed me a booklet. "I think this will resonate with you," he said.

Picking up the phone, he called a colleague who owned a publishing company to say there was a prospective doctoral student in his office who had written a book he needed to see. "Is there a time you can meet with her?" Within that year, Path of the Heart would be published. Before I took leave, Ewert encouraged me to apply for the fall semester. "It's a little late and we've already chosen our graduate cohort group, but I think we can arrange something."

Elated, I walked back through the quad and across the street to an Italian deli. Munching on an eggplant Parmesan sandwich, I opened Ewert's book, Global Spirituality: The Meeting of Mystical Paths. I was so captivated by the topic of global spirituality that I consumed the entire text in one sitting. Here was the academic equivalent of my own unlettered thoughts on the emergence of a new spiritual consciousness, a path I had been teaching in a different spiritual language for almost ten years. Crossing back to campus, I sat down on the steps of Keating Hall, and a voice, much larger than my own, said, "This is it!"

Back home, I pushed the pile of books on Teresa of Avila, Rilke, and Merton onto the farthest side of my bed. I opened Global Spirituality again, this time noting the references. The next day I contacted a religious bookstore on the Upper East Side and ordered books on my list. For the remainder of the year, I read everything I could find on the dialogue of religions, and the mystical unity of creation. Raimon Panikkar's Unknown Christ of Hinduism gripped my imagination. A master of theological inquiry, his thesis that Christ was an archetypal presence implicated in consciousness itself, and not the sole possession of Christianity, fascinated me. While I didn't agree with the undertone of Christian superiority that Panikkar would later revise with his notion of the "Christic principle," his idea that religions were intertwined and inside each other mirrored my experience.

In the fall of 1985 I was admitted into the doctoral program in Theology, and we moved to Dobbs Ferry to be closer to the Fordham campus. Since I wouldn't have a full scholarship until spring semester, I enrolled in one seminar, "Medieval Mysticism," taught by Professor Cousins, which consisted of reading and research of primary texts. I was especially captivated by the writings of Meister Eckhart, a fourteenth-century German preacher. Our seminar was lively, irreverent, and wise. I learned as much from the adult students of many nations and religions as I did from study. While Ewert dazzled us with his encyclopedic knowledge, more impressive was his transmission of mystery, of the depth of his experience. Watching him, I was given hope that one could combine a scholarly mind with contemplative insight; that one would not have to abandon critical thinking or spiritual sensitivity to survive in the world.

Halfway through my study of Eckhart's German sermons, I was floored by Sermon 52, *Beati pauperes spiritu* (Blessed are the poor in spirit).[1] Eckhart began by making a distinction between external poverty, where one voluntarily practiced simplicity, and a different kind of inward poverty, the focus of his sermon. A poor man [sic], he said, "wants nothing, and knows nothing, and has nothing." I envisioned the Meister delivering his sermon in a damp, cold church. Outside it was gray and windy, with leaden clouds darkening the early evening light. His head was bent. His eyes, like two burning embers, were cast upon the congregation of Beguines, lay Catholic women living in semi-monastic communities, to whom he ministered. Exhorting his audience to raise their hopes to a higher calling, to a more rare and profound liberation, he railed against the "donkeys" that practiced penances and external exercises in order to achieve an outward semblance of saintliness. True poverty, the kind that set the soul afire, was more demanding and raw. It required one to be free of the created will, even a will that wanted to fulfill God's will—to long for nothing, to be empty.

I heard echoes of Zen.

Lightheaded, with chills raising the hair on my skin, I realized that Eckhart, who lived six centuries before my birth, was describing one of the central insights of my October revelations: a divine plenitude beyond name and no-name. Pierced by an intuitive truth, a spiritual force fired each word directly into my soul. Turning his sermon on poverty of spirit around in my mind's eye, I saw a path of humility ahead, a way to deepen my daily prayer: *Make me empty*. I pondered the Meister's own fervent plea, "Let us pray to God that we may be free of 'God.'" His words formed an inscrutable puzzle, a Christian koan. Wow. I wondered if the Beguine women felt the same.

Meister Eckhart's explosion of wisdom didn't end with this sermon. Finding everything I could in translation and in the original Middle High German, which I barely knew how to read, a theological bridge between my own experience and Eckhart's rendering of the Christian mystical tradition began to take shape. In bold and inventive ways, he challenged spiritual complacency, forcing me to let go of preconceived ideas and limitations. Equally significant was the Meister's upending of the classical emphasis on Trinity and Christ. He did not reject their centrality, but mapped a higher path of interiority to the "naked Godhead," which he called *gotheit*. Shocking Vatican censors back then, he insisted that the innermost light of the soul left behind names and identities, even Father, Son, and Holy Spirit, to enter the quiet desert, the Source beyond distinction and difference. Here was a hymn to the Unnameable Presence.

I knew then that I would write my dissertation on Meister Eckhart. Somehow, I also knew the topic: the Desert of the Godhead as a mystical foundation for the dialogue of religions. By whatever name—Brahman, Allah, Sunyata—the unity of the cosmos was the source of planetary diversity and the variety of religious wisdoms. What I had seen and understood in 1976, that the Holy One called all to love, that segregation and division wounded the Divine Heart, was in some way corroborated by Eckhart's spirituality. I pressed myself into the pale pages of the book, making notes in all the margins, practically tasting the ink, and through an interior bond with the Meister's thought, opened a door into another liberation.

* * *

In the midst of my ruminations, I received a call from Carol that I should come to Florida as soon as possible because Pop might not live through the week. It was my birthday, October 18. Hurriedly getting my airline ticket and arranging for my friend Patricia to stay with the kids, I packed a few bags and by the next morning I was in Tampa. Sitting in the front seat of Carol's car, I reached over and took her hand. We both knew it was the end. Back at my parents' house, Pop was resting in a hospital bed set up in the living room. Hospice volunteers were tending to him, making sure the final ravages of bone cancer did not inflict further pain. In and out of consciousness, he recognized me when I drew close to his face, lifting his head off the pillow to kiss me. I climbed into bed next to him, placing my arm across his chest to hold his hand. I love you, Pop. With a strength that belied his weakness, he squeezed my fingers.

As Sunday turned to Monday, and Pop's decline became more evident, the kind hospice volunteer assured us that the morphine eliminated his pain. His kidneys were failing, but she told us his dying would continue for a few more days, his heart was so strong. Stillness, a sense of holiness, permeated the room. No longer responding, Pop was quiet. Friends and family stopped by. Unable to handle the chatter, I retreated to the guest bedroom to pray. I needed silence. No words to disrupt the sacred flow, the unspeakable unfolding. On Thursday evening, October 24, gathered around Pop's bed, we took turns holding his hands, gently touching his arms, face, and hair. By some secret fellowship, Pop waited for his oldest and best friend to arrive before he took his last breath. Right before he did, he lifted his head off the pillow, opened his eyes, and looked directly at me.

I don't have any recollection of what others felt or did, whether Mom cried or Carol wept. At the moment of his final intake of air, I saw my father's spirit lift off his body, leaving the damaged cells and years of suffering behind. I leaned over and placed my head on his chest. Whatever his foibles, fears, or weaknesses, they were dissipated like steam rising from a kettle. What was left was pure transparency; he had become scent in the air. The whole house was permeated with the fragrance of roses, Pop's favorite flower. A pulsating, luminous presence, the eternal Pop was radiating light.

Ever efficient, Mom had already arranged for undertakers from the Neptune Society to remove Pop's body for cremation. Within a short time two men arrived, dressed from head to toe in black suits and black hats. One was tall and thin with a long, sad face and the other short and plump. Carol, Mom, and I took one look at them and struggled to control our giggles. Standing next to each other at the kitchen door, they looked like Laurel and Hardy, one of Pop's best-loved comedy acts. We felt this was Pop's last message to us: Enjoy yourselves, laugh.

Later, as I lay down in bed, an intense feeling of Pop's presence washed over me. Whatever barrier had been erected to prevent our full communion was gone. Like a dance of shadows or the merging of notes in a symphony, our spirits were fully present to each other, transposed and intertwined. For the longest of moments we flowed into each other. I finally understood. Even unto death and beyond death we were joined. My pain eased, my sorrow for all that had never been or could never be, resolved. Whatever we were incapable of revealing in this earthly life was fully given in the life we now shared.

Back in New York, on the train from Grand Central to Dobbs Ferry Station, I thought about what my children felt about Pop's death. Shana's teacher found her crying in the corner of her third-grade classroom, and I needed to be home. Without funds for their airline tickets and a week of hotel rooms, I regretted that they hadn't been able to say goodbye. I decided when I got home we would create our own ceremony for Pop, lighting candles and praying together. Distracting myself from these thoughts, I pulled out a copy of *The Cloud of Unknowing*, opening to this passage: "No one can fully comprehend the uncreated God with knowledge; but each one, in a different way, can grasp God fully through love."[2] My emotions loosened, tears fell.

* * *

SPRING semester, I finally was a full-time student on scholarship. Since Pop's death in October, my mind was wavy and unfocused. Unable to concentrate on my studies or formalize a complete thought, in a desperate move I crammed a full semester of research into four intensive days of writing. With responsibility to the kids, I couldn't spend hours in the library, so daily I signed out reserve articles and books and rushed home to use the copy machine I had purchased for fifty dollars. Stuffed in a closet off the living room along with hats, coats, and assorted boots, the broken-down copier was vital to my success.

Between classes I drove Tobin and Shana to Columbia University Dental School for braces. While the orthodontic interns painstakingly secured wire thread around each errant tooth, I committed to memory passages from Ibn al-'Arabi's *Bezels of Wisdom*, allowing his poetic vision to soak my heart in light. The juxtaposition of Eckhart's exuberant breakthrough into Zen-like territory with Arabi's masterful Sufi vision of the unity of being enhanced my belief that religious dialogue was imbedded in consciousness itself.

I loved mystical theology. Before Constantine turned Christianity into the religion of empire, early church writings were mystical reflections on Scripture, prayer, and the soul's journey toward God. Among my favorite guides were the Desert Fathers and Mothers, men and women who left the cities of Asia Minor for the Egyptian and Palestinian deserts of the fourth and fifth centuries, C.E. In pithy aphorism and incisive critique of the human condition, these spiritual forbearers of the contemplative traditions of Christian monasticism deepened my practice of monastic simplicity, further establishing my soul in silence.

I began to see that the common understanding of mysticism and theology was flawed. Theology, *theos-logos* or study of God, did not have to be dry analysis of dogma or an apology for faith. As practiced by the Desert Elders, as well as Panikkar, Cousins, Eckhart, al-'Arabi, and other mystics, theology had little to do with protecting orthodoxy from questioning. Rather, it was one of the great spiritual discourses of the Abrahamic religions that probed the boundlessness and inscrutability of the cosmos. It was a way of knowing and a way of being in which metaphysical assumptions were implicated in every act of good or ill: Was the universe good, indifferent, evil? Was God on the side of human dignity and equality? How did one measure morality or ethics if not against an infinite horizon? Further, as theology became increasingly relevant to dialogue across religions, it was breaking out of an explicitly Christian or comparative context, free to engage in all manner of social, political, and ecological thought.

Similarly, mysticism was often maligned in the popular media, incorrectly associated with the occult or paranormal. Yet mystical experience differed from psychic phenomena and altered states of consciousness, its heights achieved only by loss of self. Mysticism was not a rarified state available to the few, but the depth consciousness, the intuitive capacity for awe, intrinsic to the human spirit. Its expression was not of one type or kind, but experienced throughout humanity's long history in various guises and modes: visionary, devotional, intellective, historical, nature mysticism.

Ewert in his book, *Global Spirituality*, was especially clear that mysticism was a unique interpretative perspective, not reducible to rational analysis: "It must be firmly kept in mind that mystical experience is not ordinary, everyday experience," he wrote. "In fact, mystics claim to experience God directly.... Such a claim must be taken seriously and the content of such consciousness explored on its own."[3]

In this sense, mysticism was an innate capacity within each person to access the deeper meaning of life. It was the fruit of prayer and the natural consciousness of those who ventured into the deep self. Often, a person's realization of entering a new world of perception was passive, happening without intention or forethought. At the same time, cultures throughout history taught spiritual techniques as a means of activating higher states of awareness, which were not merely a shift in perception, but referred in a broad sense to a way of *being* or state of *oneness* that reformed the whole of life.

I imagined that early human communities functioned in a mystical state of consciousness, using the metaphorical mind to track animals, study the cycles of nature, read the movement of heavenly bodies, and perform sacred rites. In fact, the great scriptural traditions of the world's religions, from the pre-written Vedas to the compilation of the sayings of Buddha and Jesus, and Mohammed's dictation of the Angel Gabriel, descended into conscious awareness through the portal of the mystic eye.

At times we are graced to receive knowledge whole. Spawned from the inner light of truth, mysticism is not the ordinary knowledge of mind or intellect, but the illuminative capacity to know, transcendent wisdom. Across traditions, mysticism asserts through love the human capacity to apprehend the unity of physical and transcendent worlds. We know through love, through being intimate with life. When we love someone or something, we know differently than when we know intellectually. If we loved our world, what would we know, what would we do?

For years I considered myself an intellectual fraud. Deep thought was never demanded of me. Good grades came easily. Education did not lead to awe. Now I knew it wasn't the subject of my studies that bored me but the limitations placed on how and what I was able to know. Previously unschooled in mystical theology, I labored to translate the October revelations into the history of religious thought. Slowly and inexorably a language was forged that would bridge the invisible universe I inhabited with concrete structures of thought. Yet, in order to translate accurately I had to assimilate into my being two or more different realities, comparing and contrasting their metaphysical assumptions and images of the divine. I was working out a comparative theology with a spiritual worldview that had been imprinted in my soul, but one that was unnamed and unrecognized by mainstream religions.

With little or no child support, and overwhelmed by student loans, I couldn't financially afford to stay at Fordham much longer. I wished I could have studied for a decade I loved theology so much. That summer, between semesters, the kids spent time with family and friends to give me an uninterrupted month of study. Enrolled in three graduate courses, I was up by 5 a.m., preparing for my 8 o'clock class. Back home by late afternoon, I dragged my books and groceries up three flights of stairs and spent the night reading and writing until 2 or 3 a.m. The first time in my adult life that I had time alone, I took a pint of Ben and Jerry's out of the freezer and ate all of it myself.

No one knows my name. Only between pen and paper dare I stoke the ashes of desire. I must be cloistered to speak. I must be hidden to write.

In stillness, you call me, whispering.

No one knows the fire that storms through my flesh at night. Word, word that seeks speech, I cannot speak you. You are hidden, veiled, a virgin bride, all hallowed in white, a tabernacle, set in motion.

I cannot speak the old words, so I am silence.

Take me as I am, empty of words, wordless. You I cannot speak.

17

Plague of Mice

I SLID INTO A PEW at the Blue Chapel in Keating Hall, joining a group of graduate students gathered for Zen-Christian meditation, a practice brought to Fordham by a Jesuit who studied with a Japanese roshi. In front of the altar, Sister Judy kneeling on a Zafu cushion sounded the gong. As its timbre reverberated through the church, silence descended like a thick balm of myrrh. Cloistered in stillness, even the stones emitted no sound.

Afterward, a few of us gathered for breakfast across from campus, swapping stories.

"When I was living in Taiwan," Sr. Judy said, "I became involved with Buddhist nuns and learned to meditate. The freedom from imagery in Zen practice and the Buddhist emphasis on non-attachment struck a cord with me."

"I had a similar experience at Tantur Ecumenical Institute in Jerusalem," Rabbi Dovid said, "participating in the Muslim call to prayer. It was amazing! The chanted words were holy."

"Did you feel you were a better Jew from the experience? I did as a Catholic."

"Absolutely. In fact, when later I was invited to spend a week at a

Benedictine Monastery, I worried I would lose my faith if I joined in community life. But, actually, it was the opposite! I felt *more* connected to my morning Torah reading. And, I *loved* the monastery."

JUDY AND I walked back to campus, carrying take-out cups. The sky was turning pink.

"You know, Judy, during the meditation I had a visceral experience of the mingling of Buddhist and Christian lineages. As if these two ancient practices fused in my inner experience, in the depths of mystic contemplation."

"What did you make of that?"

"I entered a state of absolute silence, where everything was charged with vibrancy. It helped explain the dryness, the lack of interest I've recently felt about some of my courses, which pale in comparison."

Early for our seminar, we settled in chairs, sipping tea.

"Dryness is good," she said. "Even if it lasts thirty years, so what? Embrace the fullness of now. If it is of God, it will be."

"I'm drained from study. Worry about the kids. But, I'm pulled toward solitude. Each day I affirm and deepen the monk within. And, you're right. God takes care of all our mistakes."

"You know, for seven years I wanted to be a hermit. I told my confessor and our prioress that's what I wanted. I wasted seven years defending my call! Don't defend what you want. Just do it. God will guide you."

How long have I been resisting the call of solitude? Where did the prohibition come from: society, family, religion? It didn't matter anymore. What I thought was demanded of me, even what I thought I wanted, was not demanded and I didn't want.

* *

LATER that night, propped up with pillows on my bed, I started thinking how similar my spiritual growth was to the process Evelyn Underhill described in her classic study, *Mysticism*. I, too, had traveled through awakening and purification, suffering remorse over sins that separated me from divine love. I experienced illumination, when the universe was clear and holy, and those dark nights when my soul cried out in anguish. Inexplicably, I also had been granted the gift of mystical union, of new revelation. Coded into the soul's DNA were the secret pathways of Divine return, which were activated, Underhill wrote, when "the will is united with the emotions in an impassioned desire to transcend the sense world, in order that the self may be joined by love to the one eternal and ultimate Object of love."[1] We were hardwired to participate in the grand experiment of becoming divine-like.

I realized that I had come to Fordham in part to test the moral fiber of inner knowing. How did the October revelations and their mystical teachings relate to the great systems of religious thought? Were they one with them? Different? Like other seekers before me, I sought affirmation in tradition, in elders, in the Scriptures. Now, after years of graduate coursework, I knew that my religion without religion was not *fully* contained within Christianity or any of the other wisdom traditions I studied. The gift of the October revelations was final and personal. It was not a furtive glimpse of reality, but a path of total inner transformation with its own contemplative practice and theological orientation. It was a way of being for those, like myself, longing to live a serious spiritual commitment outside a denomination, while struggling to make a living or to feed children. It was a refuge for outsiders, women and men who never found liberation or a spiritual home within religion. But, more importantly, it was a path of the heart, a source of wisdom for anyone who sought a more open, nonviolent, generous, and merciful spirituality, one dedicated to the alleviation of suffering and the flourishing of all beings.

While I continued to experience visions and mystical insights, they were tempered by a more sophisticated self-reflection, brought on by my studies. Underhill's writing, in particular, shed light on prior decisions I had intuitively chosen: why I left the meditative center, why I didn't want to be identified as clairvoyant, guru, or healer. Her contention that mysticism "is the science of ultimates, the science of union with the Absolute, and nothing else," helped clarify that my quest always had been directed toward God alone. Mysticism is "at once," Underhill wrote, "an act of love, an act of surrender, and an act of supreme perception; a trinity of experiences which meets and satisfies the three activities of the self."[2]

I had never understood the Trinity as it was explained in the Baltimore Catechism of my youth. But my ignorance was dispelled while studying the development of trinitarian theology for my doctoral exams. Quite without warning, while laboring over a difficult passage, I arrived at a sublime understanding, worked out in exquisite detail during the first centuries of the Christian era. The doctrine of the Trinity was not about three gods, but a primordial interrelationship that constituted the inner life of divinity and by extension the principles that governed the spiritual and phenomenal realms. In the divine or cosmological plan, Ultimate Reality, by whatever name, was not alone. The universe was the result of co-mutuality, interdependence. The three Persons—Father, Son, and Holy Spirit—were expressions of three divine activities united in one purpose.

Other religions explained the simultaneous plurality and non-dual nature of the cosmos through related insights: Buddhist concept of co-dependent arising of phenomena, in which all things continually influenced and conditioned each other in a non-hierarchical and self-organizing way; or Hindu *Sat-Chit-Ananda* (Being-Consciousness-Bliss), a metaphysical concept that approximated the inner nature of *Brahman*, the Absolute. In order for love or consciousness to be, there must be Being. Neither of these aspects could be present without the other.

Raimon Panikkar, in fact, had written extensively about what he called the "triadic" nature of reality in the world's religions, which he claimed was the mystic realization of the interrelationship among all things. He described this triadic intuition as "cosmotheandric," indicating that the cosmic, the divine, and the human were three dimensions of reality that characterized every moment of consciousness and of experience. Like the non-dual relationship of the three persons of the Trinity, no one element could subsist or be understood in isolation.

One did not have to be a believer to be astounded by metaphysical beauty. Here is how St. Bonaventure, a fourteenth-century Franciscan and contemporary of Thomas Aquinas, described the Trinity:

> From supreme goodness,
> it is necessary that there be in the Persons
> supreme communicability;
> … and from these supreme coequality
> and hence supreme coeternity;
> finally, from all of the above, supreme mutual intimacy,
> By which one is necessarily in the other
> in absolute lack of division
> of the substance, power and operation
> of the most blessed Trinity itself.[3]

* * *

T HE next day I was at Columbia University attending a symposium of the editors of the multi-volume *World Spirituality: An Encyclopedic History of the Religious Quest*. Seated between a Jain and a Taoist scholar, I watched a fall breeze blowing through the windows, rustling my notes. At the moment, Raimon Panikkar, an apostle of interfaith dialogue, and the Indian philosopher, Krishna Sivaraman, were part of a panel discussing the role of spirituality in religious thought.

"Spirituality is not a separate discipline," Panikkar said, "or an adjunct to moral theology. It is the first Subject; it underlies every subject. Spirituality is co-extensive with the formation of the universe."

"Exactly. This is the *tat tvan asi* ("Thou art That") of the *Chandogya Upanishad*," Krishna responded, "in which the original, primordial Self is identical with *Brahman*, or Ultimate Reality. The phenomenon of spirituality is just as real and natural as are the phenomena of heat, light, and gravity."

Their claim that spirituality was a higher state assumed by the very stuff of the universe echoed the pioneering thought of Pierre Teilhard de Chardin. If anything resonated with me, it was the shift away from the spiritual as a principle outside of and governing matter to the notion of a global force of spirit *already present within* materiality and *within* the human soul, extending over the same space and time as the universe itself. This emerging consciousness of life on earth not only drew on the ontological roots that nourished and bound together our religious heritages; it also supported the breaking through of new branches on the ancient tree of human spirituality.

The moderator asked for questions. A student wanted to know about Panikkar and Sivaraman's personal experience with cross-religious dialogue.

Panikkar talked about his travels to India and his writing *The Unknown Christ of Hinduism*, a seminal exploration of the manifestation of Christ (what he termed a "Christophany") in another tradition. During this period, he struggled with his identity as a Catholic priest and found that to be cross-cultural "is . . . to descend into the abyss and to drink from the very source where the human experience draws the water and the thirst; one might say that it is not a crossing but a cross."[4]

"The path to interreligious dialogue was easier for me," Krishna said. "Hinduism, as you know, is very inclusive, with its millions of gods and goddesses, and multiple pathways. Pluralism is central to my spirituality. Yet, the inclusiveness of Hinduism at times can be another form of exclusion. I am careful to not just embrace unity, but to live deeply our differences."

"I 'left' [Europe for India] as a Christian," Panikkar later wrote, "I 'found' myself as a Hindu and I 'return' a Buddhist, without having ceased to be a Christian."[5]

At the end of the session, Krishna and I walked to the dining hall, sharing how important Eckhart was to our personal journeys. "I have to confess," Krishna said. "When I am in despair or depressed, I don't turn to the Upanishads or the Bhagavad-Gita. I read Meister Eckhart!"

Carrying our buffet trays to the table of speakers, we joined in the ongoing conversation.

"Religious dialogue must have a contemplative foundation," Panikkar said, "or it will become bogged down in superficiality and abstraction, unable to touch the deep metaphysical rifts that fester among religious communities."

"By digging down into prejudice and hubris," Krishna added, "we arrive at a place of compassion for our shared plight. Ecological crisis and economic, political distress are evidence that religious cooperation is essential to a planetary vision of spiritual well-being for creation as a whole."

I was particularly attuned to these positions since spending time with Fr. Thomas Berry. A professor emeritus from Fordham's Theology Department, he invited me to the Riverdale Center for Religious Research to peruse his papers on the critical need for a new cosmology, mimeographed and stacked on ceiling-high metal shelves. "The natural world itself is our primary language as it is our primary scripture," he wrote, "our primary awakening to the mysteries of existence. We might well put all our written scriptures on the shelf for twenty years until we learn what we are being told by unmediated experience of the world about us."

I loved his vision of a pulsating universe, progenitor of all human endeavors. "What kind of spirituality would we have," he challenged, "if we lived on the moon? Wouldn't our imaginations be different without the natural world? The cosmos is primary. If the curve of the universe were a hair's breath different, there would be no life."[6]

* *

By now, ten years after the October revelations, a number of people had become students and pressed me to offer courses on the contemplative life. Through their steady participation and encouragement, my normal hesitancy to formalize the teachings lessened, and much of my time not in school or in study was spent assisting others in their spiritual growth. In fact, this pattern would be consistent throughout the rest of my life: dissemination of the spiritual practices and mystical theology of the October revelations would take precedent over all other endeavors.

The next weekend I was in Manhattan to lead a workshop on the recently published *Path of the Heart*. I opened the morning with a prayer:

"Most Holy and Unnamable Presence, guide us in the ways of truth, and fill our spirits with divine light. Please grant us the strength to withstand life's challenges, the compassion to confront our pain, and the patience to wait the dawning of love. We open our hearts to your emerging revelation and offer ourselves as a birthplace of your grace."

AFTER THE GROUP settled and we discussed some items from a previous class, I began the morning lecture.

"We've discussed for several weeks what it means to be drawn by faith experience to a multi-religious or interspiritual path. Many of you have shared feelings of loss and purposelessness in trying to reconcile your spiritual experience with what is offered in mainstream churches and in the media. Others have been ostracized or accused of betrayal by former friends and religious associates.

"Yet you also talked about how it was not rejection or arrogance that led you to this practice, but *faith* in this historical moment: the breaking in of new expressions of divine consciousness that draw on the collective spiritual heritage of humanity.

"This new movement of faith does not hail the emergence of a formal religion with its redacted canon of sacred texts. It is not the speaking of the angel Gabriel or the anointing of the Holy Virgin or the passage of night in which the Buddha finally found himself cosmically awake. The quickening of the divine within is not yet tangible; it is the structure of the revelatory, enlightenment moment that so many people feel but do not know how to speak."[7]

"But what about sacrament, how does that fit into this new spiritual path?" a participant asked.

"All over the world we find new expressions of sacrament—music and prayers of the Taizé Community, Dances of Universal Peace, interreligious World Day of Prayer in Assisi, Italy, to name a few. The challenge is to discover rituals of the sacred that speak to our experience, that have meaning in our lives.

"Like the Lakotas or Hopis, we can offer our newborns to the rising sun; or take the vow of a Hindu *sannyasin* that rejects social conventions for the wild horizon of renunciation. We can sanctify our marriages and authorize our priests, and pray over the dying with the fervor of conviction. We can ingest the body of Christ and find there a mysterious feeding of our souls and a forgiveness of our sins. All this and more we do. Sacrament is part of existence; only we humans can dim its light or deny its power.

"The saffron-robed Buddhists who climbed over the crooked roads and steep hills of Cambodia to anoint the trees and to ordain them monks knew this. As did Ansel Adams, scaling the cliffs of Yosemite in tennis shoes to capture a vision of Cathedral Rock. Or Georgia O'Keefe, who transfixed the hills of Abiquiu on canvases crossed by spirit-translucent light. And the pounding waves on the shore west of Mount Tamalpais, which bring us to our knees and salt away our tears. Sacrament is not confined to synagogue or mosque, but flows out into the world for those with eyes to see and hearts to feel.

"Everything that *is*, is sacramental: all that we may never feel and can never say comes from the excessive gift of love. Daily life is a domestication of this longing, perhaps a continual suppression of what animates us most, a continual curtailment or clipping of the aching generosity that breaks all bonds of convention. But even so, and even when we labor to suppress the ardent exhilaration for home, we are bearers and witnesses of the unveiled gift of glory.[8]

"To embrace the totality of this task is the path of the heart. The longing for the divine, for truth, is the primordial language of the soul, the first language of prayer. It is a way of being that cuts through daily life distractions, and focuses on the quest for meaning and love.

"We may attempt to make excuses for this state, hoping that our spiritual desire would finally go away and we would be able to function well in the 'real' world. But this longing for communion never goes away; it is the lifeblood of the mystical heart."

When I finished the morning lecture, we gathered together for silent meditation and then broke for lunch. Looking around the table, it gave me great joy to witness a kind of United Nations of religions. Some participants were devotees of a divine personage—Buddha, Jesus, Mary, Great Spirit, Allah—or a spiritual path: Yoga, Tao. Others, loyal members of their congregation, studied more than one wisdom tradition. Still others found comfort in silent practice, an indeterminate or unnamed deity, or an agnostic, even atheistic perspective.

Yet a common ground united these various pilgrims: they upheld what Mahatma Gandhi called "the manyness of truth," uncomfortable with religious languages and liturgical forms that excluded, oppressed, or patronized; they were following an authentic spiritual path, often without community support, to what impassioned them. In the process, they were giving birth to a new lineage before it was formalized and took a name—before it was co-opted and saddled with the dogmatism of the religious "ought."

Their journey of openness to other religions or to a spiritual life without religion was not a superficial entertainment or a naïve belief. Rather, it arose from a wounding felt deep within the self that calls into question and suffers over the violence of indifference, superiority, injustice, and oppression—subtle and overt—that inhabits religions and turns the heart against itself. While religious authorities and institutional structures advance or impede its flow, the spirit comes in the silence of night to teach in secret about love, true love that knows no difference of creed.[9]

*　*
*

BACK home, I dragged my briefcase and stack of papers up the narrow staircase of our three-floor walkup, leaned into the chipped wooden door, and dropped my packages on the landing, disentangling my arm from a wet shirt drying on the bannister. Our garret apartment, located in the Dobbs Ferry school district, consisted of four good-sized rooms. We lived above our landlords, Fabiano and his wife, Angela. It was while ordering a pizza slice at their café on Main Street that I casually remarked I was looking for an apartment to rent.

"I have *appartamento*. Come, I show you," Fabiano said.

I loved the place. The entire west wall of windows faced the Hudson River, affording a spectacular view of maples turning red and gold.

Things were chaotic enough as it was, with Maya and Gina in high school, Tobin in junior high, and Shana in elementary, when Fabiano decided to remodel the house, adding on an enclosed greenhouse porch and a balcony. I'm not sure what precipitated the construction or why he thought it would add value to his property. But one morning, awakened at 6 a.m. by men's voices: "Hey, bring me that ladder! No, no, over to the right!" I looked out the window, a fluffy red bathrobe tied around me. Workmen, hips hung with tool belts, erected scaffolding. One of them was lugging a boom box. Before long the radio was blasting. The kids jumped out of bed, trying to figure out what was going on. Between the noise of the men's equipment and the music, there was nothing to do, but dress, grab a quick breakfast, and get out of the house.

The next day was worse. Scaffolding up, the workmen used electric saws to remove the stucco and to make cuts in the supporting beams. Weeks went by. Usually, I handled the intrusion without much comment. But, one Friday after a particularly exhausting week, I lost it. Barely inside the threshold, I was engulfed in white haze. Plaster dust covered every surface of my bedroom, including my computer, printer, bed, dresser, lamps, clothes, and all my books and research papers. I called the foreman in from the scaffolding: "You need to clean up everything *right now*! And make sure you cover our apartment with drop cloths!"

The project lasted for five months. In the mix of this mess, I would eventually write my dissertation, sitting on the straight-backed chair I preferred, drawn up to a desk I made out of a door and two low filing cabinets. For hours each day I worked on the computer, writing, rewriting, editing, tearing up pages, and chewing packs of yellow Chicklets. My dentist said I would ruin my teeth, but this was my one vice.

When I told Ewert about my construction woes, he laughed, "It's your plague of mice!" He compared my plaster dust saga while writing my dissertation to the plague of mice that tormented St. Francis before he wrote his famous poem to nature, "Brother Sun, Sister Moon." I didn't see what was so amusing. But he was convinced that physical troubles were a good omen. "This is your catalyst to transform the base metal of theology into gold," he said, grinning.

* * *

I T was now less than a week to my doctoral exams. I was thus relieved when Fr. D called to give me the day off, tied up in meetings with the Dean. His graduate assistant, I did library research and typed his letters while he stood over my shoulder correcting me. Free of his nervous habit, I drove to the ocean. The increased hours of study had become wearying. Some days, I figuratively had to chain myself to my desk chair, forcing myself to digest volumes of theology.

Walking along the beach, Underhill's words came to mind: "The paradoxical 'quiet' of the contemplative is but the outward stillness essential to inward work."[10] Silence was deeper than prayer. I had a need for pure emptiness. How different this was than false silence, the silence deafened by what was not said, by what was not truthful! It was far grander than a still night lying under a canopy of stars in Mazatlan. Or the solitude found in the Trinity Wilderness, high in the Sierra range camping among black bears. I had had my share of lonely places. This silence pulsated within me, a depth not my own that opened out to a boundless expanse of light.

How small and insignificant is the self in comparison to All That Is!

Daily I forged a path through digressions and distractions, claiming my right to be in my own energy, in God's energy. Yet I was more involved in life than ever. I was stricken with happiness over my children's laughter and beauty. Azaleas lining Fordham campus gave rise to bubbles of joy rising in my throat. I celebrated the thought of Gregory of Nyssa, a fourth-century mystic, "inebriated" by God. The more I accepted my way, the way of silence and unsaying, the more energy flowed. Solitude, alone with the divine in my soul's hermitage, was not segregation, but intertwined in everything.

On the day of my written exams, I arrived at Fordham to pick up my sealed questions and raced home. I only had forty-eight hours to compose three thirty-page, polished essays, two from my theological major, one from my minor. The kids were staying with friends for the duration, and I immediately got to work. I must have entered an altered state of consciousness because the hours flew by and I had already completed two of the essays and was making steady progress on the third with plenty of time to spare.

During the early morning hours of the next day, I was just finishing my last essay on the development of trinitarian thought when I had a moment of insight about the Council of Nicaea, where the Christological issue of the nature of the Son of God in relationship to God the Father was settled. I could almost feel the descent of wisdom into the collective mind of the roomful of bishops in attendance at the Council, when I moved my foot slightly and brushed the computer cords on the floor. Instantly the screen went black, the computer off. Horrified, I frantically hit the "escape" button on the keyboard, but nothing happened. I tried other measures, made sure none of the wires had become disconnected, fumbled around with the disk drive. When I finally turned the computer back on (these were the days when we still used A drives) and opened my document, my entire essay was irredeemable, words scrambled in a hopeless hodgepodge. Not one sentence was in the right place!

Luckily, I was able to complete my exams on time, passing with high honors. Over the following eight months, I completed my dissertation, survived my oral examination, and stood on the very steps of Keating Hall where I had first known this is it, to receive my doctorate, with Ewert, my mother, and my children by my side. It was a glorious day.

"GET the ball! Get the ball!!" Tobin, Shana, and I shouted from the bleachers of the high school football stadium. Below us, Maya and Gina were leaning against a post in blue-and-white cheerleader's outfits, waiting for halftime. Eleventh-graders, they had boyfriends on the team. Where did the years go? How did I get so lucky to have loving, kind, terrific children?

I never paid much attention to our surroundings as long as they were clean and simply aesthetic. But I began to realize that our charmingly shabby apartment contrasted negatively with the grand homes of my children's friends. Lacking the material possessions their classmates took for granted, we measured every item in our grocery cart against the budget. Larger purchases, such as a washing machine or dental work, generated panic as I nervously calculated how much I could afford to charge on my credit card. It was only this year, 1988, that I had purchased a small color television with a monetary gift from my mother. Since my father died, my mother had remarried a widowed relative. Occasionally she visited or I travelled to her new home on the east coast of Florida.

Our relationship had changed. The pain of losing my father had mellowed us: I was genuinely open to her, and my mother had become more loving and more supportive of me. She was amazed that I managed to obtain a doctoral degree while raising four children alone, saying, "You're raising these kids better than most families with two parents. I always said you were good with children."

I had no doubt that my openness to God consciousness and my lack of fear of all things supernatural were born through her and with me into the world. That my mother taught me to love God, to seek God in all things, was her greatest gift.

Of course, she was still my mother, claiming that everything I was now laboring to accomplish she already knew when she was born.

18

Called to Silence

LATE SEPTEMBER LIGHT cast parallelograms on the floor as students rushed in from the hall and clamored to take seats, dropping their backpacks. I was standing in front of the blackboard, chalk poised midair as I thought about the day's lecture. My first semester as a college professor, I was teaching "Mysticism: East and West" to upper-division undergraduates.

At a Catholic university, among students primarily from Catholic backgrounds, I made a point of emphasizing that our study of mysticism would be philosophical and experiential, delving into some of the more profound religious experiences recorded by humans. We would investigate issues of belief, doubt, and the scope of consciousness in the weeks ahead.

But always, in one form or another, I would say, "This is an academic course. It is a time to think without restraint, dispensing with 'shoulds' and 'oughts.' You are free to have any opinion and explore your view of God or Ultimate Reality, as well as your faith, agnosticism, or atheism. Any questions?"

That was when I heard Jessica, sitting in the last seat in the middle row, stifling sobs behind an upturned book.

"Is everything all right, Jessica?" I asked while walking down the aisle.

"I'm sorry. It's just that I'm so upset." Squatting down next to her seat, I quietly asked if there was anything she needed. To my surprise, she wanted to tell us about her experience during her sophomore year participating in a spiritual group organized by Fr. T.

"Our group was having a discussion on how each person perceived God and faith," she said, blowing her nose. "When it was my turn, I told the group that God for me was in everything, a spiritual presence that I felt in an obscure way, and that I often doubted the Church's catechism.

"Fr. T became agitated. He accused me of intellectual immaturity, said my spiritual life was inauthentic; it wasn't a real Christian spirituality."

I was holding my breath, hoping she would continue.

"I was so disturbed that I stopped attending mass. For the last two years all I've been doing is questioning everything I've learned in twelve years of CCD classes and K–12 Catholic school.[1] The only reason I'm taking this class is because I have to fulfill my core requirement of nine theology credits."

With her permission, we opened a class discussion. "I know exactly what you mean," said Jacob across the aisle. "I've lost my faith, I don't know what happened, but I'm tired of being afraid of the punishing God shoved down our throats by religion. It's stupid!"

"The hardest thing for me since Fr. T's reaction," Jessica said, "was believing that I wasn't worthy to seek or know my own truth. How could I have let him do that to me? I've just substituted no faith for the Catholic faith I thought I had, but neither is going to heal the pain."

Jessica's plea for a spiritual path free of dogma, control, and subordination reverberated around the room. Many of the students, as well as adults I'd worked with from diverse religious or secular persuasions, echoed Jessica's fear of an unsympathetic and punishing God. For many, this fear, traced to scriptural images and stories, and to religious formation received as children, stifled personal spiritual exploration. While their religion extolled a God of love, too often this was purely an intellectual awareness, one that did not find correspondence between outward behaviors and inner feelings of inadequacy.

"If we are never treated with love," I said, "there is no benefit in being told God is Love. If we are traumatized by fear of divine retribution, it is difficult to know God as friend and companion. It is not our connection to God that has been severed, but our failure to bear witness to the godliness in each other that is the source of pain."

LATER THAT DAY, Trent, an engineering student who was unusually quiet in class, came to see me during office hours, wanting to discuss an experience he'd had the previous summer off the California coast.

"One evening I climbed on my surfboard under the light of the moon. The sky was clear and millions of stars were visible. I paddled out further than I had gone before, rocked by the gentle undulation of the waves and the sounds of the distant surf. Troubled by the failure of my first relationship and by my parents, who criticized my educational aspirations, I was wrecked.

"Suddenly, an intense Light illuminated my mind, stunning me. For a moment, I was really scared. But then, the Light filled me with the greatest sense of belonging I've ever felt."

Although alone, drifting in the vast ocean on nothing more than a fiberglass board, he felt united with everyone and everything. He was somehow, and in some mysterious way, immeasurably blessed. The intensity of what he felt and knew was transformative, placing his life and present troubles in a wholly different context. Unable to make sense of his experience at the time, Trent wondered if perhaps he was a type of mystic.

Like other members of the class, Trent admitted he was initially skeptical about mystical experience, which he had believed was unscientific or irrational. He harbored a common misunderstanding about mysticism—that it involved some kind of secret knowledge inaccessible to ordinary humans. But had revised his opinion after reading portions of Underhill's *Mysticism*, and the writings of the Zen monk, Bankei, Julian of Norwich, and Ibn' al-Arabi.[2]

Closely tied to this notion of a secret was what William James called the ineffability of mysticism—the inability to put into words what is experienced. The paradox of mysticism was that at the same time it was labeled "secret" or "ineffable," the enormity of humanity's spiritual archives attested that mysticism was not a rarified spiritual state but a further depth-dimension within all awareness, operating alongside other ways of knowing, including the rational, intellectual, and aesthetic.

*   *

SPRING semester, students were assigned *The Confessions of St. Augustine*, but hampered by the saint's excessive attention to the sinfulness of the body, had difficulty grasping its contribution to religious thought. One of my favorite classical authors, Augustine wrote with passion, penning the first Christian spiritual autobiography and offering a trope for centuries of theological reflection. I identified with his life struggles: abandoning the dualistic philosophy of Manichaeism, quitting his position as professor of rhetoric in Milan, and embracing celibacy. In the summer of 386, disgusted with his unruly will and in turmoil over his refusal to give up hedonism, Augustine recounts his final conversion to Christianity in a now-famous scene:

"I flung myself down, how I do not know, under a certain fig tree, and gave free reign to my tears.... Such words I spoke, and with most bitter contrition I wept within my heart. And lo, I heard from a nearby house, a voice like that of a boy or a girl, I know not which, chanting and repeating over and over, "Take up and read. Take up and read." [*Tolle, lege. Tolle, lege.*] Instantly, with altered countenance,... I checked the flow of my tears and got up, for I interpreted this solely as a command given to me by God to open the book [of Scripture] and read the first chapter I should come upon.

"So I hurried back to the spot where...I had put there the volume.... I snatched it up, opened it, and read in silence the chapter on which my eyes first fell: 'Not in rioting and drunkenness, not in chambering and impurities, not in strife and envying; but put you on the Lord Jesus Christ, and make not provision for the flesh in its concupiscence.'"[3]

Like Augustine, I had questioned my choice of sexual partners and been laid low by a conflicted will. In pursuit of a deepening commitment to God, several years ago during my second semester of doctoral studies, I vowed to remain celibate until and unless I was able to truly be myself with another person, in a relationship of mutual respect. Explicitly tied to monasticism in Christianity and Buddhism, celibacy was one of the great ascetic practices, the monk abstaining from marriage and sexual relations for the sake of God and Dharma, respectively, and by extension for all of humanity, without the constraints incurred in personal relationships. Luke's reference to celibate persons as "equal to angels" (Lk 20: 35–36) suggested their role as agents of God within the human sphere.[4]

Similarly, the Hindu renunciate or *sannyasin* was *brahmacharya*, literally "walking with Brahman." One of the cornerstones of serious yoga practice, it had two main meanings: control of the senses and celibacy, both associated with higher spiritual principles. It was mind-body-spirit training, establishing within oneself a holy vessel of peace, free from emotional and biological demands.

I didn't approach celibacy as an ascetic choice, however, but rather as a state of new innocence, of the hallowed space of nonsexual being. I wanted to formally commit to interior solitude, to experience the latitude and longitude of self without accommodation or compromise. I wanted to turn my life into a monastery. I pursued my aspiration with single-minded purpose, renouncing all that was not necessary to it. It was this heart intention, rather than a conventional asceticism that distinguished my practice from other spiritual endeavors.

Only by claiming the right of being one-in-myself, making life choices neither because of a need to please nor to be approved, would I be faithful to God and to myself. I was leaving behind a psychological dependency on what society told me I should want—whether as the counterpart to some male partner, abstract ideal, family expectation, or social norm. In the past, unhealthy external pressures had influenced me to act or think against my own integrity. Now my decision to practice celibacy was a vow made in the depth of my soul that I would protect, preserve, and honor my divine-self.

As an adherent of this new monastic commitment, the eternal wisdom guided my way. I composed prayers and canticles, developed meditative exercises and contemplative techniques, which I taught to a growing number of adult spiritual seekers. My path, which I identified as proto-religious or trans-religious, was founded on a commitment to a primordial monastic dimension prior to specific religious identity. Looking back, I identified crossroads on my journey, moments when the ancient formation process had been taking place, as I lived out the invisible horarium, its daily schedule ritualizing my longing for solitude and conforming my heart to the divine heart.

Living this way of life I perhaps was what Raimon Panikkar meant by "[t]he modern monk [who] is not interested in stripping himself of everything but in assimilating it all.... [for] the shaping of this world is a religious and even a contemplative concern not alien to or at odds with the monastic vocation...[even] the daily papers with their news have been converted into spiritual reading."[5]

Mining of the sacred from the seemingly mundane required a bodily assimilation of the totality of life experiences. As a temple of the holy, my body and all bodies—animal, insect, plant, human, mineral, water—were a cipher of the unity of spirit-flesh, the mysterious vulnerability of being born. In and through the body ever more subtle, sensuous, and intangible levels of consciousness were encoded, the entire creation possessing the holy power to transform, heal, reconcile, redeem, and liberate.

Precisely this embodied aspect of new monasticism was both exhilarating and difficult to perform. How much easier to be ascetic, to strip oneself of everything, than to be life-affirming, becoming an empty vessel through which Spirit or Allah or Buddha-mind could live and work in the world. This was my rule: Love the world, be the eyes and ears and heart and feet and hands of the divine.

St. Teresa of Avila's prayer echoed our divine responsibility in Christian terms:

Christ has no body but yours,
No hands, no feet on earth but yours,
Yours are the eyes with which he looks
Compassion on this world,
Yours are the feet with which he walks to do good,
Yours are the hands, with which he blesses all the world.

It was in this expanded sense that I had taken up the meditative-biological practice of celibacy. As a mystical state of consciousness, celibacy could be understood in two senses: as the physical absence of sexual relations, or as the maintenance of spiritual integrity, in or out of sexual relations. If this pure relationship were not present, although a person may be technically celibate—unmarried and abstaining from sex—she was not practicing mystical celibacy.

Discussing my notion of mystical celibacy with a friend, prioress of a Carmelite monastery, she solemnly remarked, "We have women here who are seventy years old and virgins who do not know what celibacy is. They allow gossiping friends to intrude on silence. Or lack emotional integrity, susceptible to praise and blame, or suffer from excessive attachment to people, food, or possessions. They are, in their own ways, just as 'married' as their sexually active counterparts outside our monastery walls." I understood her to mean that some of her sisters had never learned that celibacy was not chiefly sexual abstinence, but preservation of one's solitude with God.

Free to recover the simple health of my inner life, celibacy was not the foreboding asexual presence of popular lore, but the lively birthing place of the holiness of relations. Far from being opposed to sexuality, I practiced mystical celibacy to discover the deepest possibility of human friendship and love. Understood in its spiritual implications, solitude of self was available to all who preserved within themselves the monastic enclosure where the Divine and the self were one. Later, when I would marry, my extended years of practicing celibacy prepared me to open my heart to my partner, my children, and the whole of creation while remaining deeply faithful to my relationship with God.

* * *

DURING the academic year, I commuted from New York to Philadelphia by train, staying overnight Tuesday and Wednesday in a room rented from a college alumnus. All four children were completing a phase of their education, and I didn't want to move them until the school year was over. Together, along with help from members of my spiritual community, they managed during my absence. It was hard on all of us. Even our new mixed-Samoyed puppy, Leo, was despondent while I was away, rushing to plunk his rather large body in my lap the minute I returned home. Up at 4 a.m. to catch Metro North into Grand Central Station, cross-town on the subway to Penn Station, and then Amtrak to Philadelphia for my 9 a.m. class, the five-hour commute exacted its toll, my weight plummeting to ninety-five pounds. Worried about my health, the university provost offered me a raise concerned that my meager pay was a further strain on my tenuous financial situation.

Teaching and learning were my passion. I loved our bright and eager student body. I dearly wanted to succeed in my new career as a religious studies faculty. Yet, once again, I found it difficult to reconcile my professional responsibilities with the intensity of divine energies pressing into me. Often after teaching, I would cloister myself in my office, wondering how I was going to make it through the day. Alone, I would pray for strength and guidance. It is hard to explain, but the inflow of divine presence heightened my sensitivity to such a pitch that teaching seemed to exhaust my soul, generating a related bodily depletion. As if my being were crushed by the effort required to translate from interior, spiritual knowing to intellectual categories, and to make syllabi, order books for the library, attend faculty meetings, negotiate the million excuses students had for not turning in homework, grade exams, serve on university committees, publish new research, and function as de facto spiritual advisor to students lining up outside my office door.

Fortunate to be at a private university encouraged to teach courses on spirituality and mysticism from an experiential and not purely historical perspective, it was nonetheless true that my contemplative side had no place in academic pedagogy.[6] Intellectual life not only domesticated transcendent experience, it also was uncomfortable with scholar-practitioners who, while maintaining standard academic non-partisanship, nonetheless could not divorce the religious from religion. Our department was divided along these lines. Some faculty held that the study of religion should be approached from an outsider perspective as an artifact of culture. Others believed it was impossible to study a religion without entering into the reality of those who claimed faith.

I soon realized that "Dr. Lanzetta" was identified as a Catholic theologian, expected to adhere to the latest ecclesiastical edict, and to demonstrate compliance with Catholic moral teachings. While I had been educated at a Jesuit University and had great respect for Catholic social justice and wisdom traditions, I was not a Catholic theologian if being a Catholic theologian meant I had to abandon freedom of thought or deep faith. My commitment to interreligious dialogue and global spirituality was not an adjunct to a primary Christian identity, but foundational, ontological. I was faithfully, inexorably, a disciple of the Unnameable Perfection of the October revelations, drawn to the universality of the spiritual quest and not solely to one religion.

Yet when I shared my contemplative orientation, often people would assume I was *not* Catholic or *not* Christian. Even some of my closest friends and long-term companions on the journey still thought it was possible to repudiate one's history, or that exclusiveness could function in reverse to deny communal belonging. I did not see it that way. My path did not demand the rejection of Christianity or any authentic faith, but the inclusion of all faiths in the circle of a greater love. In a similar way, no earthly authority had the right to deny my seat at the Catholic table, shunned as a nonbeliever or an apostate. In fact, I thought the central message—God is Love—placed a special injunction on Christians to welcome every person, believer and nonbeliever alike, to the Eucharistic celebration.

In approaching Jesus' teachings from a mystical, rather than a theological or hierarchical, perspective, I found universal ethical precepts and spiritual principles that freed me to pursue truth wherever it was found. The difference lay in this: My approach was not, in the first instance, a justification for belief or religious orthodoxy, but was concerned with living out a monastic commitment, with growing closer to God. I gathered wisdom from multiple sources to deepen my understanding and integration of the radical awakening I experienced and lived.

Further, the professional theologian or academic was expected to be authoritative and articulate, facts readily at one's fingertips. There was little time to ponder or gaze. Those who spoke in tentative voice—the voice that receded, lived low, hung out with the disenfranchised—were often tromped on or ridiculed. The problem went deeper. The practice of spiritual nonviolence I followed required letting go of advantage, of being "somebody"—accomplished, recognized, extolled—to lead finally to silence, to the "palace of nowhere," or spark of the soul, which apprehended reality in its primordial vulnerability.[7]

"Woe unto you," wrote Raimon Panikkar, "you theologians and academicians, when you dismiss what others say because you find it embarrassing or not sufficiently learned."[8]

Certain hubris weighed down Christian theology with ancient enmities and exclusions, outdated moralities and, most painfully, misogyny. Male colleagues remarked on the importance of women's perspectives in the department, but the problem was more entrenched than any woman's voice could fix. Every major world religion had been founded, revised, and promulgated by males. Theology was functionally and foundationally patriarchal. In many respects, the academic enterprise was as well.

If religion had never been gender neutral, I always had imagined that mysticism and spirituality were. Now I realized that even the interior life was not exempt from oppressive politics directed at marginalized people or groups. While feminist theologians were making inroads into the bastion of male theological privilege and more women were entering the field of religious studies, it was naïve and dangerous to assume that theology escaped the interpretive limits that were suspect in every use of symbol, language, and ideology.

In addition, I found it disconcerting how each field of discourse had its own dominant rhetoric promoted by prevailing academic elites. In the late 1980s, Jacques Derrida and deconstruction were the latest rage in academic circles. I admired Derrida's brilliant philosophy, especially his attempt to stir up the guardians of orthodoxy and expose the limits of absolutist truth claims. His critique was long overdue. Derrida even found resonance with a particular type of mysticism, called negative or apophatic, which highlighted the indetermination or undecidability that was the hallmark of advanced stages of contemplation.

I won't bore you with these academic debates. But I did not agree with a major tenet of deconstruction: whether anyone could lay claim to an unmediated experience of God or Truth, a topic too close to my own life. I was not immune to the charge of postmodernism, under whose spell classical metaphysics fell. But the problem of the false god could never be solved by the intellect alone.

I wondered if the postmodern dilemma, that one never had access to Source, was just another way of getting off the hook. Of having to face what it would be like if God or Truth did knock on the door of our hearts—without possessive politics or doctrinal decrees, without demanding adherence to covenants and orthodoxies and list of sins and arch-sins. What would it be like if we let the miracle settle in, knowing it's not easy to keep the heart open in the face of (us) others who try to steal what we are too afraid to find within us, waiting to love?

ADDING TO MY turmoil, departmental politics were debilitating, riven with strictures and histories and petty quarrels and in some cases a festering resentment among tenured colleagues. As a new member of the department, it was a shock to have staked my future on a career I loved but which I feared would ultimately prove harmful to my life path.

I wanted to believe I could manage to interweave a contemplative focus with university life, much as Ewert had. But I was not able to do so. Perhaps being female and a single mother created problems that Ewert did not have to face. Or perhaps it was the intensity of contemplative experience that once again called me away.

I would remain within an academic context for almost seventeen years, initially as a full-time faculty and later, teaching part-time, presenting lectures, and building collaborative programs at several colleges. During this period, I resigned from my first college and two other tenure-track positions. My responsibility to my children and to my colleagues impelled me to stay the course. But the deeper, more radical pull of monasticism, of the feminine voice, demanded something other.

Eventually, when I made the final decision to abandon formal academic life, if not writing, teaching, and scholarship, it was not without terrific cost. It was the only community where I felt a sense of belonging, and for years afterward I continued to apply to faculty positions unable to give up their lure.

In retrospect, I understand why leaving the academy was so important. It opened the space and time for my monastic life and teaching to flourish. "Our students take up the morning hours," Augustine noted, "but what do we do during the rest of the day?... Let us put away these vain and empty concerns. Let us turn ourselves only to a search for truth."[9]

My heart was heavy for you, Holy One. I feared I had given you so little time that I had betrayed or neglected our friendship. All that I held dear was but an addendum to the bustle of daily life.

* * *

THE following evening, alone in my boarding house room, I was thinking about how much I missed the kids. Waiting for them to call me back, my mind wandered to the previous weekend when I'd attended a Chenrezig Meditation, led by a Tibetan Buddhist Rinpoche. In the Tibetan Buddhist pantheon of enlightened beings, Chenrezig (*Avalokiteśvara*, Sanskrit) is the embodiment of the compassion of all the Buddhas. The meditation involved the cultivation of immeasurable compassion, compassion felt equally for all beings.

During the day's practice, my consciousness soared to the realm of vast peace, an ocean of cessation, of brilliance. It was like an infinite breath of pure calm. Afterward, I wrote in my notebook:

Ocean of Peace: vast,
limitless
waveless

Boundless wisdom
peace

Mind arises from emptiness
Pure mind
Washed with brilliance
No thought
Pure mind
Crystalline brilliance
Empty mind
Peace

* * *

ALONGSIDE my academic duties, I continued in my private practice as a spiritual director and teacher of contemplation. One semester I offered an introductory course on the mystical tradition of health to medical and psychology professionals. To this point in my life, I had never shared or attempted to teach about the sacred art of soul healing. In a certain sense, healing cannot be taught; it arises from the work of the spirit. However, it is possible to impart how one approaches diagnosis, and the preparation, attitude, and quality of consciousness necessary to serve as a healing presence. I began the course with these thoughts:

"Some things in life cannot be bought but only freely given. They cannot be learned but only born in us. They cannot be known but only endured. They cannot be named but only lived. This is healing. While it does not succumb to the marketplace, its mysterious ways can be invoked, like the shaman calling the rains. If we long for mystery, mystery may present itself. If we open our hearts, pouring everything out, Wisdom may enter. If we honor the intimacy of life, splendor may overcome our hearts. In this way we approach the awesome truth, humbling ourselves to learn that which transcends all learning.

"As you know, in 1976, I had a life-changing series of religious experiences. At that point in my life I was not following an organized path preceded by many years of meditation practice. It was a spontaneous occurrence that broke apart reality as I knew it and, overcome by the suffering of the world, I fell to my knees and then to the ground. I witnessed the degree to which, out of ignorance or intentionality, we deny our sacred origins, trampling each other and all of creation. That day I died to the belief that I had a right to have my own life, as if there were such a thing as one's own life separate from the entire universe of beings.

"Hours later, when the suffering abated, the energies of divine love pressed into me. I was shown that we can bear suffering because love and joy far surpass anything we suffer, even, at the same time, that suffering is not illusory. Suffering and liberation form an inseparable paradox. We try to reconcile the paradox. We try to make it palatable. We try to mend it, but it is not mendable. We have to bear suffering and love in our hearts. We have to be on the floor. We have to be lost. We have to be broken. We have to be empty. We have to be bewildered, to know and to experience the Reality that transcends all thought.

"I share this story, because everything I know about healing I learned that day. We are made for healing. We are not static. We are beings of light. We are electromagnetic fields. We are energy systems. Even on cellular and subatomic levels we are in constant motion. We are beings of change. Transformation is part of our natures, intrinsic to matter and consciousness, the journey of the soul to its source.

"We are not destined to be perfect—not here, not now, yet neither are we merely flawed. We are beings born to assume suffering in order to stretch ourselves toward the highest expression of conscious love. In this sense, mystical healing attends to the wounds of the deep self, of the ways in which the soul has been separated from its beloved. The healer weaves the patient's suffering into her or his own being, until gauze knits together the place where the patient's soul is torn. And what is that gauze? It is love. It is compassion. It is justice.

"Another thing I learned that day: we always have the potential for healing because, in our depth, we are pure and untouched, of the divine light, belonging to the holy. We are adored; we are intimately one with the divine, who wants, needs, and seeks us. In the center of our beings God is always present, in search of us, and never withdraws.

"Thus, the efficacy of healing depends on soul force, on a quality of heart rather than on knowledge or technique. Who you are as a person is all-important. You may have knowledge, but if you are not a lover of truth, are not trustworthy, lack ethical standards, and don't have a prayer life, what difference can it make? You will not be able to harness soul force, which requires the cultivation of virtue. True healers practice the secret of annihilation, choosing to live on the margins of society, between worlds, whether psychologically, emotionally, spiritually, physically, or mentally. What is the secret of annihilation? It is dying while living. Soul healers live between worlds, able to pass back and forth between regions of consciousness, unafraid to journey across boundaries to mend and restore.

"Soul force is gained after years of service to others and devotion to one's God. It requires extensive training in the sacred arts, as well as an inner sense of selflessness and detachment. Without humbly opening your self to the mystery of being, communication between healer and patient or teacher and student is merely intellectual. The capacity to heal has to grow in you, transmitted soul-to-soul through the integration of body, mind, and spirit, through practicing what it means to die to the false self and open your heart to love."

* *

As the academic year drew to a close, I continued to be torn by two commitments: on the one side was my academic career and financial responsibilities; on the other Spirit was drawing me into deeper intimacy, preparing me for the time when I would devote myself fully to Silence.

With a few hours before I had to catch the train back to Manhattan, I settled under a glorious blooming magnolia tree in a nearby park. Lost in silence, my thoughts turned to an aphorism I'd read in a spiritual text: If one is deeply conflicted over two different good life choices, one of them is not from God.

PART V

THE EVERYDAY MONK

19

Garden of the Gods

IN JUNE, THE KIDS and I drove across the country in a minivan crammed with suitcases, sleeping bags, snacks, dog food, and any last-minute items we forgot to ship. While Maya, Gina, and I took turns driving, Tobin and Shana wrestled space from Leo, who at 70 pounds still thought he was a lapdog.

After much soul searching, I had resigned from my faculty position, moving our family to northern Arizona where I eventually was hired by a liberal arts college to found its religious studies concentration. At the end of the summer the twins transferred to an Arizona university, Tobin and Shana to a new high school. My first months in the high desert, the vast blue sky and open vistas dispelled a tension I'd been carrying from graduate school days, reconnecting me with joy, my center of gravity. The weight of intellectual pursuits lifted and in its place was a newfound freedom of expression. I began to write again of spiritual experiences, and to paint, something I hadn't done since childhood. Prepared for a more solitary life, I had organized my bedroom as a meditation sanctuary and pictured myself living out my later years as a monk in a desert cabin.

But circumstances would lead me in a different direction. Not long after the semester began, I was invited to southern Arizona to give a series of spiritual lectures on a Sonoran ranch. While picking up student papers in my office mailbox, I mentioned my trip to the chair of the Humanities Department, who had been instrumental in my hiring. We were slowly getting to know one another. The previous month I had shared with him about the yearly retreat I took on my holy day of October 5. Bill was easy to communicate with, so when he asked if I wanted company on the five-hour journey, I agreed.

The drive to Tucson and then south to Patagonia was beautiful, the fall landscape gleaming with translucent light. My hosts were gracious, housing Bill and me in separate suites, and my talks went well.

On the way back, we stopped at a roadside restaurant. Still vegetarian, I remembered my meal because Bill emulated my choice, later laughing at himself for believing "bird food" was going to sustain him. Afterward, Bill was driving north from Casa Grande on I-10 when I heard the familiar voice repeating in my head, *"Tell him about your life. Tell him about your life."* I'd given up sharing deeply because men often were intimidated by my self-reliance and mystical orientation. Inequality of the sexes, while perhaps evened out in certain economic and social spheres, was mostly still a reality in spiritual matters and between sexual partners.

Looking through the window, I watched the sun set below the horizon, turning the sky a deeper shade of purple and pink. Bill was plying me with questions about what precipitated my mystical experiences. "When I was twenty-nine I had a life-changing series of revelations," I said. But before I could continue my story the relentless injunction, *"Tell him about your life,"* drowned out my words and I blurted out: "I have four children with three partners." I was both nervous about and didn't care what he would think.

His response startled me. "You have had such an interesting life!" He wanted to know why I was not in a relationship.

"You know," I said, "my father asked me the same question a few months before he died. I told him, 'I haven't found anyone like you Pop, generous and kind. When you're on the other side, please find someone for me, OK?'"

A few days later when we talked on the phone, Bill asked, "Are we having a relationship?" I didn't know what he meant; we'd never been out on a date. During the trip back from Tucson, I had mentioned my monastic orientation and that I never planned to be married again or even be in a relationship. I didn't know what to say. So I said the first thing that came to mind: "It won't be easy."

"I know."

"I like to be alone. I'm wedded to solitude. I can't give up the contemplative life."

Christmas Eve, Bill came over with presents, sharing a holiday feast. Later on he would help Tobin and then Shana learn how to drive, and engage in lively conversations with Maya and Gina when they came home from college. The kids really liked him. Yet I was protecting my safe harbor from intrusion. Fifteen years since I'd had a sustained relationship, it was going to take a while.

I took my concerns into prayer. Would this be a good thing? Perhaps I simply needed companionship; it didn't have to be anything permanent. Would I be giving up autonomy? Would Bill accept that I was the founder of a contemplative community, that I had given my life to God? I had come too far and sacrificed too many opportunities to abandon the monastic call.

I needed time to ponder whether this momentous change was what Spirit wanted of me. I was not going to do anything contrary to the Divine will.

* *

A FEW weeks later, I drove to Phoenix to see Father Ernie, a Carmelite monk and scholar of St. John of the Cross. We'd met at a conference several years earlier and had been in touch by phone since. I looked forward to spending time with him, a true master of the spiritual life.

Heat from the asphalt parking lot burned through my shoes as I fast-stepped to the front door. Invited in by the church receptionist, I was told Fr. Ernie was expecting me in the meditation room. I found him seated there in an old leather chair, bent over a book. I don't recall the room having windows, but if it did, the interior light dimly illuminated the sparsely furnished space: two chairs, an icon and a candle resting on a sturdy wood side table, and a crucifix mounted on a wall. When Fr. Ernie looked up and saw me, his eyes were twinkling behind large-framed eyeglasses, his long face calm and welcoming.

After we exchanged greetings, we sat across from each other, spent some moments in silence, and then settled into discussing the reason for my visit. I shared with him my deepening friendship with Bill and my concern about future life directions.

He wanted to know more about my background and history, listening with great intensity to my story. When I had finished, I waited for him to speak.

"God has chosen you for an arduous path," he said. "It is not easy to be called by faith to a devout life outside of a formal denominational context. I imagine at times your journey has been lonely."

"It has. Especially in the beginning, when few people were interested in or understood what I was doing, I went through periods of intense loneliness. If it weren't for prayer and divine guidance, I wouldn't have made it."

"What did you find most difficult?"

"Not belonging anywhere. When I began this journey, religious dialogue was in its infancy, and people were pursuing Eastern religions and so forth. But I was outside of all that. I was on a different path."

Ernie nodded and closed his eyes. He was quiet for a while.

Then he said, "The woundedness of life is the place where God wants to heal you, your whole life experience, not only a fragment of it. Your specific history of being called by God to a solitary path, financial strain, single parenting, and emotional harm contribute to your total spiritual state. It is this that you must consider."

"Yes. I've never been in a relationship where my spiritual life was not trampled. I resist help, I want to be financially independent; it's hard for me to accept that Bill is generous, open, and loving. It's not been my experience."

Ernie waited while I wrote our exchange in my notebook. I needed to remember.

Afterward, he continued, "The violent tension you say you feel about your desire to be financially independent is a wrong form of liberation. It is not contrary to God's wish for you to be loved, cared for, and relieved of financial and emotional strain.

"Ask: What condition of life is God calling me to now? What is organic and homogenous with my life and what belongs to a different way of life, in your case, the contemplative versus the normal, secular life? What is truly compatible with God's inner call?"

"Is a relationship with Bill in conflict with a contemplative life?" I asked. "Will I be taking a wrong life path? Will I be giving up solitude, which is essential to my well-being? These are the questions that occupy me."

"Pick out things that are causing conflict, woundedness, and pain and hold them up to God. Are these compatible with Spirit or against you?"

Later that day, sitting on a bench outside the meditation room, making notes on my session, an image came to me: I was walking through a long gray tunnel, crossing from one reality to another, deeper into the mystery of contemplation. On my back I was carrying old burdens, my body bent under their weight. Trying to adjust my load, I suddenly realized I had to leave these burdens behind. I had to allow another person to help me.

*　*　*

IN March, while the kids were on a ski adventure, I drove to Tucson for the Pascua Yaqui Tribe's Deer Dance, an amalgam of American Indian and Catholic Easter ceremonies. I knew several tribal participants who were spending Holy Week in prayer and penance. I attributed my affinity with rituals of transcendence to my early life association with diverse religious practices, living in Mexico, and later attending grammar school in the predominately Jewish community of Long Beach, New York. Imbued with the spirit of Lent, Easter, Passover, and Yom Kippur, these sacramental moments seeped into my cells, becoming part of my biological code.

Phrases I'd heard growing up entered my consciousness at will: *tikkun olam* (repairing the world), *teshuvah* (repentance), *dominus vobiscum* (The Lord be with you), *chesed* and *misericordia* (Hebrew and Latin, loving-kindness). Later, when I was called upon to be a soul healer, the prayer "*lamb of God who takes away the sins of the world*" often surfaced. At the time, I didn't connect these words with the Latin mass I recited as a child, the Gospel of John, or even with Jesus Christ.

If I hadn't known that Jesus was called the "Lamb of God," what would I have thought: the lamb—gentle, quiet, adorable, and tender—without malice or artifice? The God of small things, the God of tender mercies and sweet, excruciating loveliness—this god healed the sins of the world. I wished to become more like the lamb, to me, the Mother of the World. Hidden among all names, speaking silently through all religions, leading us home.

Growing up, the Lenten season had been more about tangible austerities and rewards: sacrificing candy or television for Lent, fish on Friday and other holy days, crosses my father made from Palm Sunday fronds, and chocolate bunnies. Like most children, I didn't understand the spiritual implications of Holy Week. Yet, over the years, I'd grown to appreciate the importance of shared sacrifice and lamentation, of opening one's heart to sacramental events that shattered boundaries, scandalizing complacency. Observing the solemnity of the Deer Dancers, I ruminated on the association of the events in the hours before and including Jesus' trial and crucifixion with the word "passion," derived from the Greek verb "to suffer."

Even more inscrutable than suffering was the mystical significance of resurrection, to rise again, to enter a different form of life. Like the story of Saul (who later becomes Paul) on the road to Damascus, suffering or repentance was the catalyst for *metanoia*, a Greek word meaning "to change one's life around." Yet, to finally transcend the cross of cruelty, betrayal, and abandonment, establishing one's life on the premise of divine joy, was the promise of the Easter story. I didn't think Christianity sufficiently embraced the resurrection, as if it were otherworldly, not incarnated, not a promise for today.

Nonetheless, the earliest accounts of Christian monasticism emphasized the centrality of deification, or becoming divine-like, in one's spiritual life. Born out of reflection on Jesus' life, death, and resurrection, this ethic of perfection was founded on the promise first established in a famous phrase attributed to the early Fathers of the Church: "God became man [sic] so that man might become God." In imitation of and participation in Christ's divine-human qualities, the monk aspired to resurrect the self into a new, holy life. This mystical method involved prayer, solitude, compunction, and reconciliation. The inner way was for the sake of a higher intention: to be living representatives of Christ's triumph over death, and of his final integration of divinity and humanity.

I spent the rest of the day in contemplation. The next morning, I left Tucson before dawn, taking Fr. Ernie's questions on the road. Four hours later, I traveled north and east of Flagstaff, arriving at the Valley of the Gods in southern Utah by early afternoon. Walking into the monument, I found a secluded area to pray beneath a massive umber rock outcropping and laid my blanket down. Sitting cross-legged and spreading my arms wide, I took in the majestic landscape. I could hear Earth Mother calling me, claiming me, pulling me into her holy temple, ripe with fullness and round with reddish hue. I was born of her and held by her and would return to her one day. Overcome by the intensity of earth's intimate *presence*, I succumbed to the completeness of *being held*.

Viscerally affected, I would have given everything to gaze daily on such wonder. Silence gradually seeped into my body, my soul. Time stopped. Into the vast, windless plain ringed by red mountain gods I cast my prayer: *Please help me discern the true path for me. Will a relationship with Bill be a betrayal of my divine vow, will it distract me from the path God has chosen for me?*

Silence. Hours passed.

Then words from Spirit: *Nothing and no one can derail you from the path God has chosen. This, too, is part of your path.*

Hiking back to my car, I pondered the fragility of the line between knowing and unknowing, identity and annihilation, self and no self. If I said, like the Sufi martyr, al-Hallaj, *I am God*, was I blasphemous or prideful? I stood on the threshold between two poles, knowing that I was neither/nor, both/and, sometimes either/or, but never finalized. In the fluid space between naming and unnaming, self and no self, god and not-god, I sank into outrageous joy.

> Oh, Mother of the World, may I be worthy of your gifts,
>   my soul a mirror of delight,
>   reflecting your formless kiss.

✳ ✳ ✳

S EVERAL evenings later I was reading through my lecture notes, my mind wandering over a conversation I'd had with Bill earlier in the day, when I learned he came from a wealthy family. Although our combined salaries were meager, and he would not have an inheritance until his grandmother passed away (not expected for many years in the future), he thought I should know. I was wrestling with this information, wondering if the disparity in life experience between my family and his would be painful for my children. Also, having embarked on a simpler lifestyle, I was concerned this would be an issue between us.

During the night I had a dream. I was in a misty atmosphere, speaking to an undisclosed elder or god figure about how I couldn't have a permanent relationship with Bill because I shouldn't have a life of comfort when so many people were suffering.

The elder listened. Then like a magician he materialized in the air a succession of monasteries located in pristine settings, with sufficient food, shelter, and clothing. We swooped down into the enclosures, where he pointed out how endowments and donations supported the monastic refuge, allowing monks the relative material comfort necessary for a life of meditation and prayer. "It is acceptable for your life to be easier," he said. "You are not betraying a trust because this is your work. You have much left to do." At that moment Bill stepped out of the mist and, looking directly into my eyes, said, "Let me be your monastery."

I woke with a jolt, writing the dream in my journal. *Let me be your monastery.* Let me help preserve your solitude. Let me be in support of your spiritual journey. Twenty-three years later, it's still true of our relationship.

For several hours I ruminated on how amazing was Spirit. The inner monk, the archetype of monk, was transforming my relations, just as my life experience was transforming the traditional monastic vows of celibacy, poverty, and obedience. I sought to not strip myself of everything but to assimilate it all, to acquire by integration the fullness of human life. My partnership with Bill afforded us the opportunity to subject conventional belief about relationships, marriage, or gender roles to a greater truth. My absorption in god consciousness was a fact that had nothing particular to do with a countercultural form of life, but rather with my ability to fully open my heart.

"Stay open forever, so open it hurts, and then open some more, until the day you die, world without end, amen."[1]

Because of the October revelations I was the recipient of and radically committed to a new spiritual path; because of my history I was a mother fiercely devoted to my children. Both of these situations ruled out a traditional monastic lifeform. Yet again I was shown that if one gives one's entire being to the divine pursuit, precisely the pattern of soul development that was true and good for one's unique life situation would be revealed. All that was required was a special kind of total heart intention, as the great teacher, St. Teresa of Avila, astutely pointed out centuries ago:

> We don't give ourselves completely to this path [to be a servant of love through the path of prayer], and therefore we do not attain the blessings we desire in a short amount of time. Because: it seems to us that we are giving all to God, whereas the truth of the matter is that we are paying God the rent or giving Him the fruits and keeping for ourselves the ownership and the root.... since we do not succeed in giving up everything at once, this treasure as a result is not given to us all at once.[2]

Later that day, Bill and I talked about my dream. We both agreed that whatever relationship we had together should not be *less* than what we had alone. The freedom of one's inner life should be enhanced and preserved by one's partner, not co-opted or consumed. This is why I loved the wisdom of the poet Ranier Marie Rilke. Writing at the beginning of the twentieth century about the inequality of sexual partnerships, he believed that in the future men and women "will transform the love experience, will change it from the ground up.... And this more human love...will resemble what we are now preparing painfully and with great struggle: the love that consists in this: that two solitudes protect and border and greet each other."[3]

> She lived in solitude,
> And now in solitude has built her nest;
> And in solitude He guides her,
> He alone, Who also bears
> In solitude the wound of love.
>   —St. John of the Cross[4]

* *
* *

WHILE struggling with the possibility of a life with Bill, I was absorbed with my mission of developing an integrative curriculum that drew from a wide range of traditions and introduced students to contemplative practice at the same time. I invited a Tibetan Rinpoche to teach a semester on the *Jeweled Ornament of Liberation* and a Sufi Shaykh to offer a series of guest lectures on Islamic mysticism. We took trips to diverse religious congregations and practiced meditative techniques alongside extensive study of humanity's religious heritage. Intent on forging a global spirituality curriculum, I brought Thomas Berry and Ewert Cousins to campus, as well as other colleagues of note in eco-theology, the sociology of religion, and human rights.

I found myself reflecting on the significance of god-language and its impact on students' appraisal of ultimate reality. In an attempt to dislodge conventional thinking, I challenged them to study how the word "God" was critiqued in contemporary thought: as the personal, patriarchal, and sometimes misogynist father-god; in comparison to impersonal divine energies—*Tao, sunyata, prakti*; or with reference to mystical expressions of divine mercy, benevolence, and mother gods. Assigned to read Sallie McFague's book, *Models of God*, in which she claimed that all names for divinity were metaphorical, my students were asked to consider that whatever name we assigned to reality was never the thing in itself.

Lest students assumed divine un-naming was a modern invention, I introduced classical texts to demonstrate its usage in the world's religions. While the starkest, and perhaps clearest, example of unknowing could be attributed to Buddha's famous metaphysical silence, an anonymous sixth-century monk, Pseudo-Dionysius, was credited with placing a particular style of linguistic negation—called apophatic discourse—centrally within the Christian tradition.

The Greek word "apophasis"—to un-say or speak-away—referred to a paradoxical type of discourse that employed inscrutable phrases—"super-essential ray of divine darkness," "abyss of divinity," "luminous darkness"—to confound the mind's attempt to grasp the transcendent. Considered a higher form of contemplation, apophasis was found paired with its opposite term "kataphasis" (to say, speak-with), and the language of affirmation in Christian theology, where words praised God's attributes: goodness, mercy, compassion, love.

In terms of spiritual development, Pseudo-Dionysius associated kataphatic or affirmative theology (via positiva) with beginning spiritual stages, when one relied on religious tradition, accepted names for God, and historically transmitted prayer forms and contemplative techniques. But as one rose from the things of the world up to the divine itself, the journey shifted into negative or apophatic theology (via negativa), from known into unknown, from belief into doubt, and from intellect into mysticism. As the fuel of self-liberation, negation functioned as a disruptive element in the spiritual life, breaking down linguistic coherence and structural logic, and thereby shocking the person outside conventional notions of reality into another plane of existence.[5]

The higher the soul ascended, the more the knowledge of divinity was "too deep to be grasped in mere images," wrote Thomas Merton, "in words, or even in clear concepts. It can be suggested by words, by symbols, but in the very moment of trying to indicate what it knows the contemplative mind takes back what it has said, and denies what it has affirmed.

[For this reason] "faith sometimes mysteriously takes on the aspect of doubt, when, in fact, one has to doubt and reject conventional and superstitious surrogates that have taken the place of faith. On this level, the division between Believer and Unbeliever ceases to be so crystal clear."[6]

Students found this history fascinating. "It's helped me to consider," one man remarked, "that my unbelief is perhaps an unknowing, apophatic moment of suspension. Not necessarily a complete loss of faith. It gives me comfort."

Surprisingly, while students were receptive to the paradox of linguistic negations, they were caught short by references to God as "She." Divine metaphors were acceptable as long as they did not upset gender categories. Assigned to read about the motherhood of God in Showings by the fourteenth-century anchoress, Julian of Norwich, students came to class ready for battle. Many were outraged by Julian's reference to Jesus as Mother, a not uncommon designation by both male and female medieval Christian mystics. One woman confessed she was so disgusted she threw the book across her room. We still had a long way to go in combating stereotypical gender roles.

If students were somewhat hesitant to tackle gender, most were nonetheless in the vanguard of religious thought. For many students, the religious issues that plagued my generation and that of my parents were inconsequential. It was as if they were already living a new religious paradigm, one formed by global consciousness. Conflicts between religions over differences in philosophy or practice were met with disbelief or despair. This difference in outlook was magnified during a student-organized interfaith conversation in which a panel of senior pastors from our local religious community was invited to speak about faith.

Things were going well when a Muslim cleric asked in genuine exasperation how interfaith dialogue could reconcile the Christian claim that Jesus was the incarnation of God with the Muslim view that the idea of any incarnation of divinity violated Allah's absolute transcendence, or even for that matter with the non-theistic perspective of Japanese Zen Buddhists, who named their highest reality, sunyata—Absolute Nothing.

Other panelists accused interfaith dialogue of promoting a reductionism that was non-sacramental and connected to no distinct moment of awe or transcendence. That it was a kind of intellectual smorgasbord of religions without benefit of those enduring cycles of meaning and bereft of the mysterious grounding that formed the spirituality of the world's named religions.

After the panel adjourned, our class met to share and reflect. Students were surprised by the animated and vehement remarks made about inter-religious dialogue. They didn't understand the exclusion principle that motivated the speakers: Each religion claimed to be in possession of the one and only truth. Truth could not be multiple, in dialogue, or mutually interconnected with other truth.

In a way the reaction of our panelists didn't surprise me. It was now almost nineteen years that I had been teaching the wayless way of the October revelations to people who were essentially living and practicing a non-religious or an interfaith, interspiritual path. Yet, I still found many in and outside of the academic setting to be confused, suspicious, or fearful of this expanding vision of human devotion to God.

*
* *

SEVERAL months later, I was in Santa Fe on the eve of *Yom Kippur*. For a number of weeks I had struggled with a dry, barking cough and afraid these might be symptoms of a serious illness, prayed for healing. I have no recollection how long I prayed when the youthful face of Jesus appeared before me. Drawing closer, he extended a hand and touched my upper chest. Slowly he merged with my body and, expanding his energy, lifted the pain right out of my lungs. Almost immediately the tightness in my chest was gone.

In this heightened state of awareness, there appeared before my meditative eye an open wound located above my physical heart. Clearly outlined, like a slit cut into flesh, the skin around the wound was stretched into a bulging curve on top and bottom, similar to an eye. Inside, the wound was dark red, slightly brighter red near the surface. A bleeding, wounded heart.

I was shown that my lungs suffered an allergic irritation, but the original cause of the weakness in my chest stemmed from emotional and spiritual wounds sustained during childhood. I heard words that I must have felt but never spoke out loud as a child: *Why do you not love me? Do you not want me? Why do you hit me, and leave me to cry? Why are you so harsh and punish me so severely? Do you want me to die?*

Afterward, getting ready for bed, I felt strongly that I needed to go on a pilgrimage to the Santuario de Chimayo. The next morning, up at dawn, I ate breakfast and quickly prepared for the forty-minute drive northeast of Santa Fe. The day was glorious—full sun, warm with a tinge of autumn chill, immense blue sky, and mountains rimmed with golden aspen leaves.

I arrived at the Santuario de Chimayo early, not realizing that the chapel didn't open until 9 a.m. With ample time to spare, I walked around the grounds and down to the lower parking lot to the little river that flowed through the property. Standing near its bank, which was lined by shimmering aspens, I watched the water roiling and gushing, invigorated by its cleansing motion.

Behind the sanctuary and to the left of where I stood, Stations of the Cross had been erected, which I didn't recall noticing five years earlier when I had last visited. Placing my hand on the rock pillar into which a bronze image of Jesus' plight had been carved, I prayed for the healing of my wound—and for the healing of our wounded world. I asked that blood and tears would flow from my wound until there was no sorrow left. I asked for the grace to forgive and for the humility to be forgiven.

I circumambulated the Stations, one by one, touching each stone and the bronze relief someone lovingly had carved. I didn't know the veracity of these Biblical stories, I only knew that Jesus suffered, his suffering emblematic of the suffering taking place in that moment on our beloved earth. The Stations reminded me that suffering was not over; every day the holy slashed and burned, torn apart by troubled, violent hearts. My eyes saw the fallen, stooped bodies of humanity, struggling to lift their own cross. My ears heard cries of anguish, the defilement of innocence, in each, in all. My heart identified with the mother who mourned the dead, weaving a balm of mercy with her tears. My spirit knew the tomb was empty; we are restored, whole.

By the time I completed my meditations it was after 9 a.m. Climbing the dirt path up to the Santuario, I entered the small adobe chapel that served as a place of worship for the many pilgrims who arrived to pray and to heal. Intent on relishing the silence before the tour buses arrived, I slipped down the center aisle, stopping to study the massive wood retablos mounted on the walls depicting images of Jesus, Mary, and the saints in tones of blue, red, black, and white. When I reached the main altar, I kneeled on the altar rail and prayed: *May your wound be healed in me.*

Eventually, the sound of clicking cameras and whispered voices alerted me it was time to leave. Standing, I turned left and bent under a low arch into El Pocito, a tiny, candle-lit side chapel. Carved into the floor was a small hole that held *tierra bendita* (sacred earth), believed by the devout to have healing properties. Encouraged by a sign welcoming visitors to take a sample, I scooped a small handful of dirt into a paper bag I'd brought. As I left El Pocito, I proceeded along a narrow, dimly lit room, the walls covered by crutches, walkers, baby shoes, *milagros* (amulets), rosaries, crosses, candles, and statues of every kind and shape. Everywhere, notes of prayer or thanks-giving written on scraps of paper were rolled up and tucked in crevices. The atmosphere was permeated by a riot of color and a somber joy.

On one wall a statue of Santo Niño de Atocha, the child Jesus dressed in medieval Spanish garb, black frock, lace collar, and britches, was enclosed in a glass case. Tacked above the case was a narrative about The Holy Child of Atocha. As the story goes, during the night the child Jesus leaves heaven to bring healing water to the woes of humanity. But there are so many people to heal, the child Jesus wears out his shoes and every night has to find new ones. Inside the glass cabinet, the Santo Niño statue held a staff, a basket of fruit, and a water gourd to nourish souls, while on the wall behind it the faithful had placed innumerable baby shoes.

Leaving, I crossed into the sanctuary courtyard, uplifted by the cobalt-blue New Mexico sky. The eye-shaped wound was mending, the dried blood dissolving in the cleansing action of holy faith. Tears had not yet come, but they will if Thy will.

It was not for me to know.

* * *

ALMOST two years from the day we met, Bill and I were married. Our families and friends gathered in our home to celebrate. That same week Bill and I travelled to New York City for my ordination as an interfaith minister. Over the last year, I had completed through distance learning the ministry course I had begun and abandoned when I was at Fordham, unable to finish the two-year course at the time.

Founded in 1981 by Rabbi Gelberman, the New Seminary for Interfaith Studies was devoted to training ministers to serve people of all faiths. Because his program was based on the oneness of divine spirit, without sacrificing differences of religious history or belief, I felt philosophically and spiritual aligned with his vision. In addition to educating ministers to conduct multi-faith worship services, and to serve as chaplains in hospitals, colleges, and other institutional settings, the Seminary also opened the field of ministry to historically excluded groups, among them women, marginalized men, gays, lesbians, and people of color. Coining the expression, "Never instead, always in addition," Rabbi Gelberman explained that only through inclusion and love of each other's faith would we heal the wound of religious enmity.

The three-hour ordination ceremony was held at the Cathedral of St. John the Divine in Manhattan, co-officiated by Rabbi Gelberman and religious leaders from Buddhist, Hindu, Sikh, Hopi, Navajo, Protestant, Catholic, Jewish, Zoroastrian, Jain, and other traditions. Celestial beings bathed the cathedral in light.

Standing in a circle around the main altar with my graduating class, I watched Rabbi Gelberman solemnly perform an ancient rite of passage, anointing each forehead with oil. When he pressed warm oil into my third eye, I was lifted out of my body by a divine force, ordained to publically affirm my devotion to God and my commitment to global spirituality and to peace among religions. Following him, the other presiders one by one placed their hands on my head and offered a prayer for my vocation in the sacred language of their religion. Dizzy with joy, I returned to my seat, and to a message from the divine voice: *You will start an interfaith church.*

When the ceremony was completed, Rabbi gave Bill and me enormous hugs and offered to conduct a special blessing for our marriage. The three of us retreated into a side chapel for his blessing of Hasidic prayers, which he chanted in Hebrew. We left St. John the Divine with joyful memories and hailed a cab back to our hotel, where we packed suitcases for a short honeymoon trip.

When Bill and I returned home, our attorney initiated the process of forming the nonprofit Desert Interfaith Church. I conducted the first evening contemplative service in a small building set on a hill overlooking the mountains, offered to us by one of the town's physicians. Together we read prayers from many religions, shared bread, discussed the week's spiritual theme, and concluded the service with silent meditation.

I would continue my work as faculty, minister, and spiritual teacher, moving to a third university in another state when all four of my children were in college. But once again circumstances conspired to draw me away from this new faculty appointment and return to Arizona. Forces seemed to be propelling me toward the open space of desert, an apt metaphor for the uninhabited regions of my soul.

Forsake and give up everything. Then your hearts will become wide and deep.[7]

20

Desert Solitude

E VERY SOUL in its quest for realization passes through periods of desolation, assaulted with painful memories and unresolved beliefs. Under the gaze of the holy, the soul is pierced by an illumination of such intensity that its faculties of perception are shuttered, casting it in darkness. Yet who can explain how a soul feels or what it experiences in this time of night? Only one who has felt the tremor of the Light knows of the disorientation and anguish of the soul that has lost its bearings. For the Great Death or Dark Night by whatever name is the universal fire by which self-impediment is turned to ash. It is the time during which every spiritual crutch is removed, even faith, hope, and love, to be annihilated in a deeper way, to relinquish one's will to God.

But what happens when even the testimony of saints and mystics does not speak to the hollow pit in your gut? What happens when the spiritual processes or meditative practices designed to guide you through this very passage betray you? When you not only suffer within known categories of spiritual development, but also are pulled beyond every form of containment into a darker light? Here is where I soon found myself.

I had resigned from my third, and what would be my last attempt to lead an academic life. Unable to find work in the college town where

I was employed, Bill had been hired to head a college campus in Tucson, and I faced a new quandary: keep my faculty position, maintaining a long-distance marriage, or move back to Arizona, where I had no job. I would quickly learn, however, that this momentous change was not about my career.

Torn by the opinion of colleagues who didn't understand why I would give up a faculty position, certain to be awarded tenure the following year, I struggled to arrive at a decision. One day in late March, sitting at my desk worried about my future and about financial responsibility to my children still in college, a small gray-brown bird hopped onto the windowsill, ruffling its feathers. A passage from Matthew 6: 25–26 immediately came to mind: "Look at the birds of the air; they do not sow or reap or store away in barns, and yet your heavenly Father feeds them.... Can any one of you by worrying add a single hour to your life?"

For weeks I had been praying, and this was my answer. But, oh, if I had known in advance how much it would cost, I would not have had the fortitude to consent.

Of course, one had to constantly discern if the inner voice was from Spirit or from one's own will; if it followed the precepts of loving-kindness and emptiness of self, leading one to accomplish God's work in the world. And sometimes, as in my case, the question of obedience would be inscrutable, demanding a critical examination of intentions, of whether one was deluded by emotion, fear, or need. Presented with an obvious choice in the world's terms — keep your job! — and what might appear frivolous or unbalanced on the other, trek into the unknown, a question arose: How much does God want of me?

Everything.

I walked away from my identity as a scholar of religion and again took up my begging bowl. But this time, rather than material poverty, I would come to know another kind of impoverishment: the insufficiency of never having confronted wholly and completely what injustice does to a soul.

ONCE IN TUCSON, the consequences of the decision I had made — loss of colleagues, absence of intellectual dialogue, and lack of economic autonomy — opened an old scar. Now that I had no job, car salesmen and mortgage brokers turned to Bill and asked, "And what do you do for a living, sir?" I was the invisible "wife," and a hollow, punched-out soul pain would surface. Anything that had to do with women's rights and dignity exposed the rawness of my wound.

All of these losses forced me to address questions I had not previously considered: In what way did the ancient belief in women's physical, moral, and spirituality inferiority stigmatize my soul journey? How did global suffering, not just of my historical period but also in the genetic memory of countless generations, impact my life? Did the traditional quest for perfection really lead to freedom? Where was *my* activism?

My answer would be subtle and counterintuitive. The activism I pursued (or perhaps I should say, was pursued through me) would not follow the normal standard or model. It would begin in interiority, in the region of depth where everything not harmonious was subject to transfiguration. I would not turn away from the tragic consequences of the greed, power, and insanity exploding the serenity of the planet. Rather, I wanted to offer my soul to become evermore vulnerable to what global salvation meant: to belong to everyone and to regard everyone's suffering as my own.

I was disinterested in the grab for power and control, even under the guise of piety or liberal social agendas. Because I branded myself complicit—as a citizen of the planet—in human tragedy, I continuously fought the complacency and dishonesty that shield the deep self from the plight of others. I wanted to be a prophetic witness in the desert of modern culture, exposing my soul to the actual fate of victims through the practice of mystical solidarity.

The way I was directed in no way diminished the value of traditional activism, by which profound social movements have ameliorated poverty, racism, sexism, and other ills. But for some reason, what was required of me was mystical activism: it was my duty to stand up to injustice and discrimination, especially women's particular oppression, by mending the divide in my soul.

Jesus' statement, "If you want to have your life you must lose your life," was to become starkly real. A journal entry from 1996 reminds me that we are often the prophets of our own future, writing out of silence what we cannot yet consciously know:

In the desert solitude I am transfigured by the parched soil and the brazen blue sky. The white billowy clouds are the entrails of my hope gathering and boiling on the mountain's razor edge. I am etched by the diamond cutting light, by the relentless sun scourging out my thoughts, burning up my identity. No self-partiality survives the piercing simplicity. Against the jagged cliffs, giant-armed sentinels, and stark beauty of the hills, the magnitude of my finitude echoes in the ringing stillness. Like the beautiful mandala sands, the hand of impermanence sweeps my life away.

Every person experiences oppression differently. In my case, a root anguish that I didn't know was in me surfaced. It especially related to my capacity to communicate and afflicted my throat; I described my condition to a friend as though my center had been scattered in all directions. A new seriousness overcame me, drained by activities that used to be spiritually uplifting. Like many of my friends and colleagues, I was tired of listening to, giving in, overlooking, denying, and assuaging the constant and subtle barrage of personal diminishment directed to me as a woman.

A particularly glaring example happened when I was invited to speak about spiritual unity at an event sponsored by the local Baha'i foundation. The only woman on the panel of religious leaders, I gave a lecture on the mystical call of love in the world's religions. At the end of the session the moderator came up to the stage to congratulate the participants, shaking each person's hand and offering praise. Except to me. Instead, he went into the aisle, reached for Bill's hand, and congratulated him! Cultural differences aside, I was so stunned that my mind went blank, my gut stabbed with that dull ache.

My story was nothing new; women everywhere experienced this and more. Further, men were not the only perpetrators of patriarchy. Some of the deepest wounds came from mothers, sisters, and female friends who had internalized the violence of domination and aimed its arrow of pain with deadly accuracy.

The following Monday was the first week of October, and I left for my yearly retreat.

* *
*

FULL moon setting, sun rising, I followed a path along the edge of the monastery grounds, buoyant and awe-inspired. The previous evening, a storm had gathered on the far side of the mesa. Clouds billowed and threatened. Wind gusts rocked my little hermitage. Through the slate-blue sky a rainbow appeared, staying in the same place for over an hour. I stood on the porch hoping for a dramatic storm.

No rain. But an amazing sunset!

This rocky outcrop of hermitages, clinging to the side of a mountain range north of Phoenix, was serene. The meditation chapel in particular was spirit-filled, probably attributable to more than twenty years of Sister Josephine's fervent prayers. Seventy-seven, she tromped up and down the hills, walking stick in hand. A hermit, alone on the mountaintop, day in and day out she lived the holy office, bending down to marvel at prickly pear or salamander, in praise and gratitude.

After breakfast, I gathered my prayer shawl and journal and settled in the meditation chapel. It was October 5, 2001, my Holy Day to God. Autumn was special, this year all the more significant because the season also included Rosh Hashanah and Ramadan. Around the world, I imagined Jews preparing for the New Year, spending the High Holy Days in prayer and atonement, and Muslims fasting, turning their hearts to Allah in supplication and recitation of the Qur'an. I wondered what it would be like to belong to these centuries-old communities, I who prayed in solitude. Breaking a piece off the Challah bread resting on a plate, I raised it to the sun ascending over the horizon and ingested the grain of earth, silently speaking, *Buddha, Allah, Jesus, Moses, Divine Mother, Kuan-yin, Lakshmi, Tao, Great Spirit.*

Facing east, I cast my eyes over gold and pink mountain ranges undulating in the early-morning light and breathed in the vast silence. I offered a prayer: for my brothers and sisters around the world, the suffering and the tragedy of 9/11, victims and perpetrators, dead and survivors. Spirit filled me. Hot, molten energy burned my hands with light. I would take this love with me and offer it to our wounded nation.

Before long I heard footsteps approaching the chapel door. Probably another retreatant, I thought. I gathered my belongings and wordlessly left the altar. Outside, the sun was ricocheting off drops of dew on the desert floor. The light pierced my soul, still bruised from the portent of 9/11. In a letter to my U.S. Senator decrying the invasion of Iraq, I had written that I feared America was in danger of "losing moral ground and the very soul of our nation." Did we not know that bombs and bullets were instruments of death, endangering the Holy everywhere? Did we not realize that when the spirit was snuffed out like a flame pressed between wetted fingers, there was no life left?

I walked along the rim of the canyon, stopping to watch a hummingbird quivering midair, a family of Gambel Quail fast-stepping into a patch of sagebrush. The branches of a palo verde rustled, moved by wind rising up from the desert floor. Mesmerized by the sheer loveliness, I sat down on the ground and wrote in my notebook:

In the dappled dawn
when creation breathes a still note
we find you, Majesty.

We are your witness
We are your voice in the wilderness
Our feet tread lightly your mother ground

You made us like unto you
bodhicitta, holy spirit, atman, ruah
We are your body born in matter
gazing upon your own creation in us

Putting away my pen, I followed the path around a bend, heading for a rocking chair on the dining room porch. It was hard to believe that twenty-five years had passed since I had received the October revelations.

I never imagined a life such as this. I never imagined you would give me your very self, my self nothing but a mirror of your radiance. I never imagined how profoundly you loved me, or how much of my struggle was your grace, guiding me to my true and only vocation. Surely you have led me into the desert (Hosea 2:14), to allure me to your secret chamber, tenderly speaking in my soul.

I was overcome with gratitude for my life, for everything I had been given. In reflection, it seemed that my practice over all this time had consisted of a continual and voluntary act of surrender, of allowing my soul to be penetrated by the purifying love of God. I prayed to be empty so I might be full, to give away my small self for the great benefit of being one with that, which exceeds every self. For this is the way of all real love.

LATER DURING EVENING prayer, Josephine asked, "Where else could we be any more in solidarity with all those who suffer than here?" Often I wondered if the eremitical life was not a substitute for being in the grime, dirt, and squalor of sad places. Perhaps it was. But one thing I knew: prayer was hard work.

Outside, the stars rotated in the heavens according to an unseen order. I, too, have followed the divine order even when I knew not where I was going or if I would arrive. For was it not to you, alone, that I speak? Who else could understand the fire that consumes my soul with your joy?

I closed my eyes and heard you saying:

Abandon normal human affirmation. Reground in the contemplative. Remember the fragrant breath of mercy, how I pour myself into your soul in sweet intimacy. Write from your heart into the heart of other seekers of truth. Is it not your calling to weave my words with wine and silk and honey to intoxicate the lovers of wisdom and to feed the hungry and clothe the homeless souls longing for my light?

To be authentic is a long and lonely journey. Do not abandon the solitary path; turn inward and draw from the secret of your making, the immeasurable emptiness.

Into this mix of tears and jubilation, you will pour your wishes, desires, and cares, and all that means anything to you will be given away. Do not be afraid. Celebrate the divine words pouring forth from my life in you. Do not be distracted by the daily tumult, but stay focused on your solitary vocation. For, it is the three gifts of the spirit — humility, purity of heart, and compassion — that heal the woundedness of the world.

AS MY RETREAT drew to a close, I spent the last hours in silence. I felt profoundly hopeful about the path ahead: freed from academic obligation, I would be able to concentrate on spiritual writing and teaching. Made possible in no small measure by Bill's employment and by his enthusiastic support of my choice. How much time would I have saved by going straight ahead toward this goal? But I was not ready, not ready because of family and finances, not ready in my soul. Now God called and I answered.

Yes.

Driving home on I-10 south to Tucson I mourned the loss of the desert, which once was the last refuge from the world's commerce, "useless" it was said, and thus a place of rest which "enabled the old superficial self to be purged away and permitted the gradual emergence of the true, secret self."[1] Its stark openness pillaged, the desert wept its dry and salty tears, but where were the hearts sharing its lament?

* * *

SOON after I arrived in Tucson, I activated the Desert Interfaith Church. Normally, we held services at a chapel on the campus of the University of Arizona, but when we conducted services in our home, Leo, our beloved mixed-Samoyed, nudged himself into the center of the circle. Sitting at attention — white fur sparkling, intelligent eyes fringed by long eyelashes, mouth slightly curved in a smile — he would remain perfectly still, joining our meditation.

Fiercely unsociable with his own species, Leo was a pacifist toward other creatures, placidly observing rabbits from our front porch, unruffled by hamsters or kittens crawling over his back. He intuited thoughts.

Before I gave the slightest indication of going out without him, he would spread his body frog-like on the floor and flatten his head as a sign of heartbreaking dejection. He was an astute observer of us humans, attuned to emotional and behavior nuance. Once, when I was in bed devastated by the flu, Leo jumped up, covering me with his body and absorbing my pain. Reaching over to stroke his head, I watched a tear fall from his eye.

But not long after we moved to Tucson, Leo struggled getting up from the floor, his energy listless. Concerned, I drove him to the vet, while he sat in the passenger seat looking out the window. As I pulled into the parking lot, he started to shake and shed clumps of fur. I had to drag him into the waiting room.

Dr. G calmed him down. When he completed the exam, he said, "Leo is stoic. He doesn't want you to know how much pain he is in. But did you notice how his eyes flinched when I touched his leg?"

Yes.

"I have to run some tests, but I'm afraid he has Valley Fever."

"What's Valley Fever?"

"It's a fungal spore that lives in the desert sand. Dogs often ingest it through their noses while sniffing and digging. Humans get it too, but it's usually not fatal to them."

"You mean Leo could *die* from this?"

"I'll do everything I can to prevent that. But let's get the test results back first. Then we'll make a treatment plan."

A FEW DAYS AFTER the trip to the vet, I took a stack of flyers to a courier service to be distributed around town. Four years since I was ordained, in 1997 I founded the Interfaith Theological Seminary under the Church's nonprofit status. I had spent the last year designing the curriculum and catalog, hiring faculty, advertising on the local NPR station, and interviewing prospective students. Recently, I had admitted an initial class of twelve to the two-year program.

Dedicated to the nonviolent, contemplative spirit of ministry, the Seminary was modeled on the ancient ideal in which study of sacred texts and transmission of spiritual practices were imparted through personal mentoring by those dedicated to the meditative life. The program began with a seven-day intensive retreat, followed by weekly classes and a monthly seminar. Eventually, it also affiliated with a local college to offer a joint M.A.-ministry degree program. The Seminary's commitment to spiritual reconciliation afforded students the opportunity to publically claim their call to ministry and their devotion to the Divine. This was no small thing, given how many in our society lived as outsiders, excluded from religious office, women and LGBT persons foremost among them.

Seminary students came from every walk of life, diverse denominations and world traditions, and many professions, including nurses, physicians, college and public school educators, massage therapists, scientists, and psychologists. Whether committed to one religion or fully interfaith in orientation, they joined countless people around the globe who functioned as a collective vanguard into a new revelatory landscape. When I write these words, "new revelatory landscape," I mean they had been called to and were being called by a new or different paradigm of the sacred that made fundamental demands on their personhood and their understanding of God, self, and world. Practicing a desert spirituality outside the bounds of time and place, they were forging through a contemplative process of enlightenment as old as life itself. And even though—and perhaps because of—the absence of a formalized theology, their hearts were being transformed.[2]

PERHAPS DUE TO my outreach into the community, our Church and Seminary began to attract the attention of local religious leaders. A pastor of a conservative Christian congregation called to offer free Bibles. During our conversation it became clear that he thought our congregants were heathens who needed biblical education. That's when I responded in a gentle, respectful tone, "I feel quite hurt by your remarks, Reverend."

Caught off-guard, he asked, "What do you mean?"

"I appreciate your offer, but I feel you are presuming that if a person is not a conservative Christian, he or she is not worthy. The people who attend our services desire to understand God's meaning in their lives; they sincerely seek wisdom. They are not anti-God, but are called to a different expression of faith; they come to worship and praise, to bring to their lives something more profound and enduring.

"The multi-religious, contemplative basis of our worship attempts to heal the sin of 'otherness'—the exclusion, violence and rejection of difference—in our hearts. It diminishes spiritual and religious egoism in which one's truth, path, or scripture is secretly or overtly proclaimed to be greater, more holy, or truer than any of its competitors. This is our faith. Surely you can understand our longing."

For a few moments we were completely silent.

Eventually he said, "I do understand. I apologize for what I said earlier.

You, too, are saddened by the absence of talk about God or Jesus in secular society. Are you not?"

"I am, although I don't use the same words you do. I would say that I am saddened that the sacred is endangered in our world, and am desperate to have a public conversation about real spiritual meaning and not the superficial, trivial, or hysterical version we often see in the media."

"I'm with you on that! I really am sorry for offending you. It's exciting to learn that others in our community love God, even if it's not the same way or same God I love."

"I appreciate you saying that, Rev. K. We all suffer when the sacred dimension of life is ridiculed or ignored. We would love to have your generous gift of Bibles and I will offer them to our congregation in the spirit of our conversation. Thank you!"

* *

OVER the previous seven months, I'd been teaching a weekly seminar on the contemplative life. One of my final lectures was on images of the Divine Feminine in the world's religions, the day's topic goddess figures in Christianity. During a discussion of two Christian paths of union with God, *via negativa* (the negative way) and *via positiva* (the positive way), I spontaneously claimed there was a third way: *via feminina*, the way of the feminine, or the feminine way.

In Christian theology, *via* (Latin, meaning "road" or "way"), signified the spiritual journey toward union with God; *feminina* conveyed a quality of consciousness that included but was not confined to biological females. Thus, while the feminine was an archetype in both women and men, perhaps embodied and expressed differently in females and in males, *via feminina* was also a spiritual practice.

Having spoken the phrase, *via feminina*, a treasure trove of meaning suddenly sprung open. The conceptualization was electrifying because it was a linguistic affirmation of another mystical path, one that opened new horizons in religious consciousness. I had to stop my lecture, unable to speak. Suggesting the class take a ten-minute break, I observed fragments of insight swirl around my mind, too numerous to be captured in a coherent sentence.

By the time we reconvened, I had found my voice and continued the lecture.

As soon as I got home, I hurried to find my journal and jotted down notes. Surely, *via feminina* was a momentous unveiling of my spiritual journey. But my writing was frustrated by the insufficiency of the intellect to capture its vision. Each word caused prior words to splinter and fall. Before I could put a thought on paper, it would be gone. Fitting its truth into the ways truth has been expressed required a continual mending of the dividedness that diverted and transgressed what I deeply knew, causing intense bodily exhaustion, as if all of my energies were taxed from dredging up this insurrection of women's suppressed knowledge.

To be sure, transcendence posed a particular challenge. Even Plotinus in experiencing the One cried out, "I am in an agony of expression!" Yet something about the complete wholeness of the Divine Feminine made the passage to language especially arduous. *Via feminina* required a way of expressing that was poetic and polyphonic, its perspective organic, holistic.

More startling, structures of consciousness and whole phrases of meaning in which religions bartered meaning were transformed. *Via feminina* offered a new vantage point from which to perceive reality, one that had a far-reaching effect on our capacity as spiritual beings. It was the emergence of a truth yet unplumbed that drew us to a radical mercy, traces of which our mystic seers knew too well, challenging us to redefine what it means to be human, and what the pathways of devotion entail.

As a spiritual path, *via feminina* was attentive to the multiple wisdoms of body, psyche, and soul, placing primary importance on healing those social factors—whether of gender, culture, race, sexual orientation, or religious belief—that stigmatized persons, robbed them of dignity, wounded their souls, and betrayed the highest aspirations of the mystical life. It thus was an invitation to divest one's being of subtle forms of injustice imbedded in the categories that defined the spiritual life—redemption, salvation, *nirvana, samadhi*, soul, god—as well as in the processes of mystical ascent—purification, great death, annihilation, union—and hindered the full integration and liberation of the self.

But *via feminina's* single most distinguishing feature was its *intimate wholeness*, a vision of reality beyond feminine and masculine that included everything within its merciful, benevolent, and joyous fold. It was a specific path of reconciliation that began from a different starting point of trust and indissoluble intimacy that moved deeper into unitive states of being beyond opposites and paradoxes that simultaneously was able to sustain opposites and paradoxes, leading one to the mystery of divine-human co-creation and the birth of new forms of consciousness.

Later that evening, I was walking in the desert arroyo behind our house when I realized it was through the pain of leaving my faculty position, when I had to confront whatever collective limitation ascribed to females still lurked in my unconscious, that *via feminina* was brought into awareness. In order to be spiritually liberated as *woman*, it was not enough to affirm the universal dimension of spirituality without working to correct the injustices and violence that perpetuated sexism, racism, homophobia, and similar ills. It wasn't my universal mystical interpretation that could save me now, but the retracing of the whole journey of self-realization *again*, from the perspective of women's suppressed consciousness.

The most ambiguous thing was that I had spiraled over and again through stages of spiritual growth—the dark night of the soul was not unknown to me. But I'd never experienced, nor had I ever heard it directly expressed in religious literature, the place where I now found myself. This was a new kind of freedom and healing that went beneath the veneer of classical (male) spirituality into a realm so nameless, so elusive, that words were erased before they could slip out of my throat.

It was then that I realized *via feminina* ran parallel to the spiritual paths articulated by the great patriarchal lineages but flowed through my being more deeply and silently. For while it was related to our historical traditions, *via feminina* was not beholden to them. As long as I did not deny my foundation, classical spirituality would continue to enrich my life and to assist in the re-unification of these two eternal paths of wisdom. But since the exclusion of the sacred feminine from religious life was a violation of my full humanity, I could only pursue the process of integration by crossing the borders of other dark nights and soul sufferings that every woman experiences and knows. It was not the dark night of the soul, but the further dark night, the one I named the *"dark night of the feminine,"* that I had to surrender to now.

Living in a society that *theologically* distinguishes women over against what is pure and holy, I had to live outside myself. I could not be a contemplative in this world without addressing the violence directed at the spirit of women, without healing the wounds of my womanhood.

I realized the bridge I had built, between my inner life and the world's religions, was to some extent dangerously unfinished. Part of my impasse was precipitated by a desire to transcend my suffering, to offer it to healing before its time. It was as if I could not bear the injury to my femaleness and denied it, seeking what was higher and more holy. Only by reversing the quest for transcendence, could I lift up my womanhood to the Divine, something that felt very foreign to me both in my particular incarnation and in the history of spirituality. To be woman, and not just be able to transcend my location in history, was deeply offending, and yet was the vital link to all that I hoped to be.

While previously I had achieved equanimity when confronted with internal conflict, I now was unable to spiritualize feelings of impasse, confusion, or anger. I had to live out what felt like an erasure of consciousness that made the ability to communicate what I knew as a woman *almost* impossible. This was not a convenient intellectual thought, but an actual experience of emotional, mental, bodily, and spiritual *pain*, which extended from the rarefied dimensions of consciousness into the deepest substratum of cellular memory. The detachment of the senses, considered to be a hallmark of spiritual maturity, was inoperable in this realm.

I could only stave off the pain through an act of will. Not allowing myself to feel inflicted deeper wounds. I couldn't hope to give anything, teach anything, or prepare anything. I had to receive the labor pains of my own birth and the love that demanded with a forcefulness of its own: breath, contract, push, rest. It was not the particularity of our stories that women shared, but this labor out of silence that we knew deeply and completely. My wound was not just personal and collective, but also theological and divine. To name *only* the suffering was to remain victimized, always to be an object against which violence took control of my nature and claimed its own voice. To not name the suffering was to be a shadow of myself.

This radical turn in my life was necessary to heal the deepest violation: the denial of women's spiritual authority and wisdom. Aware that the October revelations would not be accepted by named religions as theologically *sanctioned* or *legitimate*, I needed courage to stand up to dogma, extremism, and disbelief. Yes, I was hiding.

It was common enough to assume that the recipient of spiritual insight was merely a vessel or mouthpiece for God. Certainly, my articulation of *via feminina* was a minor tremor on the surface of an infinite depth. But the supposition that one only "channeled" the spirit was a kind of false humility that ignored the participatory nature of all knowledge, and the personal commitment and self-surrender that generated divine-human co-creation. What we did or did not do with our lives, our bodies, and our souls reverberated in all worlds. The efforts we made to lead a holy life, seek truth, and practice wisdom were critical to the moral development and spiritual integrity of our world.

What I've come to is this: The fullness of what I knew and experienced, as well as my spiritual salvation or freedom, could not be actualized until I reconnected to the great mother river flowing within me, where symbols and words were not broken and women's languages and ways of knowing were holy. I would always be divided against myself unless I came to this. Of course, in retrospect I am able to assign conceptual terms to my state. But until I was brought to the lowly station of my own unbecoming, I was unable to understand, let alone speak about my broken woman self.

When I think about it now, the dark night of the feminine was a healing so embodied, so concrete, that it seemed in review to be the mending of some ancient fracture in consciousness. As I pieced together the mirror of my divine reflection, shattered in some ancient time by men's colonization of a woman ancestor I could not name, I discovered it was the theology of sexism, which condoned and perpetuated the moral and spiritual insufficiency of females that betrayed the humanity of women and men everywhere.

It was not by feminizing God or uncovering feminine images of God in our scriptures that my pain could be assuaged. It was more radical than that. I struggled to break free from the source of my unnaming, to break through the ground on the other side of which I was whole, and to revelatory realities that lived and breathed and had their meaning in some hidden place of untouched, holy silence.

* * *

CLIMBING the hill to our house, I stopped by an outdoor altar to the Divine Mother nestled in a cluster of native trees. I found solace in the Divine Feminine who, under various guises, rattled the mind and stirred the heart to seek a vast possibility, an untapped reservoir of being unseen by what is normally designated as secular or religious. Most especially to consider the spirituality of matter and an immanent cosmology in which Wisdom (Latin, Sophia) was "not a force propelling the world from without but as an ambience enfolding it and quickening it from within."[3]

Yet, all acts of worship were under a sign of contradiction, in which there was no subject who prayed or object of prayer, but a renunciation of authority and separateness. Every encounter led to the poverty of belief, to silence, and to personal limitation in the face of the Infinite. Holy Mother was not another instance of possession or exclusion, a superior god over or against historical god figures. The name, like every name, was elusive, offering glimpses of an abundance that was uncontainable.

How could I say what was different about the mystical path of *via feminina*? So much of this tender journey was interior, hidden in the sanctuary of my being. But then, spontaneously, a passage entered my mind:

> *What if the Holy One Blessed is She called us to a new contemplative path and a new way of life? What if She were drawing us closer to a deep cavern of truth that could only be found were we to give up all of our ideas and notions of god, and place all of our historical understanding of the spiritual life under a cloud of forgetting? What if the very spiritual paths we have traveled through the centuries were but a threshold for another way of being and loving? Would we not take courage, and abandon ourselves to the splendor that our Beloved Mother calls us toward?*

The Divine Feminine frees our souls in a completely astounding way; and thus, rightly so, effaces her own names.

21

Radical Wisdom

I CLOSED MY SUITCASE, wheeled it outside, and locked the kitchen door. Bill was waiting in the carport to drive me to the airport for a month's stay at a Benedictine monastery, awarded a scholarship to do research on women mystics in medieval Europe.

When I arrived at the monastery, I was guided to the scholars-in-residence program housed in a building on the west side of campus, where a small group of sisters lived in two-person apartments. Sister Amelia, tall and slender with an iconic face ringed by white curls, welcomed me with affection. Suggesting I leave my suitcase behind the reception desk, Amelia gave me a brief tour of the monastery dining room, library, exercise center, vegetable garden, and oratory where the sisters prayed the Liturgy of the Hours five times a day. When we returned, she showed me to my apartment and separate, private office space, wired with the latest technology. Jubilant over the opportunity to devote myself to writing and research, I quickly settled in.

The first evening, I was invited to dinner with several of the sisters, captivated by their stories, laughter, and toasts of red wine. It was immediately apparent that these were extraordinary women, educated, passionate, and wise. They were genuinely interested in my *via feminina* project, which led to a lengthy conversation about women mystics and contemporary monasticism. Before taking leave, Amelia said they would love for me to attend prayer in their private chapel at 7 a.m.

Before long I established a daily routine: woke at 6 a.m. bursting with energy, prayed with the sisters, biked over to the dining room for breakfast, and back to my office to write. Organizing my papers, I lit a candle on the windowsill and watched birds rustling in the tree outside my second-story perch. Engrossed in thought for several hours, I stirred only when the ringing of the chapel bells called the community to noon prayer.

Once inside the oratory, I would find my place among the rows of sisters and join in the day's liturgical cycle. After lunch, I usually walked around campus, later spending several hours in the monastic library, a cornucopia of contemporary and classical texts. If researchers from the scholarship program were presenting papers, or the sisters were offering a spiritual class, I attended. Otherwise, I spent the remaining hours before evening prayer and dinner in meditation, writing, or learning more about the monastic community.

As I got to know the sisters, I discovered that their lives were not much different than my own. Accomplished women—educators, artists, activists, psychologists, nurses—of every personality type and interest, they exuded a dignity of personhood. Life had meaning, each day devoted to prayer, service, and personal striving for sanctity. Being among a community of women who felt the same type of passion I did for all things sacred, was a miracle. This is not to say that the women religious walked around in bliss. I learned that the more contemplative sisters struggled as much as those outside the monastery to have their voices heard and their mystical orientation honored. And, like all societies, the sisters had rules and injunctions to follow, obligations to and expectations from the community, quarrels and hurt feelings to forgive and forget. A guest, I had an excess of freedom that members of the order did not.

I could write an entire book on my sabbatical, so rich and varied were my experiences. But my time away could be summarized in one word: freedom. I worked uninterrupted, in pure silence if I chose, or engaged in dialogue with other visiting scholars. What I loved most was the respectful granting of physical and psychic space to each person, without intrusion into one's solitude. We maintained gentle silence, the silence of loving respect.

One morning while folding clothes, I had a visceral, full-body sensation of divine harmony, the whole universe a hymn of praise. Paradise really existed on earth; we simply lacked the quiet, patience, and devotion to realize it. I floated through my days, mind sharp and heart full.

* *
* *

I<small>T</small> was an exorbitant morning, the vast sky and high clouds vibrant with energy. I packed a sandwich and water in my backpack, planning to spend the day hiking in the woods that extended behind the monastery grounds.

I slipped under an overhanging pine branch and entered the deep forest, reflecting on my experience since my arrival twelve days earlier. Most significant was that each person's inner life was honored and allowed to thrive. Superficial social relations were absent. A welcoming openness invited all to share in the monastic life, which was ordered around the monk's primary responsibility to seek God, holding open a place in one's heart.

I also was affected by the sisters' reverence for the mystery of faith, the Liturgy of the Hours, the Book of Scripture, and the daily efforts made to grow in grace. Invariably, a sister sitting next to me in the oratory or at lunch would share something of her life as a monk. Like many monastic communities today, the average age of the sisters was seventy, and many I met had been vowed for fifty or more years. But the responses they gave to my queries about their vocation were often similar or the same: "I am so grateful. I just cannot believe that I have had the privilege to live here for so many years seeking God, with so many good and kind women."

Occupied by these thoughts, I followed the path around a corner, coming face-to-face with a doe standing twenty feet away. Shimmering with energy, her tawny brown coat glowed in the light. She was mythical, an apparition from some heavenly realm, pure and radiant. I held my breath, awestruck. This is what the earth must have been like before humans trampled the holy, a paradise of radiant beings. For a long moment, we looked into each other's eyes. Then, with a slow, gentle grace she turned, her white tail bobbing, and bounded into the brush.

Before long I came upon a clearing, surprised by a large alabaster statue of the Madonna atop a pedestal set in a tree-shaded alcove. Sunlight and shadows danced across the statue's face. Drawing closer, I took my backpack off and dropped to my knees. Birds chirping and leaves rustling in the wind merged into a hidden wholeness, until there was only Silence. How long I prayed, I cannot say. Then from the well of silence deeper than thought, I heard the divine voice: *The path revealed to you in 1976 is the revelation of the Divine Mother, of the One. Hers is the spiritual path you have been teaching all these years, the one without name: via feminina.*

I can't express how overwhelming were these words. Stunned, I was on fire with a light brighter than the sun. My body evaporated into the air around me. I was burning up; I was freezing cold. My soul was taken aloft, rapt in deep contemplation. Unable to remain kneeling, I folded myself onto the soft earth.

I don't remember what happened next, except that I eventually wandered back to the monastery. Walking along, fragments of my life's puzzle coalesced: the namelessness of my god, the spiritual journey I had followed, which was one of taking apart worn and outdated views of self and divinity, the radicalness of practicing a new revelatory way of being. Although all these years I had followed the implicit call, it wasn't until that day did I fully realize She was the hidden voice beneath everything. I knew then that the spirituality of the Divine Feminine was essential to the future of our planet.

By the time I returned to my room, the sun had set. Unable to sleep, I spent the hours after midnight in prayer and consolation. I was still processing what I had learned, especially the association of the Divine Feminine with the revelation of the One. Not one, as in only, singular, superior, prior. But One, the unifying force of everything, the hidden wholeness, the coalescing of opposites, the one-ing consciousness of the contemplative, mystical mind. This primordial, inviolable Divine force, neither created nor destroyed, was eternally present in the pure field of silent intelligence.

* *
* *

THE next day, I was rummaging in the library stacks, intent on expanding my research on the Divine Feminine. Thomas Merton's poem, *Hagia Sophia* (Holy Wisdom), was one of my favorites, and it was to his writing I first turned. Although I'd read the poem many times, it took on an added significance since my experience in the woods.

There is in all things an invisible fecundity, a dimmed light, a meek namelessness, a hidden wholeness. This mysterious Unity and Integrity is Wisdom, the Mother of all.... There is in all things an inexhaustible sweetness, a silence that is a fount of action and joy. It rises up in wordless gentleness and flows out to me tenderly, saluting me with indescribable humility. This is at once my own being, my own nature, and the Gift of my Creator's thought and Art within me, speaking as Hagia Sophia, speaking as my sister, Wisdom [1]

I was especially interested in Merton's contention that ours was the age of Sophia when new visions of reality were brought into the world, a sentiment shared by Vladimir Solovev, a nineteenth-century Russian philosopher. Like Merton, Solovev's fascination with the archetypal feminine began with a series of visions. She was for each of them the *prima materia* of creation, the Soul of the World, Holy Wisdom, Mother of God and Blessed Virgin Mary, the erotic Bride of the Lamb (from the biblical *Song of Songs*), the Eternal Feminine, the Universal Church, and sister, wife, and playmate.

While rarely depicted as a divine person in her own right, traces of her full potential were evident as a powerful, if latent, element in the world's religions. As the heart (*lev*) of God, the Divine Feminine was exalted in the Wisdom literature of the Hebrew Bible, appearing in later Jewish mystical texts as *Shekhinah* (feminine "indwelling presence").

She is similarly expressed in the Chinese Buddhist personification of *Kuan Yin*—Bodhisattva of Compassion—as pure light, eliminating darkness and extinguishing the fire of pain. In Buddhist teachings on *Prajnaparamita*, The Perfection of Wisdom in Eight Thousand Lines, She is described as "The Mother of All the Buddhas" or "storehouse of the Supreme Dharma."

To Muslims she is the womb (*rahim*) of the All Merciful established in a famous *hadith*: "My mercy precedes My wrath." She is the sacred heart of Mary and *mater dolorosa* (mother of suffering) to millions of Catholics, her tears healing our sins and woes. Source of the ten thousand things in Taoist philosophy, she is nondual consciousness who holds creation in her womb.

Woyengi is Great Mother in Nigerian creation stories, molding human beings in Her image and breathing life into creation. In the *Laksmi-tantra*, a popular Hindu text, Creator Goddess Laksmi pervades all creation with vitality, will, and consciousness. Undertaking the entire stupendous creation of the universe with only a one-billionth fraction of herself, [she is] so transcendent...so beyond the ability of the mind to circumscribe her, that only a miniscule fraction of her is manifest in the creation of the universe.[2]

She is the wisdom that guides our souls in darkness, the night illumination, and the lesson at dawn. She offers a truth so expansive, so tender, so luminous that our minds and hearts barely can sustain her presence. She is not in the first instance sorrowful or meek. She is Pure Love, Wordless Bliss, and Breath of Benevolence. She suffers when we suffer, brightening the night sky of our despair with contagious, healing hope. She slays ancient sins and frees us from history. In her arms we are soothed by tender, gentle kisses.

* * *

THE following Saturday, dressed in my one good outfit, I walked to the main chapel to attend the rite of perpetual monastic profession of Sr. Janice. When the liturgist signaled the start of the ceremony, the massive doors of the chapel opened, and Sr. Theodore, the prioress, dressed in a white robe and holding a seven-foot candlestick, led the procession of monks. The atmosphere was serenely regal—such was the power of women's spirit. Candles flickered in the domed sanctuary as the procession slowly made its way to the center altar.

When the sisters were gathered, Sr. Theodore gave a homily on the meaning of the new monk's profession and recited ritual prayers. Afterward, Sr. Janice sang the *Suscipe* (the ancient song of monastic self-offering) three times, with the monastic community repeating after her, "Uphold me, O God, as you have promised, and I shall live: Do not disappoint me in my hope."

Then she prostrated on the ground, her arms outstretched, her body forming the shape of a cross as the community and assembly recited the Litany of the Saints. Following, the choir sang the most glorious chant until the whole congregation was lifted up in reverie.

The Prioress signaled the newly professed Sr. Janice to stand, offering a solemn blessing for her vocation, and placed a ring on her left-hand finger. Her face was a glowing ember and afterward, when we adjourned to the dining room for refreshments, she radiated Light.

The timing of the ceremony was personally auspicious. The previous evening I had had a lengthy conversation with Amelia about my desire to take monastic vows. For at least a year I had been praying about how to do this. Amelia and the small group of sisters involved with the scholars in residence were mature, masterful women and my monastic forbearers. I dearly wished for them to sponsor and witness my profession.

While we spoke, Amelia became illuminated: her translucent face glowed, love radiating from clear blue eyes. She said, "You already have a monastic heart. Profession will strengthen and stabilize your contemplative nature and spiritual mission."

Of course, from previous conversations she knew of the October revelations and my commitment to the universal monastic call. And she respected and supported my conviction. We also discussed that my vows would not be taken under the auspices of her Benedictine monastery or Christianity. I honored these traditions with my whole heart. But, I would take profession as a universal monk dedicated to the Divine Heart, to the enduring truth that preceded religious identification and institutional form. I wanted to take vows to love God the Unnameable with my whole being and to serve others through love.

I was certain that the monastic call was intrinsic to all people and was not confined to religious organizations or orders. It was a free call within the self, one born with us into the world and to which we owed allegiance. I had spent years avoiding the monk within, too busy with family and work, and perhaps afraid that it would make me more different or too pious— empty concerns. Because there was nothing more natural than to affirm one's monastic nature, living in God's time, seeking transformation into the heart of reality, and loving creation with one's whole soul.

Since I was scheduled to return to the monastery in six months to complete my research, we agreed I would use the time away to study and prepare for my ceremony of profession.

* *
*

ONCE back in Tucson, my serenity was over. I spent the next weeks moving the Seminary offices and classes to a local retreat center, where I had been hired as Associate Director. My first initiative at the retreat center was to found the Hesychia School of Spiritual Direction, an ecumenical and interfaith training course in the art of spiritual guidance. In addition to overseeing and teaching in the new program, I still had my responsibilities as founder and director of the Seminary, pastor of Desert Interfaith Church, teacher and spiritual director, and leader of our contemplative community.

Recently, I also had joined a group of academic women writers. Each month one of us presented a current project. When my turn came, I submitted a chapter from my forthcoming book, Emerging Heart, which gave a brief account of the October revelations. We were an eclectic group of writers from diverse fields: anthropology, geology, literature, sociology, feminist studies, border studies, and poetry. While I was the only participant directly writing about religious issues, a number of women had religious or spiritual affiliations.

After catching up on our adventures since we'd last met, the group settled down to discuss my project. As expected, the God language in my story affronted Ellen, a social scientist working in feminist issues. She didn't understand it and couldn't relate to its usage. This critique led to several heated exchanges between her and two other avowedly religious women, Catholic and Hindu.

But the comment that had the most impact on me was from Anahi, an American-Iranian woman and practicing Muslim.

"I read your chapter and the first thing that I thought was, 'Who does this woman think she is, a prophet? How dare she write like this!' I was so disturbed I almost tore up the pages."

"Wow. That was an intense reaction," Ellen said.

"Hold on, I'm not done. Later, my feminist consciousness came in and I thought to myself, 'Wait a minute. Isn't this what we always do to women who speak wisdom?' I mean, after all, prophets aren't only male."

I said: "You raise an important point, Anahi. I didn't think of my chapter as prophetic, but I strongly affirm a woman's right to spiritual authority. It seems that women's equality in the spiritual arena is one of the last bastions of human rights."

"I've never thought of it that way," Anahi said, "but you're right. Our religions, certainly my faith, keep women in a subordinate role despite the positive depictions of the feminine in Islamic literature. God is male, prophets are male, and men run religion. Now I'm angry!"

"I couldn't agree with you more," said Janet, a Catholic literature professor. "I love the sacraments and the spirit of Christ's message, which is why I still participate in the Mass. But I'm disgusted with the Church's position on women clergy, its paternalistic attitude toward women, and its attack on communities of religious sisters. God is still male!"

"Wait a minute," Ellen said. "I don't get the whole 'god' thing. Why do you care? What meaning do you find in a god that is against you in almost every way?"

"Isn't this the whole point?" I asked. "If God in our culture is held by most to signify the highest realm of reality, and women are not representative of that reality, then at the most fundamental levels of cultural imagination women are lesser, not equally created in the divine image. If we don't address the religious tenets that undergird violence against and oppression of women, women and men never will achieve their full potential. Whether one believes in a god or not, god-talk is imbedded in culture. We can't escape it."

"I agree," Anahi said. "We have to face the fact that women all over the world suffer, still marginalized and lacking in spiritual authority."

"Even more than according women spiritual mastery," Janet said, "can God be female? Will we respect women spiritual leaders and accord them the same authority and wisdom as a man?"

"I'm beginning to see what you mean," Anahi said. "It's almost as if the strides women are making in the university, corporations, and business mask layers of untransformed behaviors and mind-sets. It's almost like saying, women should be happy with what they've got and not want it all."

* *

SEVERAL days later, I was preparing for the arrival of two spiritual direction mentees. In my practice, I noticed that women processed experience differently than men. They seemed to have a more porous or permeable sense of self, and an often-intuitive grasp of emotional events. Yet these strengths frequently impeded the development of healthy boundaries, establishing in women an other-directed consciousness, often neglectful of their needs. I didn't know if these differences were an essential or a permanent aspect of women's nature or the result of thousands of years of social and spiritual enculturation, but in the moment of suffering the nature versus nurture debate didn't matter.

Shelly exemplified the struggle many women faced. A fifty-ish woman who had spent her life within a Christian denomination, she was widely read in the mystics, including Saints Augustine, Francis, John of the Cross, and Thérèse of Lisieux.

After hugs and silent meditation, I asked Shelley what she would like to discuss.

"Well, you know, I've spent the last thirty years devoted to feminism and Christian spirituality. I'm also a spiritual director and have witnessed the effects of violence against women, participated in women's consciousness-raising, and read every book on the subject. But now, in my own life, I can't decipher the anguish I feel; it almost makes me crazy because neither spiritual practice or mystical texts assuage the pain."

"Can you describe what you feel?"

"It alternates. Often I feel divided and distracted, up against a limit with no remedy. I'm often angry, frustrated. At other times, I have such a strong urge to be alone, to be in solitude, but I'm caught between the God taught by my religion and a future that I can't see and name. I can't tell you how distraught I am. Can you help me?"

Shelley expressed despair over her life choices, the oppression she felt as a woman in her denomination. She said, "I use to be able to transcend patriarchal elements in my religion by turning toward women's spirituality, but now this consolation feels hollow. The peace I felt in sisterhood and in our women's spiritual gatherings is gone. Even my contemplative practice is broken, marred by shattered hopes of women's equality. I get so angry, so furious, when I'm in church and the only pronoun applied to God is 'He.' I'm hauntingly divided in myself."

I listened, waiting to be guided by the inner voice to speak.

"Where is Spirit in all this?" I asked. "How is your prayer life, your relationship with the Divine?"

"Messed up. I pray and pray to find an answer but I'm in the dark, stuck."

"Shelley, I detect several interrelated threads in your life experience. I know you are familiar with the dark night experience, but I wonder if you have found remedy in the writings of the mystics?"

"Yes, of course, I love the Christian mystics. But they're not helping me. Sometimes I think I'm going crazy. Nothing works."

"May I suggest another way of looking at your situation? Have you considered you have entered a new revelatory landscape, a dimension of spiritual development not depicted in religious literature that specifically relates to your life as a woman?"

"Oh my, I never thought of that."

"There comes a time in a woman's journey when she may feel that her religion of birth or her spiritual practice impedes the development of her true self. It is during this period of inner tension that a person often experiences a spiritual oppression of the soul, a passage I call the 'dark night of the feminine.'"

"You know," Shelley said, "even after all these years of studying feminist spirituality, I never thought about it this way, that my soul experiences the pain of living in a world that marginalizes and destroys females. But what do you mean by 'spiritual oppression'?"

"The word 'oppression' signifies an unjust exercise of authority or power by one person, group, or institution over another. Whatever dominates, violates, humiliates, shames, possesses, exploits, or silences a person's spirit is a form of oppression.

"Acts of violence against a person—overt or subtle—are directed first and foremost at the core of one's nature, and are nothing less than a desire to harm or destroy a person's unique and particular embodiment of the Divine.

"The presence of spiritual oppression in a woman's life is the most significant indicator of her inability to quiet the restlessness dividing her soul, and awareness of its causes and conditions is primary in healing. Of course, spiritual oppression also is directed at men, especially those marginalized by the dominant culture."

Bending over in her chair, Shelley let out a sigh. Between bouts of her crying and laughing, we discussed why spiritual texts, even those that touched on the soul's deep transformation, did not help her now. The classical spiritual journey was an encounter with personal sins, but was not explicitly concerned with the collective sin of sexism, racism, or naming God as exclusively male, and thus superior to females.

Shelley and I talked for another hour. We discussed ways to change internalized patterns of spiritual development that limited her self-discovery. We probed how religious authorities often furthered a woman's internalized unworthiness or inferiority, distracting her from a problem with roots deeper and more primordial. Imbedded in the spiritual path were generational depictions of women as physiologically weaker, spiritually inferior, and defective in body and moral fortitude.

I read Shelley a quote from John Gerson, fourteenth-century chancellor of the University of Paris:

> The female sex is forbidden on apostolic authority (1 Tim. 2:12) to teach in public, that is either by word or by writing.... The reason is clear: common law—and not any kind of common law, but that which comes from on high—forbids them. And why? Because they are easily seduced, and determined seducers; and because it is not proved that they are witnesses to divine grace.[3]

"Oh my gosh! I've read this passage before and raged about it," Shelley said. "But I never felt like I do now: the *violence* directed at my soul. These drastic misrepresentations about women still function on our planet."

By now almost two hours had passed, and I had another mentee arriving. We spent the last moments of the session in silent prayer, ending with an agreement to meet again in three weeks.

I SOON became aware that the dark night of the feminine was not a transformative process reserved for women. In fact, many men whom I had assisted in spiritual direction were suffering from the suppression of feminine divine consciousness, a condition particularly prevalent in males who were of a contemplative nature, or who for various reasons were marginalized by the dominant culture. But even men who fit the media stereotype of the successful male frequently discovered an unexamined trove of pain and a desire to reconnect with the vulnerability that led one to God. In some ways, their struggle was more difficult because men tended to be emotionally isolated from each other, and often lacked the sharing skills that came easily to the majority of women.

For eight months I had been meeting with Carl. In previous sessions we had explored his excessive individualism, reinforced by an alcoholic father and early adult experiences of male-on-male aggression. A stockbroker in his forties who had turned to spirituality, Carl described years of unhealthy relationships based on fear and shame of vulnerability, expressed through power—over women, business partners, and nature. "I was a one-man destroyer, hiding from a repressed desire to be more intimate, and from fear of being ridiculed by other males." I had heard similar stories from other men.

During our last meeting, Carl had expressed despair and guilt about his mother's submission to domestic violence and his inability to save her, feelings he had not explored since her death two years ago. Because his pain centered on his mother, I had suggested he create an altar to the Divine Mother as a way of unlocking hidden emotion. Agreeing to the assignment with unexpected gusto, he decided to abandon his usual reticence and "go all-out."

I reached across the low table between us and took his hands in mine. "Let's have a short prayer, Carl." Afterward, his eyes were brimming with tears.

"Would you like to begin, Carl?"

He took some moments to gather himself. "On the next free weekend after we met, I packed statues of Mary, Kuan-yin, Corn Woman, and several goddess figures I'd brought back from India, a bag of photos, and other items into my Jeep and drove to the Saguaro National Forest. When I got there, I found my favorite secluded spot and parked. Then I got out all my stuff and hiked further into the desert until I was sure this was where I wanted to perform the ritual. I searched around for a stick and drew three concentric rings in the sand. In the center I arranged the statues, then photos of my mother in the second ring. The last, outer, ring I filled with items found on the desert floor: dried flowers, stones, hawk feathers, and prickly pear fruits."

"What a wonderful ritual image, Carl. How did you come up with the idea for the circles?"

"I don't know, really, because I wasn't sure what I was going to do until I got out there. Then all of a sudden I was picking up that stick."

"What did you do next?" I asked.

"Well, I sat cross-legged for a while and wondered to myself, 'What the hell am I doing?' At first I felt awkward, wasn't sure why I was wasting a Sunday in the desert when I could be watching football or golfing. But, I followed your instructions, honoring the land and my ancestors, meditating the way you taught me, keeping my mind open, not thinking.

"Then an odd thing happened. You figured that, right? I was *forced*—like someone was pushing my hand—to reach for my favorite photo of my mother and me taken when I was about three years old. My mother was gentle, but to protect me, she took the brunt of my father's rages. Something about her arm around me, and my head pressed against her leg tore me up. I started to cry, and then these huge heaving sobs erupted. I couldn't stop myself. I'm just glad no one was around!"

"How long did this last? Did you experience any special feeling or awareness?"

"I didn't have my watch, and my cell phone was in the truck, but it was a while. All kinds of feelings were pouring out of me. It's hard for me to describe. But afterward, when I calmed down and allowed myself to relax, I felt this shadow side of the masculine that ridiculed my deepest longing. It had its own voice, speaking in my head, like my Dad's, like men I've known, taunting, dismissive, crude. I felt completely done in by that voice. I wanted to bang my head, roar.

"Instead, I got up and walked clockwise around the circle, breathing. While walking, a cool wave like my mother's hand touching me brought me back. I saw how my father had shunned me for loving my mother, for being vulnerable. A series of images assaulted me: my rage against him, guilt about not protecting my mother, anger at myself for violating my marriage vows, the hollow failure of divorce, and my denial, denial of it all, unable to confront my complicity. I was truly afraid that I would not be able to contain or heal the waves of grief inside me."

"Thank you for sharing this powerful experience with me, Carl. What has happened since?"

"Something has changed in me. I've thought a lot about it: my father's brutality, my fear of him, shrinking away, and then vowing I'd never let myself be vulnerable again to violence. But the damage had been done. I'd closed off my emotions, refused to acknowledge my anger. I've hurt a lot of people, mostly women. But you know what? I want to take off the mask of masculinity. I want to keep the positive attributes of maleness. I'm not giving up."

* *

A FEW days before Christmas, I was finishing a gift for my mother, who had recently moved to Tucson. Several years after my father died, she had remarried. Twelve years later, she was a widow again. I spoke to her frequently on the phone, and within several months she moved from Florida and bought a townhouse a mile away, reconnecting with my children, growing closer to Bill, and enjoying her new great-granddaughters. Almost eighty years old, she was amazingly energetic and determined to "find a man."

Despite the desert heat, my mother dressed like she was going to the opera: high heels, black stockings, black or beige chiffon blouse with matching slacks, gold necklace and earrings, and a wide-brimmed hat—not the attire of the casual retiree. It was not surprising to us that she found it difficult to meet a suitable partner.

During weekly dinners together, she would regale us with stories about the sorry lot of available senior men: too cheap to buy her coffee, with dirt under their fingernails, or wearing beltless, baggy shorts and flip-flops. My mother had a great sense of humor. We laughed a lot. Yet I worried constantly about her increasingly impetuous behavior, hysterical crying fits, and nighttime fear of being alone. Later, looking back, I would recognize these changes foreshadowed her impending health crisis.

During this same period, we lost Leo. One evening, finally unable to ward off the ravages of Valley Fever despite aggressive treatment with antifungal medicines, Leo was gasping, choking for breath. I rushed to his side, stroking his head, whispering, "It's OK, boy, it's OK."

Beseeching me with those perceptive brown eyes, he exerted whatever energy he had left to raise his front paw and place it on top of my hand. It killed me. *I love you, Leo.* We stayed that way, looking into each other's eyes.

A flood of Leo memories rushed through me: a tiny puppy yelping so much that the kids and I had to sleep with him on the floor. Sitting on the third-floor landing waiting for us to carry him down the stairs for a walk. Dragging Shana around the block. Maya or Gina chasing after him when he escaped without his leash. Playing tug-of-war with Tobin over a sock. Bill and Leo racing up a forest trail behind our home. Sitting on the sofa, like a human, his back legs and rump on the cushions, two front paws on the floor. Meditating during interfaith services. Barking and laughing, running and jumping, hiding under the bed, terrified of lightning. Ferocious protector. Tender companion. Pure love.

A dam broke, and everything inside me poured out in raspy, anguished sobs. I never cried so long or so hard in my life.

OTHER CONCERNS PRESSED into me. Battling exhaustion, dizziness, and dangerously low blood pressure, I was urged by my health providers to change my vegetarian diet. Twenty-five years since I had tasted animal food, I didn't want to break my vow. But after intense prayers, trying numerous alternative food sources, vitamins, B-12 shots, homeopathic remedies, and herbs, I had to consider that my body had its own wisdom, a lesson that would be repeated during my sojourn in the Sonoran desert.

In many ways, the eleven years we lived in Tucson was a blessed period of spiritual productivity. But after thirty years of overwork, I was physically and mentally depleted.

One afternoon in late January, I stood up from my desk and collapsed. I was unable to stand, so Bill helped me into bed and took my vital signs: blood pressure 60/40, heart rate 45. The room became startlingly calm, as if the atmosphere had been compressed into a still point. I felt myself leave my body, dissipating into space. Everything was so peaceful. I was like a leaf in the wind floating away. For six weeks, I barely could lift myself out of bed.

When the latest Seminary class was ordained, I took a month off to restore my health and think through my options. I didn't want to close the Seminary, but doubted I'd be able to continue the program without financial backing. While my daughter Gina was an exceptional administrator and others volunteered their time, most of the responsibility for its success fell on my shoulders. Over the next weeks, I prayed. I had another stack of admissions. It was such a good program, and many people depended on me.

Normally when I prayed, I waited for guidance. But this time I decided to pose a question and seek an answer with body, mind, and spirit: Should I continue the Seminary and admit a new class? Immediately, my heart and my mind said, "Yes." But my body refused. Its No was urgent and definite. I knew if I continued working this hard, I wouldn't live to see my grandchildren grow. I would have to take care of myself. To be true to that voice was all that mattered now.

Recognition of the power of the body to communicate spiritual wisdom became vital to my well-being. For years, advanced meditative states and other type of soul powers had been integral to my spiritual practice and healing rituals. Now I would become even more alert to how bodily signs—emotional reactions, ethical concerns, soul sufferings, and physical pains—provided insight into the subtle movement of spirit. The labor of reading these signs occupied my efforts to map the mystery of embodiment, how body excesses and worldly pains affected the spirit, and how the spirit broke through into body awareness.

I learned a difficult truth: spirit could be depleted. There was a dark side to throwing my whole self into everything I did, holding the Seminary together with my bones and my cells.

Every day was not ecstatic, but a slow working out of the mystical capacity to restore my bodily connectedness with the whole divine cosmos. To do this required a turning inward to listen with a still heart to the body-mind-spirit teachings that infused my whole being.

I also learned another lesson: For the majority of students, school, whether my own creation or an institutional one, was a means to achieving a certain material outcome, however worthy or noble. It always would represent an exchange of goods. The deepest truths could not be shared this way. It was only heart to heart and soul to soul, without thought of personal gain, that Holy Mystery was transmitted.

Before my month retreat was over, I decided to focus on something that gave me pleasure. For longer than I could remember, I had wanted to travel to Italy. I began to study travel brochures and map out an itinerary, even though I knew we wouldn't be traveling for another year.

* 22 *

Pace e Bene

ANOTHER SEASON HAD PASSED, and it was time to return to the monastery. I arrived in June, scheduled to offer a weeklong conference on the mystical path of contemplation to the community of Benedictine sisters. The rest of the month I planned to continue my writing project and prepare for taking monastic vows.

The conference title I had chosen was "The Longing Heart," and that particular morning I had completed the sixth of my ten lectures, based on Meister Eckhart's notion of the God beyond God. As part of my participation, I had been asked to serve as spiritual director for any sister who wished to have a private session.

While I waited in the small room off the oratory assigned for this purpose, Sister Agnes slowly walked in and sat down. Physically frail and dressed in black, she looked to be close to ninety years old. Her eyes were bright and her face, although wrinkled with age, was a study in the attentiveness that comes from years of prayer.

"Welcome, Sr. Agnes. May I ask what you would like to discuss today?"

In a quiet yet animated voice, she immediately confided her reason for wanting to speak with me. "When I was a novice and through the first decade of my profession, my vows and faith in the Benedictine vocation I had chosen came easily. I would arise in the dark of night to say *matins*, and then follow the liturgy of the hours with joy throughout the day. There was such certitude in dedicating my life to Christ.

"Yet for so many years, maybe it's been fifty or more," she said, "I have not been able to pray to Jesus or the saints. I've thought this was so terrible of me, and it has troubled me and caused me great pain. I don't understand myself or know why I have been unable to find solace in our prayers and liturgy.

"I don't know God in the way I suppose I should; I only seem to find God in silence and darkness—in what you called today the Desert of the Godhead. Often I suffer, wondering if the Presence I feel is real because I am not content with the frills we assign to God.

"But this week your lectures brought peace and helped me understand that there is another way to love God. And what I wanted to ask you: Is it OK to pray to God with no name? Am I on a true path if I follow the *unnamed*?"

* * *

DURING the following weeks, I continued my research on women mystics, making steady progress on the book. I walked around campus, visited with the sisters, and luxuriated in silence.

I was coming full circle back to the child who roamed the moss-covered paths of Great South Bay, the child who relished silence and listened to trees.

Since my last visit, I had spent many hours reading the history of monasticism and studying vows and rituals of diverse monastic communities. In each, I sought universal percepts. I took particular interest in Gandhi's "The Eleven Observances" that he designed as a rule of life "to heal the hurting indifference which keeps one human being from another."[1]

From 1904 until his death in 1948, Gandhi founded and lived in religious communities. His experiments in applying spiritual principles to the social sphere radicalized the otherworldly attitude of the traditional *sannyasin*. He felt with extraordinary intensity the plight of India's masses and the brokenness of the world, and sought ways to create a society without suffering. As the twentieth century's most famous karmic yogi, Gandhi inspired others to advocate for nonviolent social change in India and around the world.

The first of his observances or vows was "Truth is God, the one and only Reality. All other observances take their rise from and the quest for, and the worship of, Truth." Truth was the way to God. "What I have been striving and pining to achieve these thirty years is self-realization, to see God face-to-face, to attain *moska* [salvation]. I live and move and have my being in pursuit of this goal. All that I do by way of speaking and writing and all my ventures in the political field are directed to the same end."[2]

Prayer was at the center of Gandhi's pursuit of truth, which he approached as a process of self-purification leading to a conscious realization of the Presence of God. By surrendering to prayer and to the inner voice, Gandhi found the moral courage to leave behind social convention, stand against British rule, and fight for the dignity of India's untouchables and women. "Prayer has been the saving of my life," he wrote. "Without it I should have been a lunatic long ago."[3]

Gandhi lived by the vow of *ahimsa* or nonviolence, the most well known of his spiritual precepts. In Sanskrit, *ahimsa* means non-harm or non-killing. Gandhi employed the term not passively, as the absence of something, but as the active performance of total love for life and for humanity. From the physical to the mystical level, nonviolence referred not only to external action, but also to the thoughts, emotions, and perceptions of the inner life.

Especially relevant to the spirituality of nonviolence and central to my vows was Gandhi's insistence that persons of faith must not harbor a superiority of salvation. This quest for non-possession of truth formed the basis of his ashram hymnals, which contained prayers from Muslim, Christian, Buddhist, Sikh, and other sources. In *Young India*, he wrote: "I came to the conclusion, after prayerful study and discussion…that all religions were true, and also that all had some error in them,…So we can only pray, if we are Hindus [that] we broaden our Hinduism by loving other religions as our own."[4]

But, finally, what was most coincident with my monastic orientation was a sentiment shared by the sisters and Gandhi: the complete surrender of the heart to God. Monasticism was an opportunity for intense spiritual development, a model of loving concern for the turbulent world, and for pursuit of total, inner transformation. It was purity of heart, an undivided heart longing for God alone, that the monk sought.

"Happy is that person of love who has caused God," wrote Martyrius, a seventh-century Syriac monk, "who is love, to dwell in his heart. Happy are you, O heart, so small and confined, yet you have caused him whom heaven and earth cannot contain to dwell spiritually in your womb as in a restful abode. Happy that luminous eye of the heart which, in its purity, clearly beholds him before whose sight, the seraphs veil their face. . . . Blessed are you, O heart that is luminous, the abode of the Divinity; Blessed are you, heart that is pure, which beholds the hidden Being."[5]

I SPENT THE EVENING before my ceremony of monastic profession in prayer, first in the oratory and later before my personal altar. For several weeks I had recorded my spiritual journey, joys and repentances. Amelia had sat with me, listening and pointing the way.

I had been born with a contemplative soul, and only Spirit knows why I was called (often against my own will) to a new monastic way. I have followed the call in darkness, determined without understanding, seeking without knowing what was sought, having faith in the light when there was no light. Devoted to the divine in the everyday holiness of matter, I turned inward toward silence, never abandoning the quest.

I become a monk not through acts of personal will, or even through communal anointing, but through a divine yearning in my soul that overtakes my whole being and leads me to a new way of life.

I take vows to remind me that as a citizen of our planet, I am not on earth for myself alone. In our sentient universe, every utterance, every deed is recorded in the cosmic memory. My actions or inactions profoundly affect my relationship with all beings. Thus my soul cannot be shielded from small and great sufferings, from injustices and wars, which strike more deeply into the sacred web of creation.

At the core of my monastic profession is a vow: to place Divine Mystery and the earthly realm and its entire human and more-than-human inhabitants on an altar of devotion and consecrate my life each day to their benefit.

I was ready for my ceremony of monastic profession the next day.

*
* *

CANDLES flickered in the dusky evening light, casting creamy shadows on the Madonna statue in the corner of the prayer room. Prostrate on the floor, arms outstretched in the ancient posture of the postulant, my body formed a tree of life, intersecting lines of spirit and earth. Standing around me in a circle, eight women monks began to chant the service of profession. As voices rose in anticipation of the antiphon, a quivering stillness descended upon the room. Soon, the chords of *Veni*

Creator Spiritus intensified, causing my spirit to soar above the great arc of creation, until my soul, swept along its perimeter, dissolved. It is for this that I had waited.

My body now melded with the sweet, round earth, I silently prayed for grace, for descent of Spirit. Alert to every sound, my soul trembled as the sisters' rich soprano voices chanted the Litany of the Saints I had chosen for this holy day, which began:

Holy Mother, Mary, Skekhinah, Laksmi, Kuan Yin,
Woyengi, Corn Woman, and All Named and Unnamed
Female Prophets, Goddesses, and Saints
Pray for Us

Dear God, Jesus, Lord Buddha, Tao, Allah,
Great Spirit, Krishna, and All Named and Unnamed
Male Prophets, Gods, and Saints
Pray for Us

After the full chant was completed, Amelia invited me to stand and receive the invocation of prayers.

Gracious God, look mercifully upon Beverly. Grant her the gift of
  your Spirit as she seeks to live this monastic way of life. Amen
May she commune with the earth and all creatures in a humble
  awareness of our relationship with God and all things. Amen
May she serve God with the good things she has been given. Amen
May she seek peace and nonviolence in thought, word, and deed.
  Amen
May she be patient and steadfast in time of trial. Amen
May she be faithful in prayer and attentive to the presence of God
  in all of creation and all of life. Amen
May she support her sisters and brothers in mutual love and esteem.
  Amen
May she walk in the tradition of monastic women and men who
  have gone before her. Amen
May her family and friends and all who support her be blessed.
  Amen
May those with whom she shares her life, and all those who have
  shared life with her, be blessed. Amen

> Ever-loving God, Divine Mother and Father of us all, accept our
> prayers and all our lives. Amen

Following an ancient order of service, the ring I'd chosen was blessed
by the sisters and slipped onto my finger. "May this ring be a pledge of
steadfast love and a sign of your commitment to a new monastic way of
life," Amelia said.

I signed the Promises of Vows, written by my own hand and witnessed
by the sisters gathered around the table.

My turn to read, I recited from the Magnificat: *My soul trembles in the
presence of the loving Creator.* Then sharing a sign of peace with the sisters, I
surrendered my heart to the closing prayer they read:

> Loving Creator of the world and of all people, we honor you with
> praise and thanksgiving. Today, it is right that your house should
> echo with a new song of thanksgiving for this sister of ours who has
> listened to your voice and responded in faith and love. We pray that
> in the freedom of her heart she may bring comfort to your people.
> May she look upon the world and see it ruled by your loving wis-
> dom. May the gift she makes of herself hasten the coming of peace
> on earth and make her one with you and your saints forever. Amen.

⁎⁎⁎

SEVERAL months after returning from the monastery, Bill and I were
invited by our *santero* (painter of saints) friend to attend Easter Week
services of the *Penitentes*, a lay Catholic brotherhood. Every Friday during Lent, members of his brotherhood gathered at a tiny hilltop *morada*
(dwelling, chapel) in northern New Mexico. Devoted to the crucified
Christ, their spiritual practices were especially intense during Lent, which
consisted of all-night prayer vigils on their knees, recitation of the rosary,
praying the Stations of the Cross, and private ceremonies of penance.

Holy Thursday we drove north to spend the evening with the *hermanos*
chanting the rosary in the darkened *morada*, statues of Jesus, Mary, and
saints illuminated by candlelight. We felt honored to participate in this
sacred ritual, the energy of the chanting reverberating in our cells, our
souls. Wiped out by the intensity, we barely remember the drive back to
our hotel and fell fast asleep.

On the way to breakfast the next morning, we ran into Pasquale, a friend who was just preparing to walk with thousands of other pilgrims along the highway to the *Santuario de Chimayo*, a journey of over thirty miles. As we waved goodbye, Bill reminded me that we had another friend from the Zia Pueblo who also was preparing for a solemn Good Friday, when his pueblo was closed to the public in preparation for the Kachina Dancers to come down from the hills. Each of these expressions of communal devotion lent sweetness to the atmosphere.

By 8 a.m., we were standing in the courtyard of a Catholic church north of Santa Fe. Joining other visitors, Bill and I waited behind a wooden fence for the *Penitentes* to emerge from their all-night penance in the *morada*. Soon, a man bearing a large wooden cross solemnly led the procession of *hermanos* ringing bells and shooting muskets counterclockwise around the *morada* and onto the dirt road, stopping to lean the wooden crucifix against the church's adobe wall. Joining other visitors, we formed a line behind the *hermanos* as one by one we fell to the gravel-covered dirt, walking on our knees to venerate the cross and kiss Jesus' wooden feet. The atmosphere was rich with devotion, hearts full of longing, open to mystery.

Charged with light, my soul was joyful to be in a community willing to give of its time and profit to re-enact a moment so out of time, so out of the normal commerce that passes for religion or faith. To participate in pure giving for its own sake was the "scandal" of the cross.

Yet the events of the week also brought pain, as I reflected on the many sufferings and crucifixions going on in our world. While I had no way of knowing what the *hermanos* experienced in their acts of penance, I witnessed something profound and deep in them—they who had solemnly pledged their lives to share in the Pascal mystery. In imitation of Christ's suffering on the cross, they participated in a mystical death, when the deliverance God offered from pain was not no pain, but the pain was actually a gift. For sacrifice was a condition of life built into the structure of reality itself, what makes things what they are.

The Easter ceremonies over, we took leave from Santa Fe, my soul nourished by having shared with others a deep love of the Holy.

ONCE HOME, I started work on an icon of St. Francis, birds fluttering around his head, anticipating our upcoming trip to Italy.

* * *

AFTER a long flight, we finally arrived in Rome. Sister Helena, who had taken my spiritual direction course in Tucson, met us at the airport and drove us to *Immaculata*, the convent where we were staying. Two Spanish and two Indian Franciscan sisters ran the guesthouse and were so welcoming that we felt at home right away. After dropping suitcases in our room, Helena guided us through the bus and metro systems to the Vatican. That afternoon we went into St. Peter's, floored by its size and scale, and by Michelangelo's *Pietà*.

Up early the next morning, by 7:30 we were on line with our guide for a tour of the Sistine Chapel and the Vatican Museums. Bill and I barely had time to absorb the genius of Michelangelo's frescoes before we were herded down corridors lined with marble statues gleaming under ornately carved and gilded ceilings. When the tour was over, we jumped on a bus to Piazza Repubblica and walked the rest of the way to Santa Maria della Vittoria to see Bernini's *Ecstasy of St. Teresa*. But when we got there the church was closed for siesta. Welcoming the midday rest, we returned to the chapel several hours later.

To the left of the main altar was Bernini's masterpiece. Golden spires meant to illustrate heavenly light created a backdrop for the sculptures, which depicted a vision described by St. Teresa in her autobiography of an angel piercing her heart with a golden dart, causing her both immense sweetness and pain. Bernini portrayed Teresa's body in a contorted posture, her face in ecstatic trance, the overall effect highly theatrical.

If I wondered whether Teresa would have approved of Bernini's representation, I nonetheless celebrated the grandeur of the artist striving to portray the intensity of the visionary world St. Teresa described:

> I saw close to me toward my left side an angel in bodily form.... the angel was not large but small; he was very beautiful, and his face was so aflame that he seemed to be one of those very sublime angels that appear to be all afire.... I saw in his hands a large golden dart and at the iron tip there appeared to be a little fire. It seemed to me this angel plunged the dart several times into my heart and that it reached deep within me.... The pain was so great that it made me moan, the sweetness this greatest pain caused me was so superabundant that there is no desire capable of taking it away; nor is the soul content with less than God. The pain is not bodily but spiritual, although the body doesn't fail to share in some of it, and even a great deal.[6]

A few days later we took the train to Florence. After checking into our hotel, I turned onto *via dello Studio*, breathing in the soft, sage-tinted air of ancient olive groves. Walking the cobblestone streets, I couldn't dispel the sense that here was the landscape of my soul, where many of the mystics I had spent my life studying and teaching were born. This spiritual geography, like my biological one, reached across Italy and into Spain, for somehow and in some way my being was rooted in these places.

I found myself kneeling in blue-washed churches and praying before gilded statues of Mary. The genius of Caravaggio and Fra Angelico enticed from canvases mounted on hidden side altars and frescoed on ceilings like portals into a divine realm.

At the Uffizi and nearby Accademia Galleries, the transcendent vision of Renaissance artists nourished a deep current in my soul. Michelangelo's statue of David seemed to embody the mysterious idea of incarnation, when the divine became human and the human became divine. A large altarpiece, the Ognissanti Madonna painted by Giotto around 1310, took my breath away. The religious theme in these works was culturally significant, but it was the artists' rendering of the emotional complexity of the human figures that radicalized my attention.

In the Basilica of Santa Croce, I paid homage to the tombs of Michelangelo, Galileo, and Rossini, later wandering through the *mercato centrale*, stalls piled with leather goods and souvenirs, straining to have my halting Italian heard above the din. On another street corner, on the sidewalk in front of a church, a placard announced an upcoming Mozart concert conducted by Giuseppe Lanzetta. The phone book listed pages of residents with the surname, Bettini, like that of my maternal ancestors born in the region. On my way to meet Bill at *Casa di Dante*, I stopped on the *Ponte Vecchio*, watching the Arno River flow under the famous bridge, simply awed by a feeling of *home*.

OUR LAST DAY in Florence, by one o'clock Bill and I were on board Trentialia to Assisi, the birthplace of St. Francis. Perched on top of a hill, Assisi was a jewel of medieval architecture. No sooner had we stepped off the train and climbed three flights of stairs to our rental apartment, when a buried remembrance ignited intense feelings in me. Unpacking my suitcase I wondered if these stirrings were the result of reading St. Bonaventure's *Life of Francis*.

Or was my knowing deeper and more primary?

When Bill took off to photograph the area, I decided to explore San

Damiano, the chapel Francis was inspired to rebuild. Following a line of pilgrims, I descended a steep staircase outside the wall of the village, and walked along an overgrown meadow path. The countryside was stunning; no wonder Francis celebrated nature! I entered the little oratory rebuilt by Francis, who one day in 1205 heard a voice that seemed to come from a crucifix in the small rundown church: "Francis, Francis, go and repair my house which, as you can see, is falling into ruins." He immediately got to work.

An earthen structure with plastered walls, the small arched chamber welcomed me into its warm cocoon. Aroused by the serene atmosphere, I sat down on a narrow wooden pew and looked up at the crucifix suspended above the nave, a replica of the original cross Francis found between the crumbling stones.

Closing my eyes, I felt Spirit pressing in. After a period of contemplation, my vision flooded with a golden light so bright that I opened my eyes to see if someone had turned on a spotlight. But the Light radiated out from the heart of the crucifix, widening as it approached me. I was shown my path: wide and direct, illuminated by blazing light, no detours, no curves.

Praying for direction on the next phase of my life in God, I saw the heavens open, and from the heavens many angels came forth to gather me into the divine fold. The golden angels seized my heart to heal whatever impeded the fullness of generosity, simplicity, humility, and poverty.

Before sunrise the next morning, Bill and I climbed the slope of Mount Subasio to the caves outside the walls of Assisi where Francis and his band of followers often retired to pray. Here at the *Eremo delle Carceri* (Carceri Hermitage), I looked out on the valley below as a white dove flew across the sky, followed by two more white doves. Something deep within me broke open. Collapsing against the ancient stone structure, I wept, overcome with gratitude for the life I had been given and for the gift of knowing God. Here, again, an intense recognition flooded my consciousness. For the first time, I realized—no, I knew—why my spiritual awakening had occurred in Northern California, in a landscape not dissimilar from the one where I now stood.

Back in the village, I could almost hear Francis greeting passersby in the narrow streets, with the expression *Pace e bene!* (Peace and all good!). I walked to the Basilica di San Francesco, the serenity in Assisi palatable. The Upper Basilica was alive with color, the massive cross-vaulted ceiling an intense blue, the walls of the transept and the nave adorned with vibrantly hued frescoes by Giotto and Cimabue. A testament to high art and intense spirituality, the Basilica would have scandalized Francis, who preached and lived a simple life of renunciation in devotion to God.

I took the stairs down to the Lower Basilica, and halfway along the nave another stairway downward to the crypt containing the remains of St. Francis. Nothing adorned the walls of the crypt. There were no frescoes here. The tomb was made of stone. I believe Francis would have liked the simplicity, and this is where I came to pray.

EVER SINCE I'D read St. Bonaventure's *The Life of Francis*, I had wanted to visit Mount La Verna in the Apennines, where Francis received the stigmata in September 1224. Several days into our stay, we hired a local driver to take us there. Slightly under two hours northwest of Assisi, it was late morning when we arrived at the *Santuario Francescano*, which sat atop a mountain with a breathtaking view of the valley below.

In August 1224, frustrated by changes in the Order of Friars Minor, Francis withdrew to La Verna for a forty-day fast in preparation for the Feast of Saint Michael the Archangel. One morning while praying on the mountainside he saw a seraph with six wings gleaming like a fire descending from heaven. After a mysterious and intimate conversation, the vision vanished, leaving Francis with the marks of crucifixion impressed on his feet and hands, and a blood-red wound on his right side.

A friar attached to the monastery offered to show us several sites of special significance to Franciscan spirituality. He told us that in 1263, a small chapel was built over the spot where Francis received the stigmata. It was reached by a long corridor lined with frescoes depicting the life of the saint and bas-reliefs of the way of the cross. From what I understood of the friar's Italian, the friars walked along this route to the chapel daily as their forefathers had since 1341. Halfway down the corridor was an ancient door that accessed a dark grotto. This was the place where St. Francis slept, using a rough piece of stone as his bed.

In 1225, some six to ten months after he received the stigmata, Francis was in Assisi spending his days in a small hut adjacent to the church of San Damiano. Blind and frail, he was tormented by mice. One night, feeling deeply depressed and sorry for himself he inwardly prayed to bear his troubles patiently. Then he heard a voice assuring him, "Brother, be glad and rejoice in your infirmities and tribulations since henceforth you are as secure as if you were already in my kingdom."

The next morning he told his companions he should rejoice for even in the midst of his sufferings God had assured him of salvation. It was on this day that Francis composed "The Canticle of Brother Sun."

Praised by you, my Lord, with all your creatures,
Especially Sir Brother Sun,
Who makes the day and through whom you give us light.
And he is beautiful and radiant with great splendor,
And bears the signification of you, Most High One.[7]

The following day we packed our suitcases and left Assisi. In the weeks ahead, like other tourists of this ancient land, we were awed by the lengthy stretch of Roman history that insinuated itself into the drama of the last two thousand and more years. Within the span of a few blocks, ancient, classical, and modern civilizations rested side by side or on top of each other. The sacred was not cloistered in churches and museums but spilled over into the streets, where the sensuality of art, nature, and aesthetics coalesced in such a way to raise the material to the spiritual and to bend the spiritual toward earth.

Unseen worlds were everywhere present in Italy, weaving the threads of my life together. Unprepared for how much the land and people affected me, I dreamed of Italy every night for six weeks after we returned home.

* * *

SEVERAL years now have passed. So much has changed: the mysterious anchoring of my being in Great Solitude; the unshakeable sense of belonging; the serenity of earth-inspired transcendence. More grounded in this world than ever before, I was also more at peace with the daily tumult. It was as if a magnetic force of love pulled me into a hermitage interior to the divine enclosure, from which action and nonaction radiated.

I worked to accommodate my busy schedule with this new iteration of self, observing the moorings of my soul. Such was the depth or extent of this transformation that it became more hidden as I became simpler.

Trailing behind "me" were multiple representations of lives lived and lost. Like vapors in mist, they were ephemeral. Generational, which some called karmic or past, lives, were insubstantial—they were an energetic co-mingling of thought and emotion and deed and culture. They were empty in the true sense of being without form.

"I" was the consciousness of self-sacrifice, of stepping outside the circle of dharma.

"Monk" was another code for freedom, paradise, dissolving in the ocean of being.

The mystical heart was the true meaning of my humanity, a breaking light at dawn.

This is how devotion to God worked.

My personality still in play, perhaps even intensified, was merely a shield protecting the sacred depth.

But the river of silence coursed through everything, gathering in its mighty waters the yearnings of a soul.

EPILOGUE

FLYING OVER THE ATLANTIC, about two hours from Barcelona, I
had enjoyed a blessedly quiet flight, which allowed me to complete
my talk for the conference I was attending on "Emerging Images of
God." With pen poised over the page, I wondered about the image of God
as *emerging*. I could never say whether the path I had taken was ancient or
new, if I were not speaking a secret that should not be told. I only knew
that I loved instead what I could not fully know, privy to a longing and a
wonder that rivaled my soul.

Twelve years have passed since I had taken monastic vows. As an out-
growth of my commitment, I developed a program of monastic profession
for the contemplative, interspiritual journeyer, initiating the formation
of The Community of a New Monastic Way. Together with students from
my earliest days of teaching, we remain faithful to the original revelation
received in 1976 and continue to explore its many and varied expressions.

At least once a year our members gather as a community for an extended
period of study, prayer, reflection, and solitude. We discuss the meaning
of belonging without boundaries, being committed to a new expression
of monasticism that is rooted in silence and practices its wisdom in and
through everyday life in the world. But more than this, we are bond by our
love of the Divine, by seeking total interior transformation to the best of
our abilities and in the context of our contemporary lives. In this way, we

aspire to be true monks; mystical monks open to the world.

In thinking back over almost forty years of teaching, I can see the path that I have been forging is gently taking form. Yet, even as I continue to articulate the revelations, especially the subtle formlessness of *via feminina*, these efforts are but a fraction of the whole. The vast majority of what I have experienced about this rare evolution in spiritual consciousness is not in the public domain. I imagine my future will be devoted to a further synthesis of the mystical path of the feminine, including its implications for planetary peace and social justice. And, of course, I hope that my work will contribute, in some small way, to the many other voices advancing a contemporary lineage of sacred literature.

MUCH HAS CHANGED in our family. Bill retired from his academic position. We moved to New Mexico and then moved again to the California coast after I discovered Santa Fe's high altitude was adversely affecting my health. My children are thriving in their careers, and we have five granddaughters now. And not long ago my mother passed away after a long illness.

Several days before she fell into a coma, Bill and I rushed to Florida to be with her. Immobilized by another stroke, unable to roll over or lift her arms, my mother's eyes lit up when she saw us. Inclining her head toward several religious statues on her dresser, she spoke about God. "Bev, I've learned so much since I've been in this bed. You can't believe how much I've learned." Squeezing my hand, she closed her eyes.

This she taught me: There is no death for one who believes in the White Light of the Holy Spirit.

Our family gathered at the ocean for her memorial service. I imagined her with us, wearing mascara and high heels, and a wide-brim hat to keep away the sun. I could almost hear her voice, calling the kids "Sweetie" or "Handsome," plying them with questions about lives and loves.

I took out the small vial of Pop's ashes my mother had entrusted to me for safekeeping: "When I die, Bev, mix our ashes together and free us into the sea."

Watching their grayish remains swirl in an ocean eddy, I prayed into the wind, "We had great parents."

Looking back over the span of my life, there always had been a part of me that was ready to take up a begging bowl and follow wherever I was led. Because the whole path of enlightenment hinges on this: Trust the inner voice, love God with one's whole heart, and be empty of self.

In my sixth decade, daily I practice bringing myself to zero in preparation for my great transition into the life of spirit. I realize that this taking of flesh is the truest preciousness. I pray for strength, radical self-honesty, and compassion for others. I pray to be worthy of the gift.

Not so long ago, while meditating, my hands became blazing, fiery orbs, my whole body one illuminated mass of light. Then the ten-winged archangel descended in a pillar of fiery wings, piercing my soul with love's longing. I saw the imprint of fire blazing in the soul of the world, igniting a new path of divinity.

I do not know what waits on the other side of everything known, or whether the human heart will abandon self-interest and learn to love our beloved earth and the unimaginable gift of life.

Until my last breath, I will yearn to help more, do more, and give more toward healing the wounded heart of the world.

But I am at peace.

I have spent my life loving the Unnameable.

ACKNOWLEDGEMENTS

To GREG GLAZNER, award-winning poet and professor of writing, I cannot begin to express my gratitude for our friendship and your masterful editorial guidance. Without your gentle manner and poetic sensibility, I would not have learned how to integrate my transcendent experiences with personal life events in a fluid, narrative style. The first to read aspects of my life I never before had shared, you were my anchor during the difficult early years, encouraging me to dig deeper and to say more. Without doubt, whatever clarity and ease of style exists in this work is, in large measure, the result of your respect for the sanctity of words.

To Christine Salem and Susan Weckesser, our monthly writing group was the highlight of my time in Santa Fe. You were such passionate readers and expert editors, especially patient dealing with book chapters I submitted out of sequence and in rough draft. As we shared chocolates and iced tea, your earnest concern that the story live up to its potential helped me to expand on areas that lacked specificity or were inadequately covered, and to clarify issues in religion, theology, or the mystical life that would benefit the general reader. Five years later, we live in different states, but meet via conference call, our friendship deepening.

To my dear friends—Pamela Johnson, Nelson Kane, Corinne Martin, Gregory Perron, Margaret Riordan, Theresa Schumacher, Sarah Stein—who read earlier drafts of the manuscript—how can I thank you for your loving hearts and sound advice, especially when I resisted publishing Nine Jewels at all? You, who know intimately the joys and struggles of a contemplative life, your sensitivity and loving support of my life's journey, mean everything.

To my sister, Carol DeAgazio, who had faith in this project, helped excavate childhood stories, and has been my family confidant all these years, I am in awe of your resilience, compassion, and gentle presence.

And to members of our monastic community, whose prayerful souls have been a source of grace for so many years, I am profoundly grateful for your dedication, close friendship, and affectionate care. I cannot imagine how lonely my heart would have been without the benefit of our shared experience!

As the manuscript was being readied for publication, I am thankful to have worked with Laurie Gibson, a superb copyeditor and proofreader. If I ever doubted whether the placement of a comma could elevate the meaning of an idea, it was dispelled by Laurie's ardent love of the written word.

To my daughter, Shana Lanzetta, who is the content and media manager of my personal website, and that of Blue Sapphire Books, I am touched by your insight, generosity, and passionate commitment to ensuring that this book and my other writings reach a wider audience. What could be better than spending time each week speaking with you—who loves with your whole heart—about spiritual matters!

In forming Blue Sapphire Books, I am indebted beyond measure to Pamela Johnson and Nelson Kane, who have given of their energy, time, wisdom, and compassionate hearts to the publication of this book. How fun has it been to confer on the smallest detail of book design, production, and marketing! I am in awe of their spiritual depth and professional experience, how even the smallest aspect of book production is approached with a holy intention.

Pamela, your gentle, but firm belief that Nine Jewels needed to "walk out into the world" was my guidepost throughout the publishing process, especially when I was tempted to abandon the task. Our monthly spiritual discussions always astounded me, as we discovered over and again parallel paths. And your understanding that the marketing of a book is an organic process of reaching those of like-heart is a continual source of blessing to me and to those whom this book speaks.

Nelson, I've never known anyone who brings to graphic design such a passionate respect for visual detail, realizing that every element is a reflection of the divine in form. Our frequent phone conversations were the highlight of my week, as we worked through a wide-range of spiritual and artistic issues, your steady wisdom and gentle soul a wondrous gift. Your beautiful cover design and book layout enhance the spiritual reading of the text and are, in themselves, a contemplative exercise.

It was the collaboration with all of these people that has made the writing and publishing of Nine Jewels of Night such a joyful endeavor.

And finally, to my children and grandchildren, without whom none of this would be possible, who are the strength and joy of my life, and to Bill, who has championed this book, encouraged me to write, and holds my heart,

Thank you.

I love you, all.

ENDNOTES

CHAPTER 1

I Counted My Solitude

1. Hermann Hesse, Demian (New York: Dover Publications, 2000), 1.

CHAPTER 2

Hidden Hand of Fate

1. A Yiddish word used often by my mother and her Jewish friends, meaning to spread, as in cream cheese on a bagel, but also used to refer to a smudge, a mess.

CHAPTER 4

Freed from the Known

1. J. Krishnamurti, Freedom from the Known (San Francisco: HarperSanFrancisco, 2009), 10.

2. Ibid. 69.

CHAPTER 5

Motherhood of Mercy

1. Dietrich Bonhoeffer, in Eric Metaxas, Bonhoeffer: Pastor, Martyr, Prophet, Spy; A Righteous Gentile Vs. the Third Reich (Nashville; Thomas Nelson, 2010), 296.

CHAPTER 6
Love's Benediction

1. St. Isaac of Niniveh, in Thomas Merton, *The Climate of Monastic Prayer* (Kalamazoo, MI: Cistercian Publications, 1969), 43.

CHAPTER 7
Pure Mind

1. http://www.jkrishnamurti.org/about-krishnamurti/the-core-of-the-teachings.php

CHAPTER 8
Ray of Sublime Light

1. Sri Aurobindo, *Savitri: A Legend and a Symbol*. "Canto II: The Way of Fate and the Problem of Pain" (Twin Lakes, WI: Lotus Press, 1988), 461.

2. Julian of Norwich, *Showings, The Classics of Western Spirituality*, translated by Edmund Colledge and James Walsh (New York: Paulist Press, 1978), 204–5.

3. "Neti, Neti," is a Sanskrit term found in the Hindu Upanishads. As a meditation on the nature of Brahman, it reveals the paradox of what Brahman is not. It corresponds to the Western *via negativa*, which negates rationalizations in order to affect a non-conceptual direct experience of reality.

4. Thich Nhat Hanh, *Love in Action: Writings on Nonviolent Social Change* (Berkeley: Parallax Press, 1993), 104.

CHAPTER 10
Secret Teachings of Love

1. Adapted from Beverly Lanzetta, *Emerging Heart: Global Spirituality and the Sacred* (Minneapolis: Fortress Press, 2007), 13–19.

2. Ibid. 18.

3. Teresa of Avila, *The Way of Perfection, The Collected Works of St. Teresa of Avila* (vol. 2), translated by Kieran Kavanaugh and Otilio Rodriguez (Washington, D.C.: Institute of Carmelite Studies, 1980), 21.2, 117.

CHAPTER 11
Leap of Faith

1. John of the Cross, *Living Flame of Love. The Collected Works of St. John of the Cross*, translated by Kieran Kavanaugh and Otilio Rodriguez (Washington, D.C.: Institute of Carmelite Studies, 1991), 3.47, 692.

2. Thomas Merton, *The Wisdom of the Desert: Sayings of the Desert Fathers of the Fourth Century* (New York: New Directions, 1960), 18.

CHAPTER 12

The Friends of God Suffer

1. Rebbe means master, teacher, or mentor and is a Yiddish word derived from the Hebrew, rabbi. In Hasidism, "rebbe" refers to the head of a Hasidic group.

2. Rabbi Nathan of Bratzlav, *M'Shivath Nephesh: The Teaching of the L-rd is Perfect* (Winnipeg, Manitoba, 1970).

3. *The Book of the Poor in Spirit: By a Friend of God*, translated by C.F. Kelley (New York: Harper & Brothers, 1954), 229.

4. The *Zohar*, a Jewish mystical text, considers Friday night, the Jewish Sabbath, the most propitious occasion for the reunion of the Shekhinah the Sabbath bride and her mate. Intercourse is believed to produce a new soul and thus Sabbath is the time for a righteous man and woman to have sexual contact.

CHAPTER 13

Nine Jewels of Night

1. Teresa of Avila, *The Interior Castle*, *The Collected Works of St. Teresa of Avila* (vol. 2), 1.2.3, 289.

CHAPTER 14

Night Vigil

1. Augustine, *The Confessions of St. Augustine*, translated by John K. Ryan (New York: Image Books, 1960), 189. 8.5.10

2. Thomas Merton, *New Seeds of Contemplation* (New York: New Directions, 1961), 258.

3. Teresa of Avila, *The Book of Her Foundations*, 31.46, translated by Antonio Perez-Romero, *Subversion and Liberation in the Writings of St. Teresa of Avila* (Amsterdam, Atlanta: Rodopi B.V., 1996), 181–82.

CHAPTER 15

No Hunting Except for Peace

1. Reza Baraheni, *God's Shadow: Prison Poems* (Bloomington: Indiana University Press, 1976), 59.

2. Terrence des Pres, *The Survivor: Anatomy of Life in the Death Camps* (New York: Oxford University Press, 1976), vi.

3. Eric Hobsbawm, "War and Peace in the 20th Century," *The Guardian* 24: 4–21 (February 2002), 16.

4. Abraham Joshua Heschel, *The Prophets: An Introduction* (vol. I), (New York: Harper & Row, 1955), Idem, *The Insecurity of Freedom: Essays on Human Existence* (New York: Farrar, Straus and Giroux, 1966), 183.

5. Thomas Merton, *Contemplation in a World of Action* (New York: Image Books, 1973), 36.

6. Thomas Merton, *Introductions East & West: The Foreign Prefaces of Thomas Merton*, edited by Robert E. Daggy. Preface to the Japanese edition of *The Seven Storey Mountain*, August 1963 (Greensboro, NC: Unicorn Press, 1981), 45.

7. Rainer Maria Rilke, in *Sunbeams: A Book of Quotations*, edited by Sy Safransky (Berkeley: North Atlantic Books, 2012), 51.

CHAPTER 16

Blessed are the Poor in Spirit

1. German mystic and theologian Meister Eckhart's writings are refreshingly radical, a fact that no doubt contributed to his posthumous condemnation of heresy by the Vatican Curia in 1329.

2. Anonymous, *The Cloud of Unknowing* and *The Books of Privy Counseling*, edited, with an introduction by William Johnston (New York: Image Books, 1973), 50.

3. Ewert Cousins, *Global Spirituality: Toward the Meeting of Mystical Paths* (Madras, India: Radhakrishnan Institute for Advanced Study In Philosophy, University of Madras, 1985), 26.

CHAPTER 17

The Plague of Mice

1. Evelyn Underhill, *Mysticism: A Study in the Nature and Development of Man's Spiritual Consciousness* (New York: New American Library, 1974), 71–72.

2. Ibid. 84.

3. *Bonaventure: The Soul's Journey into God, The Tree of Life, and the Life of St. Francis*, introduction and translation by Ewert Cousins (New York: Paulist Press, 1978), 104.

4. Raimon Panikkar, "Some Words Instead of a Response," *Cross-Currents* 29 (1979), 196.

5. From my personal notes of conference presentations, 1987. Raimundo Panikkar, *The Intra-Religious Dialogue* (New York: Paulist Press, 1978), 2.

6. Thomas Berry, from his private papers and conversations. New York: 1987–89. See Thomas Berry, *Thomas Berry and the New Cosmology* (Mystic, CT: Twenty-Third Publications, 1988); Idem, *Befriending the Earth: A Theology of Reconciliation Between Humans and the Earth* (Mystic, CT: Twenty-Third Publications, 1991); and Idem, *Evening Thoughts: Reflecting on Earth as Sacred Community*, edited by Mary Evelyn Tucker (San Francisco: Sierra Club Books, 2006).

7. Adapted from *Emerging Heart*, 22.

8. Ibid. 25–27.

9. Ibid. 55–56.

10. Underhill, *Mysticism*, 83.

CHAPTER 18

Called to Silence

1. CCD (Confraternity of Christian Doctrine) classes, or Catechism, provide religious education to Catholic children.

2. Adapted from *Emerging Heart*, 34–35.

3. Augustine, *The Confessions of St. Augustine*, translated, with an introduction by John K. Ryan (New York: Image Books, 1960), 8.12.28–29, 202.

4. Historically, in Christian monasticism celibacy is abstinence from marriage and chastity abstinence from sexual relations. In practice, the two often are taken to be synonymous in monastic communities, with the monk vowing to abstain from marriage and sexual relations. In this chapter, I use the term "celibacy" to convey both senses.

5. Raimon Panikkar, *Blessed Simplicity: The Monk as Universal Archetype* (New York: Seabury Press, 1982), 33–34, 43, and 50.

6. Today, contemplative studies are a burgeoning field in colleges and universities. Nonetheless I contend the mystical question remains a neglected sphere of study and influence in the academy.

7. Thomas Merton, "Where is Tao," in Thomas Merton, *Thoughts on the East* (New York: New Directions, 1995), 6: "Therefore come with me to the palace of Nowhere where all the many things are One."

8. Raimon Panikkar, *The Intrareligious Dialogue* (New York: Paulist Press, 1999), 1.

9. Augustine, *Confessions* 6.11.18, 149.

CHAPTER 19

Garden of the Gods

1. Joel Lovell, "The Beautiful, Brutal Vision of George Saunders," *New York Times Magazine*, January 6, 2013, p. 47.

2. Teresa of Avila, *The Book of Her Life* (Washington, D.C.: Institute of Carmelite Studies, 1987) 11.2, 111.

3. Ranier Maria Rilke, *Letters to a Young Poet*, translated by Stephen Mitchell (New York: Vintage Books, 1987), 78.

4. John of the Cross, *The Spiritual Canticle*, Stanza 35.1. *The Collected Works of St. John of the Cross*, 476.

5. For a superb study of the apophatic traditions of the Abrahamic traditions, see Michael A. Sells, *Mystical Languages of Unsaying* (Chicago: The University of Chicago Press, 1994).

6. Thomas Merton, *New Seeds of Contemplation* (New York, New Directions, 1971), 1; and Idem, *Faith and Violence: Christian Teaching and Christian Practice* (Notre Dame, IN: University of Notre Dame Press, 1994), 213.

7. *Hadjewijch: The Complete Works*, trans. Mother Columba Hart (New York: Paulist Press, 1980), 212.

CHAPTER 20

Desert Solitude

1. Thomas Merton, *The Wisdom of the Desert* (New York: New Directions, 1960), 8.

2. Adapted from *Emerging Heart*, 20.

3. Barbara Newman, *Sister of Wisdom: St. Hildegard's Theology of the Feminine* (Berkeley: University of California Press, 1987), 64.

CHAPTER 21

Radical Wisdom

1. Thomas Merton, *Hagia Sophia* in *A Thomas Merton Reader*, edited by Thomas P. McDonnell (New York: Image Books, 1974), 506.

2. Adapted from, *Radical Wisdom: A Feminist Mystical Theology* (Minneapolis: Fortress Press, 2005), 44–46.

3. Cited in Caroline Walker Bynum, *Jesus as Mother: Studies in the Spirituality of the High Middle Ages* (Berkeley: University of California Press, 1984), 135–36.

CHAPTER 22

Pace e Bene

1. Mohandas K. Gandhi, *Vows and Observances*, edited by John Strohmeier (Berkeley: Berkeley Hills Books, 1999), 15.

2. Ibid. 29. And, *The Essential Gandhi: His Life, Work, and Ideas*, edited and with an introduction by Louis Fischer (New York: Vintage Books, 1962), 4.

3. Mohandas K. Gandhi, *Prayer*, edited by John Strohmeier (Berkeley: Berkeley Hills Books, 2000), 41.

4. Mohandas K. Gandhi, *Young India*, January 29, 1928, cited in *The Essential Gandhi*, 212.

5. Martyrius' *The Book of Perfection*, cited in *Purity of Heart in Early Ascetic and Monastic Literature*, edited by Harriet A. Luckman and Linda Kulzer (Collegeville, MN: The Liturgical Press, 1999), 42.

6. Teresa of Avila, *The Book of Her Life*, 29.13, 252.

7. *The Canticle of Brother Sun*, translated from the Italian by Ewert H. Cousins. Cited in Ewert Cousins, *Christ of the 21st Century* (Rockport, MA: Element Books, 1992), 137–38.